Big
Sky
Mind

Big Sky Mind:

BUDDHISM AND THE BEAT GENERATION

Carole Tonkinson, ed.

Introduction by Stephen Prothero

Thorsons

An Imprint of HarperCollins*Publishers*

Thorsons
An Imprint of HarperCollins*Publishers*
77–85 Fulham Palace Road,
Hammersmith, London W6 8JB

First Published by Riverhead Books, New York 1995
This edition published by Thorsons 1996
10 9 8 7 6 5 4 3 2 1

A catalogue record for this book
is available from the British Library

ISBN 0 7225 3330 6

Printed and bound in Great Britain by
Caledonian Book International Manufacturing Ltd, Glasgow

Contents

Editor's Preface

"When everything exists within your big mind, all dualistic relationships drop away. There is no distinction between heaven and earth, man and woman, teacher and disciple. . . . In your big mind, everything has the same value."

—SHUNRYU SUZUKI ROSHI

In the Big Mind of Buddhism, the Beats found an antidote to the paranoia and conformity that were at the heart of fifties culture. Big Mind, or panoramic awareness, as Tibetan teacher Chogyam Trungpa Rinpoche described it, is "a state without center or fringe" in which there is no watcher or perceiver, no division between subject and object; in this view all phenomena are acknowledged as temporary, dependent on causes and conditions, and utterly devoid of any fixed identity or self-existing nature. Seeing the sky through the "bamboo tube" of everyday awareness, it looks separate, discrete, but in Buddhism's Big Mind the boundaries between self and other are dissolved in the experience of the empty sky itself. The elimination of that distinction and the recognition that all such dualistic perceptions are illusions offered an irrefutable rebuke to the sense of hierarchy fundamental to the social and political structures of the fifties and rendered meaningless the Cold War catchwords of *us* and *them*, *ally* and *enemy*. Other fundamental teachings of Buddhism were also apropos: the acceptance of the impermanence of all life provided a new context in which to examine the fear of death and suffering that were further intensified by the development of the H-bomb and the Korean War, and Buddhism's advocation of a mendicant, homeless path suggested a practical alternative to the rapidly accelerating cycle of work, produce, and consume that was the engine driving the culture of the fifties.

Forsaking bargain homes and gleaming machinery in favor of the freedom of the road, the Beats found their corollary for the open space of Buddhism in the vast empty space of the Western sky. During extended stays on the northern California coast and lookouts in the Cascades, the Beats experienced the limitless expanse of blue that had been inspiring pioneers and artists for centuries; there, they began to forge an American brand of mountain mysticism based on Buddhist sources as well as on American models—Whitman's sense of the open road, Thoreau's immersion in nature at Walden Pond, and the journey of the train-hopping American hobo. Not only did the Beats adapt the wisdom teachings of the East to a new, peculiarly American terrain, they also articulated this teaching in the vernacular, jazzy rhythms of the street, opening up what had been the domain of stuffy academics and stiff translators to a mainstream audience. With Jack Kerouac's runaway bestseller *The Dharma Bums* and a paperback pocket-poet series published by Lawrence Ferlinghetti, the voices of American poets recounted the teachings of the Buddha to the general public for the first time.

Only now with the emergence of some long unpublished work and a revival of popular interest in the Beats are we beginning to appreciate the pivotal role these writers played in the transmission of Buddhism to America; the purpose of this volume is to document that contribution. Rather than purporting to be a Buddhist reader or a Beat reader, this collection is a conflation of the two. For that reason, certain essential Beat texts ("Howl," for example) and some central Buddhist teachings (the Eightfold Path) are not to be found in these pages. Instead readers will find perhaps lesser known work alongside familiar poems and passages of prose. The selections are limited to the writings of those who had sustained interest in and contact with Buddhism, as well as some work by a very few "fellow travelers." There are some notable omissions from the core group of Beat authors: Gregory Corso, Herbert Huncke, Amiri Baraka (LeRoi Jones), and others, as well as those from the ranks of Buddhist poets who are not directly connected with the Beats. The exclusive focus of this volume is on those authors who explored Buddhism extensively in their work. For any oversights, I offer by way of comfort the hope that this book will open the conversation about Buddhism and the Beats rather than utter the last word.

Technically, the Beats were considered an East Coast phenomenon, and the first section of this book features the writers who hailed from that coast. The second section focuses on the Buddhist poets of the San Francisco Literary Renaissance. The two groups came together in what became known as the "Beat Generation," the dates of which run roughly from 1944 and continue through the early sixties. The third section, "Echoes," includes those Beats who were not formally affiliated with Buddhism, yet were influenced by it. The final section, "Like Minds," concentrates on two poets who fall outside the perameters of the "Beat" chronology, but who were closely affiliated with the Beats: a member of an older generation of San Francisco Poets, Kenneth Rexroth, who translated Japanese and Chinese poetry and acted as an early mentor to the movement, and Anne Waldman, who grew up reading the Beats, and later went on to cofound the Jack Kerouac School of Disembodied Poetics at Naropa Institute, which is dedicated to combining the spontaneous composition pioneered by the Beats and Buddhist meditative practices. While this section of the book might have included many poets, we chose to focus on the two writers who were central to the dissemination of Buddhism in America and who, in a way, bracket the Buddhist

Beats: Rexroth who acted as an ancestor to the Beats and Waldman who has been and continues to be instrumental in encouraging another generation of practitioner-poets.

The pieces included in this collection are not confined to those written during the "Beat" period. Instead each author's selection includes work spanning the writer's career from the Beat time period to the present in an attempt to explore the persistent influence of Buddhism. Consequently, in selecting work from so many writers with long and varied careers, there was much to choose from—too much to be able to offer a representative sample of the full career of each writer. For this reason, readers are directed to investigate the author's own collections and novels. In each author's selection the pieces are arranged, roughly, according to the date of composition, except for those cases in which an author has proposed an alternative chronology in collected works.

Minimal notes have been provided. In most cases the author has composed the work for public consumption, letting the action of the poem itself be a clue to the meaning of unfamiliar words and foreign terms, some of them Buddhist. In some cases, brief explanations have been offered in a note preceding the poem or passage, and in most instances in which the author provided his or her own notes to text, they have been reprinted here. All original spellings and style have been retained. Any editorial mistakes or factual errors are mine alone.

—C. T.

Big
Sky
Mind

Introduction by Stephen Prothero

In a passage buried in the book that would eventually make him famous, American Transcendentalist Henry David Thoreau mused, "How many a man has dated a new era in his life from the reading of a book." Thoreau never informed the readers of *Walden* (1854) which book or books played this role in his life, but in reflecting on his own life, Beat poet and novelist Jack Kerouac did. In the winter of 1953–54, he sought out a copy of Thoreau's *Walden* and was so inspired by its discussion of Indian philosophy, especially the *Bhagavad Gita,* that he was prompted to read other Hindu scriptures. However, like Thoreau's Transcendentalist colleague Ralph Waldo Emerson, who once described the *Gita* as "the much renowned book of Buddhism," Kerouac apparently had some difficulty discriminating between the Hindu and Buddhist traditions. When he went to the library in search of Hindu holy books, Kerouac picked up instead an English translation of

Ashvaghosa's fourth-century *The Life of the Buddha.* A few months later, while visiting friends Neal and Carolyn Cassady in California, Kerouac ensconced himself in the San Jose Library, where he became entranced by Dwight Goddard's *A Buddhist Bible* (1932), an anthology of Buddhist scriptures. Soon he was devouring everything he could find on Eastern religions, including the Vedas, Patanajali's *Yoga Sutras*, and writings by Lao-tzu and Confucius. But Buddhist sutras, especially those included in Goddard's *A Buddhist Bible,* remained Kerouac's favorite Asian texts.

Kerouac's reading of *Walden* and, later, of Buddhist teachings, clearly marked a new era in his life, but it also marked a new era in the life of the nation, since Kerouac's awakening to Buddhism stirred similar searches in other members of the Beat Generation and in the hippies of the sixties, thus helping to bend postwar counterculture eastward. Just as Kerouac, in a mood of desolation over a lost love and a large pile of unpublished manuscripts, had turned to Thoreau and to Buddhist texts, many young people disenchanted with Cold War America and the atomic age ushered in by World War II sought solace in Kerouac's *The Dharma Bums* (1958). In turn, *The Dharma Bums* soon proved itself capable of marking new eras in individual lives, thus sparking something of the "rucksack revolution" of wandering "Zen lunatics" that it had prophesied.

Other members of the Beat Generation also came to Buddhism by way of books. Philip Whalen may have been the first of the Beats to read about Buddhism. In an investigation of religion prompted by questions about his own Christian Scientist upbringing, Whalen visited the Portland Public Library in the early 1940s, while still a teenager, and discovered the writings of theosophical Buddhists A. P. Sinnett and Helena Petrovna Blavatsky. Gary Snyder, who was a student at Reed College in Portland, Oregon, with Whalen in the late forties and early fifties, had become interested in things Asian as a boy when he saw Chinese landscape paintings in the Seattle Art Museum; but his more formal decision to study Buddhism was made in 1949 after he first read translations of Chinese classics by Ezra Pound and Arthur Waley. Soon Snyder,

Whalen, and fellow Reed College student Lew Welch (all of whom were to become members of the San Francisco Poetry Renaissance) were reading R. H. Blyth's four-volume translation of *Haiku* (1949–52) as well as various works on Zen Buddhism by D. T. Suzuki that Blyth had recommended.

These literary encounters define a lineage of sorts in the transmission of Buddhism to America—from Thoreau, who in 1844 in the Transcendentalist periodical *The Dial* published Elizabeth Palmer Peabody's translation from the French of the *Lotus Sutra* (the first time a Buddhist sutra appeared in English); to Dwight Goddard, a former American missionary to China who founded the Followers of the Buddha in 1934; to Jack Kerouac, the Beats, and the writers of the San Francisco Literary Renaissance; to today's American Buddhists, many of whom were brought up in other traditions and who first learned of Buddhism by reading *The Dharma Bums.* This anthology takes one moment in this history—the moment when the Beats discovered and practiced Buddhism—to explore how a new Buddhism began to take shape in the America of the fifties and sixties and how that has transformed, and is transforming still, the landscape and culture in which we live. This collection of letters, poems, excerpts from novels, essays, artwork, journal entries, interviews, and even a sutra, makes an implicit argument that the Beats were significant not only in terms of their literary legacy, but also in terms of their spiritual legacy. Furthermore, this collection testifies that the Beats constitute an important branch in the lineage chart of Buddhism in America, and asserts further that the Beat encounter with the Buddhist tradition was as serious as it was sustained.

In the midst of a lifetime of considering how spiritual lineages are constructed and ancient wisdom handed down, Gary Snyder has noted that in traditional communities, wisdom is passed down orally from teacher to student, from grandparent to grandchild, without the intervention of texts. But in Western culture, Snyder has remarked, that same wisdom is often transmitted from author to reader, from book to book. Books are our elders, asserts Snyder, and libraries our repositories of spiritual insight. This observation can certainly be applied to Buddhism in America, which until very recently propagated itself largely through books.

While Americans had encountered Buddhists in the China trade of the late eighteenth century, and Buddhists crossed the paths of American Protestant missionaries as early as the beginning of the nineteenth century, neither the traders nor the missionaries took Buddhism seriously enough to sit down with these Buddhists, to learn firsthand what they had to teach. And while Chinese immigrants began arriving on American shores in the mid-1800s and Japanese immigrants made their way here closer to the turn of the century, very few outside of these Asian communities took sufficient interest in their Buddhism to enter into dialogue with them about their beliefs and practices.

Buddhism began to make its way into mainstream American culture only when an odd mix of Unitarians, Transcendentalists, theosophists, and Orientalists picked up the Buddhist scriptures and began, first, to read about the Buddhist tradition and, later, to write new books themselves. In fact, despite the arrival of Buddhist missionaries in the late nineteenth century, and most notably the presence of Anagarika Dharmapala from Ceylon and Soyen Shaku from Japan at the Parliament of World Religions in Chicago in 1893, the American encounter with Buddhism remained largely confined to Asian-American communities. Among Americans brought up in other traditions, Buddhism remained for the most part a literary and intellectual enterprise until the sixties and seventies.

Against this backdrop, the Beats can be appreciated as transitional figures constructing a "middle way" between the early era of armchair Buddhism and contemporary Buddhist practice, which usually involves a formal setting and study with a teacher. In an America short on English-language texts and English-speaking teachers, the Beats helped to foster the interest that would support the subsequent establishment of dharma centers and *sanghas*, or communities. For example, when Gary Snyder vowed in the early fifties to sit and meditate, he had only a book as his guide. And when he decided to seek out a Zen master, he determined it was necessary to go to Japan.

Beats who looked for Buddhist teachers later in life did not have to travel so far. Allen Ginsberg, for example, came across his Tibetan Buddhist teacher Chogyam Trungpa Rinpoche on the streets of New York City in 1970. And, after living in Japan, Philip Whalen discovered his American-born teacher, Richard Baker-roshi, in northern California in the early seventies. The Beats also adopted an Emersonian ethos of self-reliance and a Thoreauvian appreciation of solitude in nature; many of them went beyond books and embarked on a contemplative path by taking jobs—as loggers, sailors, and fire lookouts—that placed them in the midst of nature. The Beats had succeeded in picking up the thread of the Transcendentalists' interest in the wisdom traditions of the East and in nature and began to weave it seamlessly into the fabric of American life.

The Beats and Transcendentalism

Nearly half a century ago historian Perry Miller contended in an introduction to *The Transcendentalists: An Anthology* (1950) that American Transcendentalism, a school of thought influential among New England writers in the mid-1800s, was not primarily a literary movement. Transcendentalism, he argued, was essentially a "religious demonstration" and as such demanded the attention not only of students of American literature but also of scholars of American religion. Contemporary readers familiar with the writings of Emerson and Thoreau, not to mention the work of "second-cycle" Transcendentalists such as James Freeman Clarke and Elizabeth Palmer Peabody, might be surprised to learn that this matter was ever in doubt. For instance, very early in his life, Emerson described in a letter to his aunt Mary Moody Emerson "the treasures of the Bramins [sic] and the volumes of Zoroaster" as "learning of El Dorado." And as a young man writing essays such as "Compensation" and poems such as "Brahma" he worked at his desk with the *Bhagavad Gita*, the *Laws of Manu*, and the *Puranas* opened out before him. Thus, the spiritual concerns of the Transcendentalists now seem self-evident, but Miller's argument needed to be made for two reasons. The first is that the Transcendentalists were rebels against religious orthodoxies. They rejected not only traditional Christianity but also Unitarianism, the unofficial orthodoxy of Boston and its environs. They did so, moreover, in unequivocal terms. Unitarian ministers, Emerson concluded, were "corpse-cold," and his Transcendentalist colleagues added that Unitarianism's sacred center of Harvard Divinity School was an "ice house." Many critics of the Transcendentalists saw their rejection as incontrovertible evidence that they were uninterested in religion in general. A second factor that made Miller's argument necessary was that the Transcendentalists' interests in a variety of Asian religions were typically seen as proof that whatever minimal religious concerns they might have had were as shallow as they were wide.

For a long time, the Beats suffered a similar reputation as anti-religious enemies of god and country, or, at best, as dilettantes, fashionable dabblers in the exotic East. And while a recognition of the Beats' contribution to literature has now been established by Allen Ginsberg's winning of the National Book Award and Gary Snyder's Pulitzer Prize, their interest in religion and their contribution to American religious history is still largely ignored. This is all the more surprising, given the fact that nearly every one of the Beats have claimed not simply to be writers, but to be religious writers with abiding spiritual interests. Early in his career, Jack Kerouac characterized the Beat Generation as "a 'seeking' generation." And when a reporter, the young Mike Wallace, asked him what he was seeking, Kerouac replied, "God. I want God to show me His face." In an influential *Esquire* essay on "The Philosophy of the Beat Generation" (1958), Beat author and observer John Clellon Holmes recast Kerouac's remarks into the claim that the undeniable kinetic imperative of the Beats—their urge to go, go, go and "burn, burn, burn"—was motivated not, as critics claimed, by adolescent flight but by spiritual searching. "The Beat Generation," he argued, quoting Kerouac, "is basically a religious generation."

Given the claims of Kerouac, Holmes, and many other Beats that their work was essentially spiritual, the failure to view the Beat movement as religious cries out for explanation: one explanation is that this failure has been motivated by the same biases that led critics to view the Transcendentalists in exclusively literary terms. Set aside for the moment the many other intriguing parallels between the Transcendentalists and the Beats—their romantic longings for lives led apart from the unnatural rhythms of city life, their certainty of the correspondences between the natural and the supernatural, their sense of the prophetic role of the poet, and their disdain for "foolish consistencies"—and consider only these two key facts: first, the Beats, like the Transcendentalists, were rebels against entrenched religious orthodoxies, and, second, the Beats and the Transcendentalists looked to the East for spiritual inspiration.

While the Transcendentalists spurned "corpse-cold" Unitarianism, the Beats rejected what they saw as the unfeeling Protestant-Catholic-Jewish faith of Eisenhower's icy-hearted America. During the period that bridged World War II and the Cold War and gave birth to the Beat movement, Protestants, Catholics, and Jews were converging in a spiritual synthesis exquisitely suited to what historians have described as "the placid decade." Rabbi Joshua Liebman's *Peace of Mind* (1946), Monsignor Fulton J. Sheen's *Peace of Soul* (1949), and Reverend Billy Graham's *Peace with God* (1953) constituted something of the canon of this emerging generic faith. Although these books were written by a Jew, a Catholic, and a Protestant, respectively, their messages were as strikingly similar as their titles. Like Norman Vincent Peale, the author of *The Power of Positive Thinking* (1952), another best-seller of the time, each of these authors was convinced that the faithful could will their way to spiritual and material success in postwar America. This cheery outlook seemed almost surreal to the early Beats, who were downcast and alienated not only by the looming Cold War but also by the bomb, the Holocaust, and World War II.

Not surprisingly, critics of the Beats, like critics of the Transcendentalists, viewed this rejection not as a refusal to participate in the fifties versions of various religious traditions but as a wholesale rejection of religion. In fact, the most persistent criticism of the early Beats was that they repudiated not simply religion but meaning itself. Cultural icon *Life* magazine depicted the Beats' refusal to "accentuate the positive" as an attempt to undermine all that was sacred in postwar America—"Mom, Dad, Politics, Marriage, the Savings Bank, Organized Religion, Literary Elegance, Law, the Ivy League Suit, and Higher Education, to say nothing of the Automatic Dishwasher, the Cellophane-wrapped Soda Cracker, the Split-Level House and the clean, or peace-provoking H-bomb." Even *Playboy* called them "nihilists." This line of interpretation became an orthodoxy of its own with the publication of Norman Podhoretz's strafing of Jack Kerouac's *On the Road* in *Partisan Review* in 1958. "The Bohemianism of the 1950s is hostile to civilization; it worships primitivism, instinct, energy, 'blood,'" Podhoretz fumed. "This is a revolt of the spiritually underprivileged and the crippled of soul." In a note in the successive edition of *Partisan Review,* Podhoretz asked, "Where is the 'affirmation of life' in all this? Where is the spontaneity and vitality? It sounds more like an affirmation of death to me."

To this sort of question, the early Beats responded in one voice. "The Beat Generation is insulted when linked to doom, thoughts of doom, fear of doom, anger of doom," Ginsberg, Gregory Corso, and Peter Orlovsky complained. "It exhibits on every side, and in a bewildering number of facets," John Clellon Holmes added, "a perfect craving to believe." Responding to a critic who described his poetic manifesto "Howl" as a nihilistic "howl against civilization," Allen Ginsberg contended that the poem was a prophetic utterance—a protest in the original sense of "pro-attestation, that is testimony in favor of Value." *Howl and Other Poems* (1956), he added, "is an 'Affirmation' by individual experience of god, sex, drugs, absurdity. . . . The poems are religious and I meant them to be." Echoing Ginsberg, Kerouac responded to a claim advanced in *The Nation* that the Beats were "nay-sayers." "I want to speak *for* things," Kerouac explained. "For the crucifix I speak out, for the Star of Israel I speak out, for the divinest man who ever lived who was German (Bach) I speak out, for sweet Mohammed I speak out, for Buddha I speak out, for Lao-tse and Chuang-tse I speak out."

Unfortunately, these testimonials did little to persuade critics that the Beat movement was, as Beat poet Michael McClure once argued, a "spiritual occasion." In fact, the interest in Buddhism and other Asian religions made plain in Kerouac's litany only reinforced the perception promoted in magazines such as *Life* and *Time*, as well as in more sophisticated literary publications including *The Saturday Review* and *Partisan Review*, that the Beat movement was areligious at best. Just as the Transcendentalists' forays into Asian religious texts did little to persuade critics of Transcendentalism that religious concerns were integral to their movement, the Beats' efforts to incorporate Asian meditation techniques into their lives and Eastern religious teachings into their writing only reinforced the widespread conviction that the Beats were, in Podhoretz's terms, "spiritually underprivileged and . . . crippled of soul."

Champions of Beat spirituality may take heart in knowing that advocates of Transcendentalist spirituality have won their argument. It is now scarcely defensible to teach a course in American religion without discussing Emerson's "Nature," Thoreau's *Walden*, or some other "scripture" in the emerging Transcendentalist "canon." And there are now a handful of scholarly books (*Hindu Scriptures and American Transcendentalists, Emerson and the Rhetoric of Revelation, American Transcendentalism and Asian Religions, Zen and American Transcendentalism,* etc.) and one anthology (*The Spirituality of the American Transcendentalists*) devoted exclusively to Transcendentalist spirituality. Together these books document how the Transcendentalists' interests in Asian religious traditions paved the way for future generations of Hindu and Buddhist sympathizers in the United States—the Beats included.

This anthology emerges out of the conviction that, like the Transcendentalists, the Beats have been appreciated for their contributions to literature at the expense of their spiritual offerings and influences. *Big Sky Mind* brings together in one volume what amounts to an unrelenting testimony to the Beats' deep, persistent interest in Buddhism, challenging negative judgments of the Beats' religious interests. It makes the case for viewing the Beat movement as, in Miller's words, a "religious demonstration" and prepares the way for future considerations not only of the role played by Buddhism in the Beat movement but also of the role played by the Beats in popularizing and transforming Buddhism in America.

The Beat Movement and a "New Consciousness"

But who exactly were the Beats and what exactly is the Beat movement? First of all, the Beats did not, strictly speaking, comprise a generation. During the fifties, journalists, who eagerly exploited the Beats in order to sell magazines and newspapers, and Hollywood moguls, who also attempted to cash in on the Beat vogue with films such as *The Beat Generation* (1959) and *The Beatniks* (1959), fiercely promoted the idea that the Beats somehow stood for an entire generation of disaffected youth. But the attempt to sell the friends and followers of Kerouac, Ginsberg, and Burroughs as a unified "Beat Generation" was like today's attempt to turn so-called "slackers" into a "Generation X," a vast overgeneralization devised by marketing executives rather than careful historians. Diane di Prima, who wrote *Memoirs of a Beatnik* (1969), once remarked, "As far as we knew, there was only a small handful of us—perhaps forty or fifty in [New York City] . . . We surmised that there might be another fifty living in San Francisco, and perhaps a hundred more scattered throughout the country." So the Beats, in short, comprised not so much a generation as a movement; but the impact of the Beats can be seen in terms of generations that followed—the counterculture of the sixties and seventies. The Beats created the role models, the language, and the ideals that set off the "rucksack revolution."

The Beat movement is frequently dated from the famous poetry reading held on October 13, 1955, at the Six Gallery in San Francisco—a reading that according to announcements for the event promised "free satori"—during which Allen Ginsberg offered the first public delivery of his brooding and prophetic "Howl." But the Six Gallery reading functioned more as a coming-out party than as an inaugural meeting. A more reasonable time to begin the Beat story is 1944, the year that Jack Kerouac, Allen Ginsberg, and William Burroughs first met in New York City. These three characters—a working-class Catholic with French-Canadian roots, a middle-class Russian-American Jew from New Jersey, and a well-to-do Anglo-American Protestant from the Midwest, respectively—stood at the center of the early Beat drama, which soon included a large and diverse supporting cast of novelists, poets, and hangers-on.

Although the Beat movement was clearly centered on Kerouac, Ginsberg, and Burroughs, early on it incorporated other East Coast writers such as John Clellon Holmes, Lucien Carr, and Gregory Corso; as they criss-crossed the country, the Beat impulse made its way westward, embracing the poets of the San Francisco Literary Renaissance, among them Gary Snyder, Philip Whalen, Lew Welch, Michael McClure, Joanne Kyger, Lawrence Ferlinghetti, Philip Lamantia, Bob Kaufman, and others, and then back east again, incorporating poets and novelists such as Diane di Prima, Amiri Baraka (then LeRoi Jones), and still others, all writing in the jazzy Beat style, many of them interested in Buddhism. The Beat movement proper came to an end in the early sixties, a victim of media overkill. Once you could "Rent a Genuine Beatnik" for a "bash" at your "pad," it was clear that the movement was over. Still the Beat impulse marched on—steadily if no longer manically, surviving the deaths of Neal Cassady in 1968 and Jack Kerouac in 1969.

What united the work of the early Beats and defined them as a movement was not so much a common political stance or even a shared literary style but a distinctly spiritual quest for a "new consciousness." This quest was most pronounced in Kerouac and Ginsberg, but even Burroughs claims he was in search of something: "Since early youth I had been searching for some secret, some key with which I could gain access to basic knowledge, answer some of the fundamental questions," Burroughs wrote in *Naked Lunch* (1959). "Just what I was looking for, what I meant by basic knowledge or fundamental questions, I found difficult to define. I would follow a trail of clues."

The trail the Beats traveled in the early fifties led to different understandings of "Beat" over time and thus to different understandings of Beat spirituality. Epitomizing one of these understandings was Herbert Huncke, one of Kerouac's "desolation angels," who according to Ginsberg "was to be found in 1945 passing on subways from Harlem to Broadway scoring for drugs, music, incense, lovers, Benzedrine inhalers . . . encountering curious & beautiful solitaries of New York dawn." Huncke symbolized for the early Beats a social and spiritual type that Oswald Spengler had described in *The Decline of the West* (1939) as the "fellaheen." According to Spengler's sprawling history, which the Beats devoured in the 1940s, the fellaheen are characterized by "a deep piety that fills the waking-consciousness . . . the naive belief . . . that there is some sort of mystic constitution of actuality." The Beats may well have been romanticizing Huncke, but they saw him as the embodiment of the "second religiousness" of the "fellaheen." "In his anonymity & holy Creephood in New York," Ginsberg observed, "he was the sensitive vehicle for a veritable new consciousness." This "new consciousness" was "Beat" in the sense that its living saints, like the Times Square hustlers from whom they borrowed the term, were both "beat-up" and "beat-down." At least in the gospel according to Huncke, who was by legend the first of the group to have used the term "Beat" to describe himself, Beat spirituality was a dark and dreary matter that, depending on your point of view, either gracefully articulated the First Noble Truth or veered dangerously close to the amoral, apocalyptic nihilism that critics were so eager to pin on the Beat movement. Many of the Beats worked feverishly to distance themselves from this definition of "Beat" and its stereotyped nihilism, but, nonetheless, the image stuck.

Another version of this "new consciousness" was epitomized by Neal Cassady, who arrived in New York City in 1947 and was later immortalized as the irrepressible Dean Moriarty of Kerouac's *On the Road*. If Huncke was a classic representative of what philosopher William James once described as the "sick soul," Cassady was the epitome of James's "healthy-minded" type. "His criminality," Kerouac noted, "was not something that sulked and sneered; it was Western, the west wind, an ode from the Plains, something new, long prophesied, long-a-coming (he only stole cars for joy rides)." The recasting of "Beat" exemplified by Cassady celebrated the adhesiveness of comrades prophesied by Walt Whitman and preached the sacramentalization of everyday life—the sacred splendor of cosmic companions digging the open road.

The literature that emerged from this definition of "Beat" was, in Ginsberg's terms, "a clear statement of fact about misery . . . and splendor." And authors informed by this definition crafted literature that embraced the unalterable reality of suffering yet affirmed wholeheartedly, in Kerouac's words, "the holy contour of life." This holiness was further refined by Kerouac's redefinition of the term in 1954, when he had a vision in a church in his hometown of Lowell, Massachusetts, and saw "Beat" as part of the word "beatific." This understanding came after Kerouac was already studying Buddhism, when he began to go beyond an appreciation of suffering on its own terms and started to see the possibility for the cessation of suffering, for liberation from it. With Kerouac leading the way, Beat literature came to concern itself with spiritual emancipation and the cultivation of a vast view, a Big Sky Mind. As Gary Snyder once said, "In a way the Beat Generation is a gathering together of all the available models and myths of freedom in America that had existed before, namely: Whitman, John Muir, Thoreau, and the American bum. We put them together and opened them out again."

Tilting East

More than a century earlier, the Transcendentalists' quest for a "new consciousness" of their own had led Emerson and Thoreau, most notably, to the sacred writings of Hindus, Buddhists, Confucian ethicists, and Persian poets. But the Beats turned primarily to Buddhism, rather than focusing on Hinduism as Emerson and Thoreau had. "Primarily" is an important qualifier here because the Beats' spiritual interests were in no way confined to Buddhism. Kerouac's Catholicism remained strong throughout his life; Ginsberg's Judaism has never ceased to inform his writing; and Snyder has carefully studied Native American religion and culture.

In a decade in which other Americans were boasting of overcoming tensions between Protestants, Catholics, and Jews, the Beats were cultivating a much more radical ecumenism. This ecumenism was epitomized by Kerouac, who was born and died a Catholic but nonetheless identified himself as a Buddhist for a significant period in his life and once even fasted during Ramadan. His ecumenism is expressed in a creed from *Mexico City Blues:*

I believe in the sweetness
        of Jesus
And Buddha—
        I believe
In St. Francis,
        Avaloki
Tesvara,
        the Saints
Of First Century
        India A D
And Scholars
        Santidevan
And Otherwise
        Santayanan
        Everywhere

Ginsberg, a self-proclaimed "Buddhist Jew," was even more eclectic. In this litany from "Wichita Vortex Sutra" he invoked spiritual beings from Buddhism, Hinduism, Christianity, Judaism, and Islam:

                million-faced Tathagata gone past suffering
        Preserver Harekrishna returning in the age of pain
Sacred Heart my Christ acceptable
        Allah the Compassionate One
                Jaweh Righteous One

all Knowledge-Princes of Earth-man, all
ancient Seraphim of heavenly Desire, Devas, yogis
& holyman I chant to—

While it is clear that Beat spirituality was not committed exclusively to one religious tradition, it was inspired more deeply by Buddhism than by any other. And while we know *how* individual Beats came to study Buddhism, just why so many individuals were attracted to it at that time and why such a diverse flowering occurred independently across the country is not entirely clear. Among the East Coast Beats, William Burroughs claimed in a number of letters that he had studied Zen Buddhism and practiced some sort of yoga long before meeting up with his fellow Beats, and Allen Ginsberg has noted that Professor Raymond Weaver of Columbia University suggested in the 1940s that Kerouac and he look at the writings of Egyptian Gnostics and Zen Buddhists. Burroughs, Ginsberg, and Kerouac were also exposed to Asian thought in the mid-1940s through their reading of Spengler. But it was not until the fifties, when Ginsberg encountered Chinese paintings in the New York Public Library and Kerouac read sutras in translation for the first time, that they began to look seriously at the Buddhist tradition.

Not surprisingly, the West Coast Beats came to Buddhism earlier and more easily. Asian immigration was both more longstanding and more sustained in California than in New York. The discovery of gold at Sutter's Mill in 1848 had lured thousands of Chinese to the States, and by 1853 San Francisco boasted its first Chinese temple. Japanese immigrants did not begin to arrive in significant numbers until the 1890s, but shortly after the turn of the century important Japanese Buddhist teachers such as Nyogen Senzaki and D. T. Suzuki arrived in the United States. At least one future Beat, Japanese-American Albert Saijo, actually studied with Nyogen Senzaki, with whom he had been interred at the Heart Mountain camp for Japanese nationals and Japanese-Americans during World War II. This Japanese and Chinese presence contributed to a climate that was conducive to introducing Buddhist influences into the culture at large. The climate encouraged the interests of men such as Lloyd Reynolds, who taught calligraphy at Reed College and encouraged Welch, Whalen, and Snyder to investigate Buddhism while they were students there, and Kenneth Rexroth, a poet and activist well read in Asian philosophy and literature who, on his weekly radio broadcast on San Francisco's KPFA radio, frequently discussed Asian texts and Buddhist thought.

Kenneth Rexroth was also the one to suggest that Allen Ginsberg make the acquaintance of Gary Snyder; the meeting of the East Coast Beats and members of the San Francisco Literary Renaissance that resulted from this suggestion transformed the Beat impulse into a national movement that would soon be dubbed the "Beat Generation." That meeting and the Six Gallery reading it gave rise to reconfirmed in the minds of all participants the importance of their artistic and spiritual experiments, including their mutual attractions to Buddhism. From this point on, the Beats were well on the way to carving out a path for Buddhism in American culture.

Gary Snyder, who came to the San Francisco Bay Area in 1952 in order to study Asian languages at the University of California at Berkeley, left for Japan in May of 1956 to study and practice Zen, eventually becoming a disciple of Rinzai Zen master Oda Sesso Roshi, Head Abbot of Daitoku-ji in Kyoto. Snyder and Kerouac provided the two points around which Buddhism and the Beat Generation came together. Snyder, who was becoming more immersed in formal Buddhist practice than any other Beat, would no doubt have exerted even more influence on the Beat movement if he had remained in the United States. Instead, it was Kerouac who, as the most prolific of the Beat Buddhists, became their official spokesperson. Buddhism commended itself to Kerouac because rather than denying suffering and death, it faced squarely up to both. Moreover, by tracing the origin of suffering and death to craving, desire, and ignorance, Buddhism also offered a way to transcendence. Finally, and perhaps most important, Buddhism seemed to be teaching that the phenomenal world was dreamlike and illusory. All of these teachings comforted Kerouac, especially the notion that the apparent world is "mind-only." "Happiness consists in realizing that it is all a great strange dream," he wrote in *Lonesome Traveler* (1960). And he echoed the sentiment (though in a decidedly biblical grammar) in *The Dharma Bums:* "Believe that the world is an ethereal flower, and ye live."

Although the popular press would come to associate the Beats with Zen Buddhism, Kerouac was not drawn to Zen but to a diffuse Mahayana Buddhism. He resisted Zen because of his conviction that it emphasized attaining mystical insight rather than cultivating compassion. "It's mean," Kerouac's alter ego of Ray Smith complained to Japhy Ryder [Gary Snyder] in *The Dharma Bums,* "All those Zen masters throwing young kids in the mud because they can't answer their silly word questions." "Compassion," he concluded, "is the heart of Buddhism." Kerouac, whom Burroughs would describe condescendingly as "a *Catholic*-Buddhist" [emphasis his], was also put off by Snyder's apparent hostility toward Christianity. Like Kerouac, Ray Smith happily conflated Jesus Christ with Avalokitesvara, the bodhisattva of compassion. "After all," he explained, "a lot of people say he is Maitreya [which] means 'Love' in Sanskrit and that's all Christ talked about was love."

Unlike the Transcendentalists, whose Asian religious interests remained largely textual, Kerouac translated his intellectual curiosity about Buddhism into actual practice. In the mid-1950s he chanted *The Diamond Sutra* (his favorite Buddhist scripture), meditated daily, and attempted for months at a time to live the ascetic and celibate life of a Buddhist monk. He also translated Buddhist scriptures from French to English and took notes on his Buddhist studies that soon swelled to an unpublished manuscript called *Some of the Dharma.* Inspired by Ashvaghosa's life of the historical Buddha, Kerouac wrote *Wake Up*, a biography of Shakyamuni Buddha clearly informed not only by his reading of the ancient account but also by his Catholic upbringing. Neither of these texts have yet been published, but a book of Buddhist poems, *Mexico City Blues* (published in 1959), and a sutra called *The Scripture of the Golden Eternity* (which came out one year later) did provide early published evidence of his Buddhist concerns, as did novels such as *The Dharma Bums, Visions of Gerard* (1963), and *Desolation Angels* (1965).

Kerouac's Buddhist interest faded in the early sixties—just as Ginsberg was beginning, however gradually, to study more rigorously the wisdom traditions of the East. And here again the parallels with Transcendentalism may be instructive. Students of Transcendentalism have noted for some time that Thoreau's interest in Asian religions was intense but fleeting, while Emerson's was slow to germinate but ultimately longer-lived. At least on this score, Kerouac was the Beat movement's Thoreau and Ginsberg its Emerson. Like Thoreau, whose Asian interests faded, Kerouac ultimately turned away from the Buddhist tradition. And like Emerson, whose Asian interests deepened over time, Ginsberg's affinity for Buddhism has grown stronger as he has grown older. Although he exchanged letters about Buddhism with Kerouac in the mid-fifties, it was not until he traveled in India and Japan in the sixties that Ginsberg became serious about Buddhist study. And it was not until May of 1972, nearly a full ten years after his first trip to India, that Ginsberg formally became a Buddhist by taking refuge vows with Tibetan lama Chogyam Trungpa Rinpoche.

If Snyder, Kerouac, and Ginsberg are the most celebrated Beats to take up the Buddhist path, they are not the only Beats to have been influenced by Buddhism. In fact, Albert Saijo was one of the Beat poets with the most extensive Buddhist training. As the first of the Beats to receive formal instruction in zazen, Saijo helped Whalen, Snyder, and others to correct their self-taught sitting posture in the mid-fifties. Saijo is described by Kerouac in *Big Sur* as George Baso, "the little Japanese Zen master hepcat" who in a 1959 trip across the country with Kerouac and Lew Welch sat in the lotus position on a mattress in the back of a Jeep composing spontaneous haiku.

Other poets drawn toward Buddhism include Joanne Kyger and Diane di Prima, both of whom studied Zen with Shunryu Suzuki Roshi of the San Francisco Zen Center, and later investigated Tibetan Buddhism. The work of Lenore Kandel has been influenced by the tantric traditions of Hinduism and Buddhism. Kandel claims to have been attracted to Buddhism at the age of twelve, and she practiced zazen at New York City's First Zen Institute for much of 1959. Philip Whalen, meanwhile, was ordained a Zen monk in 1972 and in the mid-seventies became head monk at the Zen Mountain Center in Tassajara Springs, California. He now serves as the abbot of the Hartford Street Zen Center in San Francisco. And a generation of younger poets similarly felt drawn to Buddhism, inspired in part by the writings of the Beats. Among these poets is Anne Waldman, who met Chogyam Trungpa Rinpoche in 1970 and has since studied with other Tibetan Buddhist teachers.

Conclusion

When Allen Ginsberg was asked, "Were the Beats first and foremost artists, or first and foremost spiritual seekers?" he saw the trap and refused to enter. The two, he answered, are inseparable, and he cited the example of the Milarepa school of Tibetan Buddhism, where in order to be a lama one must reportedly also be an archer, a calligrapher, or a poet. "The life of poetry," he added is "a sacramental life on earth."

This sentiment circles back again, in a way, to the Transcendentalists, specifically to their understanding of the poet as prophet. Like the Transcendentalists, the Beats were far more than literary innovators or social critics; they were also wandering seekers of mystical visions and transcendence. They went on the road because they could not find God in the churches and synagogues of postwar America. They saw human beings as enmeshed in a vast network of connections with other human beings, with animals, and with life itself. They saw intimate correspondences between the human mind and the life of the universe. Like Emerson, the Beats aimed to make contact with the sacred in moments of indescribable intuition and then to transmit at least some of what they had experienced into words. Like Thoreau, they insisted upon the sanctity of everyday life, the sainthood of the nonconformist, and the awesome sacredness of Nature. And like those socially minded Transcendentalists who aimed to transform land at Brook Farm, Massachusetts, into an occasion for the cultivation not only of vegetables but also of the kingdom of God on earth, they aimed to create a spiritual brotherhood based on shared experiences, shared property, shared literature, and an ethic of what Kerouac called "continual conscious compassion." With Transcendentalists of all stripes, the Beats gloried in eliminating distinctions between matter and spirit, divinity and humanity, the sacred and the profane.

The Beats, like the Transcendentalists, were committed to sharing these insights with others through their words even though it is widely accepted among practicing Buddhists that experience is untranslatable, that it cannot be captured accurately in words, that language can only hint at, point toward it. As it says in the Pali canon, "When all conditions are removed, all ways of telling are also removed." All sermons, and all books, therefore, are doomed, at best, to be exquisite failures. Certainly Shakyamuni Buddha was aware that words could never come close to describing the reality of the world as he saw it. Certainly he knew that the students he would gather around him would misunderstand his spoken words, and that students of theirs would perpetuate those misunderstandings in volumes upon volumes of books. But still he committed himself to teaching, content, perhaps, that at least some of this transmission, recorded in a few books perhaps, would mark new eras in the lives of individuals. Perhaps he hoped, as well, that these individuals would be smart enough to read these books and then toss them aside in the name of an even deeper understanding. This sentiment, at least, was reiterated by one of the Beats: "When you've understood this scripture, throw it away," Jack Kerouac wrote in *The Scripture of the Golden Eternity.* "I insist on your freedom."

—Stephen Prothero
Philosophy Department
Georgia State University, Atlanta

PART ONE

The Beats

Jack Kerouac
(1922–1969)

"The empty blue sky of space says 'All this comes back to me, then goes again, and comes back again, then goes again, and I dont care, it still belongs to me'—The blue sky adds 'Dont call me eternity, call me God if you like, all of you talkers are in paradise: the leaf is paradise, the tree stump is paradise, the paper bag is paradise, the man is paradise, the sand is paradise, the sea is paradise, the man is paradise, the fog is paradise.'" — JACK KEROUAC

Jack Kerouac met Lucien Carr, William Burroughs, and Allen Ginsberg in New York where he attended Columbia University on a football scholarship; in 1944, the four friends formed the core of what was to become known as the Beat Generation. Kerouac published his first novel, *The Town and the City*, in 1950; it was a straightforward story told in a language reminiscent of Thomas Wolfe. By 1951, however, Kerouac was pioneering a stylistic revolution, forever changing the nature and content of his writing. Abandoning conventional techniques of editing and revision, Kerouac committed himself to a new method, the practice of spontaneous prose. Unsatisfied with simply creating a stream of consciousness in the characters of a novel, as the modernists had done, Kerouac wanted to take that idea further and use the movements and patterns of his own mind as his subject matter. His aim was to create an honest record of the writer's modes of perception. In a three-week, Benzedrine-enhanced spontaneous writing experiment, Kerouac produced his first novel by this technique, *On the Road.* For six years, the manuscript languished, unable to find a publisher; during that time Kerouac, unbowed by market pressures, stuck to his resolve and committed himself to spontaneous writing, producing novels, sketches, dream visions, and poems.

In 1954, Kerouac's reading of Thoreau's *Walden* led him to pursue a serious, self-taught program of Buddhist study, and his affinity for the teachings was immediate. Both Kerouac's sense of compassion for the down-and-out, the "beat," who populated his novels, and his revolutionary new method of "spontaneous bop prosody" found full expression in Buddhist thought. The *Surangama Sutra,* for example, affirmed Kerouac's own commitment to spontaneity; in the sutra, the Buddha counsels: "If you are now desirous of more perfectly understanding Supreme Enlightenment and the enlightening nature of pure Mind-Essence, you must learn to answer questions spontaneously with no recourse to discriminating thinking." Kerouac had discovered a version of this text in a San Jose library; shortly thereafter he went north, where he wrote *San Francisco Blues,* his first book of "blues"-inspired poetry and a work that reflects his newfound spiritual interest. Kerouac returned to his mother's home in April of 1954 determined to pursue a monastic, contemplative style of life. He then began an ambitious program of sitting meditation and sutra reading and incorporated Buddhist understanding into his own observations about the nature of consciousness, later describing the mind as a "beating light" that reveals the fluctuation, and hence the falseness, of all it illuminates.

Kerouac's discovery of Buddhism also coincided with his redefinition of the term "Beat." Not long after his initial reading of Buddhist texts, Kerouac went to visit his birthplace, Lowell, where he had a vision in a church. Having already coined the phrase "Beat Generation," he now came to understand the word "Beat" as meaning not simply down-and-out but also "Beatific, trying to be in a state of beatitude, like St. Francis, trying to love all life, being utterly sincere and kind and cultivating 'joy of heart.'" This flash of insight propelled Kerouac to attend to his Buddhist studies with still more fervor and despite acute phlebitis in his legs he immersed himself in the practice of sitting meditation. He also embarked on two Buddhist works, a life story of the Buddha, *Wake Up,* and a book of notes and translations based on his Buddhist readings, which he called *Some of the Dharma.*

Kerouac's hermetic, meditative existence intensified while he lived at his sister's home in North Carolina, but his practice of spending nearly all of his time in silent contemplation came under fire from his family, who equated his behavior with laziness. When in July of 1955 *On the Road* was finally accepted for publication, Kerouac immediately took his publisher's advance and set off for Mexico City in the hope of finding a more peaceful setting for his meditation. There he wrote the Buddhist-inspired poem *Mexico City Blues* and *Tristessa,* a novel that Kerouac thought exemplified Buddhism's First Noble Truth, the truth of suffering.

In August of 1955, he wrote to Allen Ginsberg from Mexico: "All I want as far as life-plans are concerned from here on out, is compassionate, contented solitude—Bhikkuhood is so hard to make in the West—it would have to be some American streamlined Bhikkuhood, because so far all I've done is attract attention . . ." But this was only the beginning of the attention Kerouac was to receive. In the fall, Kerouac went on to Berkeley, where he found Ginsberg busy planning what was to become the legendary Six Poets at the Six Gallery reading, the event that launched the Beats into mainstream consciousness. It was at this time, after Kerouac had already enjoyed sustained periods of practice and solitary study, that he met the "dharma bums," the West Coast poets who shared his interest in Buddhism, among them Gary Snyder, Philip Whalen, and Lew Welch. For the first time, Kerouac was exposed to other

Buddhists, ones who had been informed not only by reading but also by contacts with teachers and Asian-American communities. When Kerouac attended one of Kenneth Rexroth's famous literary evenings, he announced to everybody that he was a great Buddhist scholar, but, according to Rexroth, promptly quieted down after learning that everyone in the room spoke at least one Asian language.

Buddhist themes continued to dominate Kerouac's creative work; during this time he produced *Visions of Gerard* as well as adding to *Some of the Dharma.* In the spring of 1956, Kerouac returned to the West Coast to spend time with Gary Snyder before Snyder's departure for Japan. At Snyder's suggestion, Kerouac tried his hand at writing a sutra, *The Scripture of the Golden Eternity,* before ascending to a peak in the Cascades for an eight-week stint as a fire lookout. Kerouac had been looking forward to this experience of solitude as an opportunity to practice meditation and write, dreaming of "Zen lunatics" and solitary mountain mystics such as Han Shan (or "Cold Mountain"), the seventh-century Chinese poet. His taste for Buddhism in a formal setting was limited, and he envisioned instead a new American Buddhism—a meditation center without rules, where wandering bhikkus could rest and meditate during their journeys on the road. He confided to friends his desire to found a monastery in Mexico, starting with his own "dobe hut," or, alternatively, to find a cave where he and Snyder could spend summers practicing "like Milarepa" (a Tibetan saint). After his stint on Desolation Peak, however, it became clear that such heavy doses of solitude did not agree with him. He was only too happy to return to the frenetic activity of the city.

In September 1957, *On the Road* was published and greeted with tremendous media attention—both positive and negative. Unwittingly, Kerouac succeeded in becoming the symbol of a generation. The life of a solitary Buddhist wanderer now an impossibility, Kerouac became increasingly overwhelmed by the pressures of celebrity, and began to take refuge in alcohol. In November of 1957, while *On the Road* was on the best-seller list, Kerouac, at the urging of his publisher, wrote *The Dharma Bums.* Again the reactions that his work provoked were extreme. Support from some corners was strong. *The American Buddhist,* the organ of the Buddhist Churches of America, ran a review of the novel that said, "As a book *The Dharma Bums* is an answer to the literature of disillusion, petulant sensualism and indignation against dry-heart bourgeois hypocrisy. . . . As an alternative to the packaged way of life it should be taken seriously by youth and taken as a threat by our policy makers on the east coast." But, by the mainstream press, Kerouac was condemned as an enemy of the American way and his literary talents were dismissed as not writing but "typing." Amid hostility from the scions of the literary establishment, outrageous demands from a reading public that gave him no privacy, and a rising tide of "beatniks" who had less and less to do with Kerouac's beatific vision, he sank into alcoholic despair. Only a few years after their initial meeting, Kerouac wrote to Snyder that his Buddhism was dead. In his later years he turned toward the Catholic faith in which he was raised and continued to shy away from publicity, becoming more isolated even from his friends. In 1969, at the age of forty-seven, Kerouac died of cirrhosis.

This selection of Kerouac's work focuses on pieces written during the height of his involvement with Buddhism. For many years Kerouac's treatment of Buddhist themes was actively discouraged by editors and colleagues, a reaction not unique to his work. As he wrote to Philip Whalen in 1956: "Meyer Schapiro the art critic read your work one night when Allen [Ginsberg] visited him, and said it was good except when it dealt with enlightenment per se. . . . I dont agree that we should not discuss Buddha . . . who says? I like your poetry and Gary's [Snyder] because it discusses enlightenment. . . ." This resistance to the Buddhist material proved so strong that Kerouac's two works that deal most extensively with Buddhism, *Wake Up* and *Some of the Dharma*, have yet to be published, more than twenty-five years after the author's death.

While Kerouac envisioned all of his novels forming one great autobiographical chronicle, "The Legend of Duluoz," he wrote the books out of sequence; therefore, some of the works that recount the early part of "the legend"— Kerouac's childhood, for example—are influenced by Buddhist thought, while those that cover later periods in Kerouac's life, such as *Visions of Cody,* a novel about Kerouac's friend Neal Cassady, are not. For that reason, the work is arranged not in order of Kerouac's own treatment of his life story, but in a chronological order according to the approximate date of composition, so that the reader may chart the influence of Buddhism on his work. Because *Some of the Dharma* and *Wake Up* have not yet been published (at the time of the compilation of this volume), they are not represented in this selection.

. . . .

Kerouac drew up this streamlined description of his spontaneous approach to writing at the insistence of Allen Ginsberg and William Burroughs, who were so impressed with The Subterraneans, *written in three nights in 1953, that they urged him to share his method. Kerouac later included this version of his "essentials" in a letter written on May 28, 1955, to Arabel Porter, the editor of* New World Writing, *so that she could respond to one of his critics with his prediction that "the method of the modern jazz instrumentalist" would influence "the development and flowering of Western Letters."*

LIST OF ESSENTIALS

1. Write on, cant change or go back, involuntary, unrevised, spontaneous, subconscious, pure
2. Scribbled secret notebooks, and wild typewritten pages, for your own joy
3. Submissive to everything, open, listening
4. Be in love with your life every detail of it
5. Something that you feel will find its own form
6. Be crazy dumbsaint of the mind
7. Blow as deep as you want to blow
8. Write what you want bottomless from bottom of the mind
9. The unspeakable visions of the individual

10. No time for poetry but exactly what is
11. Visionary tics shivering in the chest
12. In tranced fixation dreaming upon object before you
13. Remove literary, grammatical and syntactical inhibition
14. Like Proust be an old teahead of time
15. Telling the true story of the world in interior monolog
16. Work from pithy middle eye out, from the jewel center of interest, swimming in language sea
17. Accept loss forever
18. Believe in the holy contour of life
19. Write in recollection and amazement of yourself
20. Profound struggle with pencil to sketch the flow that already exists intact in mind
21. Don't think of words when you stop but to see picture better
22. No fear or shame in the dignity of your experience, language, and knowledge
23. Write for the world to read and see your exact pictures
24. In Praise of Character in the Bleak inhuman Loneliness
25. Composing wild, undisciplined, pure, coming in from under, crazier the better
26. You're a Genius all the time
27. Writer-Director of Earthly Movies produced in Heaven, different forms of the same Holy Gold

. . . .

This poem was composed for Allen Ginsberg in 1954 as part of Kerouac's campaign to get him interested in Buddhism.

How to Meditate

—lights out—
fall, hands a-clasped, into instantaneous
ecstasy like a shot of heroin or morphine,

the gland inside of my brain discharging
the good glad fluid (Holy Fluid) as
I hap-down and hold all my body parts
down to a deadstop trance—Healing
all my sicknesses—erasing all—not
even the shred of a "I-hope-you" or a
Loony Balloon left in it, but the mind
blank, serene, thoughtless. When a thought
comes a-springing from afar with its held-
forth figure of image, you spoof it out,
you spuff it off, you fake it, and
it fades, and thought never comes—and
with joy you realize for the first time
"Thinking's just like not thinking—
So I dont have to think
        any
    more"

. . . .

In an unpublished notebook from 1954, Kerouac outlined his plans to attain nirvana by the year 2000.

Modified Ascetic Life

1954 No chasing after women anymore.
No more drunkenness or alcohol, no more "sipping" [. . . .]
1955 No more rich or/& expensive foods—elementary diet of salt pork, beans, bread, greens, peanuts, figs, coffee (and later grow everything & pick acorns, pinyon nuts, cacti fruit myself).
1956
Finally (after 5-volume LIFE) no more writing for communicating and other SKETCH books of wilds, no more writing

or I art-ego of any kind, finally no I-self, or Name; no shaving of beard.

1970

No possessions, finally, but wilderness Robe, no hut, no mirror, begging at houses of village.

2000 Nirvana and willed death beyond death.

. . . .

Written in August and September 1955, during a stay in Mexico, Mexico City Blues *has been hailed as the great religious poem of the twentieth century. The following is a selection from the poem's 242 choruses.*

119TH CHORUS

Self be your lantern,
        Self be your guide—
                Thus Spake Tathagata
                    Warning of radios
                        That would come
                            Some day
                                And make people
                                    Listen to automatic
                                        Words of others

and the general flash of noises,
forgetting self, not-self—
Forgetting the secret . . .

Up on high in the mountains so high
        the high magic priests are
                swabbing in the deck
                    of broken rib torsos
                        cracked in the rack
                            of

Kallaquack
tryin to figure yr way
outa the calamity of dust and
eternity, buz, you better
get on back to your kind
b o a t

126TH CHORUS

Like running a stick thru water
The use and effect
Of tellin people that
their house
is burning,
And that the Buddha, an old
And wise father
Will save them by holy
subterfuge,

Crying: "Out, out, little ones,
The fire will burn you!
I promise to give you fine
carts
Three in number, different,
Charming, the goat cart,
The deer cart, and
The cart of the bullock

Gayly bedecked—With oranges,
Flowers, holy maidens & trees,"
So the children rush out, saved,
And he gives them
The incomparable single Greatcart
Of the White Bullock, all snow.

226TH CHORUS

There is no Way to lose.
If there was a way,
    then,
        when sun is shining on pond
        and I go West, thou East,
        which one does the true sun
        follow?
        which one does the true one
        borrow?
        since neither one is the true one,
        there is no true one way.
        And the sun is the delusion
        Of a way multiplied by two
        And multiplied millionfold.
Since there is no Way, no Buddhas,
No Dharmas, no Conceptions,
Only One Ecstasy—
        And Right Mindfulness
        Is mindfulness that the way is No-Way—
            Anyhow Sameway—
Then what am I to do
        Beyond writing this instructing
        Poesy, ride a magic carpet
        Of self ecstasy, or wait
        For death like the children
        In the Funeral Street after
        The black bus has departed—
        Or—what?

. . . .

From Visions of Gerard, *a novel written in January 1956 about Kerouac's older brother Gerard, who died at the age of nine from a rheumatic heart. "Ti Jean" is Kerouac and "Ti Nin" is Kerouac's sister Caroline.*

[. . .] Gerard comes slowly ruminating in the bright morn among the happy children—Today his mind is perplexed and he looks up into the perfect cloudless empty blue and wonders what all the bruiting and furor is below, what all the yelling, the buildings, the humanity, the concern—"Maybe there's nothing at all," he divines in his lucid pureness—"Just like the smoke that comes out of Papa's pipe"—"The pictures that the smoke makes"—"All I gotta do is close my eyes and it all goes away"—"There *is* no Mama, no Ti Jean, no Ti Nin, Papa—no me—no *kitigi*" (the cat)—"There is no earth—look at the perfect sky, it says nothing [. . .] "

. . .

[. . .] Gerard was inward turned like a chalice of gold bearing a single holy host, bounden to his glory doom—He sits on the little wall contemplating the kids, and the bum in the field, the nuns in the window, the little girls hopskotching beyond and where Ti Nin is screaming with the rest—"Little crazy, look at her gettin all excited—she doesnt understand the blue sky this morning, she doesnt care like a little kitty—But look—" he looks up, mouth agape—"There's nothing there, not a cloud, not a sound—just like it was water upside-down and what's the bugs down here?" The air is crisp and good, he breathes it in—The bell rings and all the scufflers go to shuffle in the dreary lines of class by class with the head nun overlooking all, the parade ground formation of the new day, latecomers running thru the yard with flying books—A dog barking, and the coughs, and the gritty gravel under restless many little shoes—Another day of school—But Gerard has eyes up to sky and knows he'll never learn in school what he'd like to learn this morning from that sky of silent mystery, that heartbreaking sayless blank that wont tell men and boys what's up—
"It's eye of God, there's no bottom—"

"Gerard Duluoz, you're not in line—!"

"Yes, Sister Marie."

"Silence! The Mother *Supérieure* is going to talk!"

"Ssst! Mercier! Give me my card!"

"It's mine!"

"It is not!"

"Shut your trap! (*Famme ta guêle*)."

"I'll fix you."

"P r r r r t"

"Silence!"

Silence over all, the rustle of the wind, the banners of two hundred hearts are still—Under that liquid everpresent impossible-to-understand undefiled blue—

. . .

Hearken, amigos, to the olden message: it's neither what you think it is, nor what you think it isnt, but an elder matter, uncompounded and clear—Pigs may rut in field, come running to the Soo-Call, full of sow-y glee; people may count themselves higher than pigs, and walk proudly down country roads; geniuses may look out of windows and count themselves higher than louts; tics in the pine needles may be inferior to the swan; but whether any of these and the stone know it, it's still the same truth: none of it is even there, it's a mind movie, *believe* this if you will and you'll be saved in the solvent solution of salvation and Gerard knew it well in his dying bed in his way, in his way—And who handed us down the knowledge here of the Diamond Light? Messengers unnumberable from the Ethereal Awakened Diamond Light. And why?—because is, is—and was, was—and will be, will be—t'will!

. . .

[. . .] death is the only decent subject, since it marks the end of illusion and delusion—Death is the other side of the same coin, we call now, Life—The appearance of sweet Gerard's flower face, followed by its disappearance, alas, only a contour-maker and shadow-selector could prove it, that in all the perfect snow any such person or thing ever did arrive say Yea and go away—The whole world has no reality, it's only imaginary, and what are we to do?—Nothing—*nothing*—*nothing.* Pray to be kind, wait to be patient, try to be fine. No use screamin. The Devil was a charming fool.

In his last days Gerard had little to do but lay in bed and stare at the ceiling, and sometimes watch the cat. "Look Ti Jean, the little nut—look, he looks one way, he looks the other—Lookat the crazy face, what's he thinkin?—Everytime he sees something what does he think?—Look, he's goin in the other room. Why? What's he thinkin that makes him go in the next room? Look, now he stops, he looks—he licks himself—there, he yawns—well, now he's comin back—he's crazy—O CRAZY KITIGI! Bring him!" and I'd bring him the little grey tiger cat and we'd biddle and fwiddle with his crazy nose and stroke his head and he'd set in purring and glad. "Look at him, a little crazy ball like that, a little white belly as soft and as smooth as a heart—God made kitties I guess for us—God sent his kitties everywhere—Take care of my kitigi when I'm gone," he adds holding kitigi to his face and almost crying.

"Where you goin?"

No answer.

. . .

I dont remember how Gerard died, but (in my memory, which is limited and mundane) here I am running pellmell out of the house about 4 o'clock in the afteernoon and down the sidewalk of Beaulieu Street yelling to my father whom I've seen coming around the corner woeful and slow with strawhat back and coat over arms in the summer heat, gleefully I'm yelling "*Gerard est mort!*" (Gerard is dead!) as tho it was some great event that would make a change that would make everything better, which it actually was, which granted it actually was.

But I thought it had something to do with some holy transformation that would make him greater and more Gerard like—He would reappear, following his "death," so huge and all powerful and renewed—The dizzy brain of the four-year-old, with its visions and infold mysticisms —I grabbed Pa and tugged his hand and glee'd to see the expression of likewise gladness on his face, so when he wearily just said "I know, Ti Pousse, I know" I had that same feeling that I have today when I would rush and tell people the good news that Nirvana,

Heaven, our Salvation is *Here* and *Now,* that gloomy reaction of theirs, which I can only attribute to pitiful and so-to-be-loved Ignorance of mortal brains.

"I know, my little wolf, I know," and sadly he drags himself into the house as I dance after.

. . . .

From The Scripture of the Golden Eternity, *written in May 1956 in response to Gary Snyder's suggestion that Kerouac write a sutra.*

1

Did I create that sky? Yes, for, if it was
anything other than a conception in my mind
I wouldnt have said "Sky"—That is why I am the
golden eternity. There are not two of us here,
reader and writer, but one, one golden eternity,
One-Which-It-Is, That-Which-Everything-Is.

2

The awakened Buddha to show the way, the
chosen Messiah to die in the degradation
of sentience, is the golden eternity. One that
is what is, the golden eternity, or God, or,
Tathagata—the *name*. The Named One.
The human god. Sentient Godhood.
Animate Divine. The Deified One.
The Verified One. The Free One.
The Liberator. The Still One.
The Settled One. The Established One.
Golden Eternity. All is Well.
The Empty One. The Ready One.
The Quitter. The Sitter.
The Justified One. The Happy One.

3

That sky, if it was anything other than an
illusion of my mortal mind I wouldnt have said
"that sky." Thus I made that sky, I am the
golden eternity. I am Mortal Golden Eternity.

. . . .

27

Discard such definite imaginations of phenomena
as your own self, thou human being, thou'rt a
numberless mass of sun-motes: each mote a shrine.
The same as to your shyness of other selves,
selfness as divided into infinite numbers of beings,
or selfness as identified as one self existing
eternally. Be obliging and noble, be generous
with your time and help and possessions, and be
kind, because the emptiness of this little place
of flesh you carry around and call your soul,
your entity, is the same emptiness in every direction
of space unmeasurably emptiness, the same, one,
and holy emptiness everywhere: why be selfly and
unfree, Man God, in your dream? Wake up, thou'rt
selfless and free. "Even and upright your mind
abides nowhere," states Hui Neng of China.
We're all in Heaven now.

. . . .

46

O Everlasting Eternity, all things and all truth
laws are no-things, in three ways, which is the
same way: AS THINGS OF TIME they dont

exist and never came, because they're already gone and there is no time. AS THINGS OF SPACE they dont exist because there is no furthest atom than can be found or weighed or grasped, it is emptiness through and through, matter and empty space too. AS THINGS OF MIND they dont exist, because the mind that conceives and makes them out does so by seeing, hearing, touching, smelling, tasting, and mentally-noticing and without this mind they would not be seen or heard or felt or smelled or tasted or mentally-noticed, they are discriminated from that which they're not necessarily by imaginary judgments of the mind, they are actually dependent on the mind that makes them out, by themselves they are no-things, they are really mental, seen only of the mind, they are really empty visions of the mind, heaven is a vision, everything is a vision. What does it mean that I am in this endless universe thinking I'm a man sitting under the stars on the terrace of earth, but actually empty and awake throughout the emptiness and awakedness of everything? It means that I am empty and awake, knowing that I am empty and awake, and that there's no difference between me and anything else. It means that I have attained to that which everything is.

. . . .

62

This world has no marks, signs or evidence of existence, nor the noises in it, like accident of wind or voices or heehawing animals, yet listen closely the eternal hush of silence goes on and on throughout all this, and has been going on, and will go on and on. this is because the world is nothing but a dream and is just thought of and the everlasting eternity pays no attention to it. At night under the moon, or in a quiet room, hush now, the secret music of the Unborn goes on and on, beyond conception, awake beyond existence. Properly speaking, awake is not really awake because the golden eternity never went to sleep: you can tell by the constant sound of Silence which cuts through this world like a magic diamond through the trick of your not realizing that your mind caused the world.

. . . .

In Old Angel Midnight, *Kerouac attempted to use automatic writing to achieve a kind of Joycean experimental prose, one that followed sound more than sense. He used port wine and the meditative technique of letting go of his thoughts to loosen him up to write in this free-form style. In this passage, in which Kerouac muses on warrior ants, he seems to be improvising on a theme that Thoreau explored in* Walden. *Watching the struggling ants, Thoreau wrote, "I was myself excited somewhat even as if they had been men. The more you think of it, the less the difference."*

The black ants that roosted in my tree all winter long have just emerged to meet an army of enemy ants (same breed) & a big war is now taking place, I just looked with my brakemans lamp (by sunlight) (brake the day sun) warriors are biting each other's sensitive rear humps & killing each other with more intelligence about murder than my boot knows—I squashed one wounded warrior whose poor right front armorer was missing & he just croualtad coupled there, I hated to see him suffer & he was open (ow) for attack too, bit safe a mo on a flat rock used for lady's flagstones in the pink tea world which ignores ant Wars & doesnt know that when the first space ship lands on the planet Amtasagrak (really

Katapatafaya in other galuxies) the ship will immediately be swarmed over by black ants, even the window obscured, they'll have to turn their X-Roentgen Gun Ray on it to see & what they'll see'll make em wish Von Braun had stayed in brown germany: one sextillion sextillion idiot insect fiends a foot deep eating one another endlessly the top ones scuffling, the next layer dead & being nibbled, the next layer belly to belly cant move from the weight, & the bottom layer suffocated at last—& the lady ants have wings & fly to little tiny planets that hang six feet above the moiling black shiny ant sea, where they hatch, push the grownup kids off (into the Mess) & die Sighing for Paradise O ye singers of War & Glory

After seeing a thing like this who wd dare not ask for enlightenment everywhere? Who will deny ant war with me?

Meanwhile in my yard the triumphant winning warrior ant stands over his defeated dying brother & you see his little antled helmet waving in the glorious breeze like How Ta Ra the trumpets of Harfleur & (you know what I was going to say there—hm—) no compassion in these little febrile finicular skeleton—O Ant Soup!

. . . .

In early May 1954, Kerouac had written to Allen Ginsberg proposing that he become Ginsberg's guide to Buddhist teaching. He urged him to "listen to me carefully and implicitly as tho I was Einstein teaching you relativity or Eliot teaching the Formulas of Objective Correlation on a blackboard in Princeton." He also provided Ginsberg with an extensive reading list of Buddhist texts in translation. In this letter, which dates from January of 1955, Kerouac adopts a more humble attitude and suggests that he is not yet qualified to instruct Ginsberg but predicts that someday he and Ginsberg will both teach the dharma.

. . . Now, as to my being master, and you disciple—I'm only a Junior Arhat not yet free from the intoxicants. The danger of my being a Teacher is twofold:

1) I'm too ignorant still to give the true teaching and am only in the early stages of vow-making, not actual turning-about within.

2) The teaching may & will be appreciated by intelligent but insincere poseurs who will use it for their own terrestrices and evil and heretical ends—This includes myself—i.e. a poet using Buddhist images for his own advantage instead of for spreading the Law. As if you would bruit Buddha abroad in Rome. In the Sutra it says that you must vow to rebirth in all forms and keep your Bodhisattva-Mahasattvahood a secret speaking not without discretion (as I've been doing) before those who are not practising meditation, "except toward the end of your mortal life you may disclose to your most worthy fellow disciples the secret teachings and instruction lest the evil heretics disturb and lure them away by their lies." The Sixth Patriarch story, as you may not know, ends with the fifth Patriarch secretly rowing him across the river on that same night and bidding him run and hide among the hunters in the caves, saying, "You may start on your journey now; go as fast as you can toward the South. Do not begin preaching too soon; Buddhism is not to be easily spread." EVIL-DOERS DO PERSECUTE. This is clear to me now. I've recently been informed on to the police, by phone, and again arrested. The culprit is some fool of ignorance.

We are fellow disciples before the Awesome Law, not master and student.

Besides, I'm too young and bashful at present to take on the role of Master and too softheaded and fearful to undertake the burdensome job of officially rowing the Yana-ferry back and forth across the spectral stream. Later I will do so, and so you also. I know this. We will be justified in Heaven. In the living world, I am like an Imbecile. (I am, at least, while you make psychiatric efforts to "straighten out" and "adjust" to Ignorance.) In the Bright Room, I am not an Imbecile, but the Holy Tathagata whose body is not measurable and is all the universe, who knows that all this is but a Mental Womb.

. . . .

From a letter written to Allen Ginsberg on January 18, 1955. In it Kerouac tries to answer Ginsberg's request for more specifics as to what "signposts" to look for when meditating.

Now let me give you this: on the subway yesterday, as I read the Diamond Sutra, not that, the Surangama Sutra, I realized that everybody in the subway and all their thoughts and interests and the subway itself and their poor shoes and gloves etc. and the cellophane paper on the floor and the poor dust in the corners was all of one suchness and essence. I thought, "Mind essence loves everything, because it knows why everything is." And I saw that these people, and myself to a lesser extent, all were buried in selfhood which we took to be real . . . but the only real is the One, the One Essence that all's made of, and so we also took our limited and perturbed and contaminated minds (hankering after appointments, worries, sorrows, love) to be our own True Mind, but I saw True Mind itself, Universal and One, entertains no arbitrary ideas about these different seeming self-hangs on form, mind is IT itself, the IT . . . The cellophane, when I looked at it, was like my little brother, I really loved it . . . so saw that if I sat with the True Mind and forgot myself and its limited mind and imagined and set-up sufferings (that as you know vanish at death) (like Melville's loomings on street 100 years ago in dark America with ice and snow on sidewalk that if he didnt have BODY he'd a fallen through endless space) (no sidewalk even) (all empty, hallucination of forms). If I sit with True Mind and like Chinese sit with Tao and not with self but by no-self submission with arms hanging to let the karma work itself out, I will gain enlightenment by seeing the world as a poor dream.

This is not bullshit I really believe this and not only that I will prove it to you at some time or other. As to your going to desert, it ain't necessary (scorpions in yr. pockets). It is for me, if it turns out to be the way of really Samboghakaya [the bliss of the Buddha] staying-with-it all the time then I'll tell you and then it will be time to say you should do it. But nothing I can do to change your own vision of sad love which is after all Sebastian's and the other night I realized that when Sebastian died on Anzio he probably did so by rushing through bullets to aid wounded comrade (he was medic) and died a Tathagata [enlightened being] in his sad Charles Boyer Algiers hospital. Who knows? Yet there is no other way but sitting. The trick is dhyana [sitting meditation], twice a day. That's the trick. I'll hip you, as you ask, on "specific bodily and mental insight signposts."[. . .]

Drink a small cup of tea. Lock door first, then place pillow on bed, pillow against wall, fold feet, lean, erect posture, let all breath out of lungs and take in new lungful, close eyes gently and begin not only breathing gently like little child but listening to intrinsic sound of silence which as you know is the sea-sound shh under noises which are accidental. It's the sound of the imaginariness of the scene—the mind-sound of mind-stuff everywhere. This is Tathagatas singing to me. To you too. This is the only Teaching. Babes hear it. It never began, never will end. Tathagata means "He who has thus come and thus gone." That is, the essence of Buddha-hood. The first signpost is, that after 5,10 minutes you feel a sudden bliss at gentle exhalation and your muscles have long relaxed and your stomach stopped and breathing is slow. This bliss of out-breathing means you are entering samadhi. But dont grasp at it. The bliss is physical and mental. Now you're no longer interested in sounds, sights, eyes closed, ears receptive but non-discriminatory. Itches may rise to make you scratch; dont scratch them; they are imaginary, like the world; they are "the work of Mara the tempter" in yourself, trying to delude you and make you break up your samadhi. As the breathing is blissful, now listen to diamond sound of "eternity," now gaze at the Milky Way in your eyelids (which is neither bright nor dark, entertains neither arbitrary conception of sight). Body forgotten, restful, peaceful. I mention the tea, it was invented by Buddhists in 300 B.C. for this very purpose, for dhyana. As bliss comes realize by INTUITION (this is where we leave the X) the various understandings you have concerning the day's activities and the long night of life in general, their unreality, eeriness, dream-ness, like Harlem Vision [a mystical vision Ginsberg had in 1948 in which he heard the voice of William Blake reciting a poem] again. Then if you wish, use a lil tantrism to stop thought; to stop thought you may say "This thinking is Stopped" at each outbreath or "It's all Imaginary" or "Mind Essence loves Everything" or "It's only a Dream" or "Adoration to the Tathagata of No-Contact" (meaning no contact with thoughts). By cutting off contacts with thoughts, their clinging ceases; they come and go, certes, like dreams in sleep, but you no longer honor their forms, because you're honoring Essence. By a half hour of this a further bliss seeps in. But then there are leg-pains. Try often to stand the leg-pain as long as possible to dig that when it seems unbearable; at that instant, you can take it just one minute more, and suddenly during a few seconds of that minute, you forget cold about the pain, proving their imaginariness in Mind. But hung with body you have to come out. Try continuing with legs out, or better, rest, rub them, and start again . . . Practice ONE long dhyana a day, because it takes 20 minutes to quiet the machine motor of the mind. It's simply by dhyana that you'll come to what you seek to find because that in itself is, like in my vision of the subway, abiding "in self-less oneness with the suchness that is Tathagatahood" (emptiness, rest, eternal peace).

. . . .

Kerouac begins this letter, written to Allen Ginsberg on July 14, 1955, by insisting that Ginsberg abandon his studies of Ezra Pound and learn instead to translate sutras from Sanskrit: "How many times do I have to tell you that it's a Buddhist, AN EASTERN FUTURE ahead." In the following excerpt, Kerouac goes on to envision a solitary, hermetic life for himself. There is no reference in any existing biographical studies to indicate whether or not Kerouac ever made his planned visit to the Buddhist monastery that he mentions in this letter.

Turns out that all my final favorite writers (Dickinson, Blake, Thoreau) ended up their lives in little hermitages . . . Emily in her cottage, Blake in his, with wife; and Thoreau his hut . . . This I think will be my truly final move . . . tho I don't know where yet. It depends on how much money I can get. If I had all the money in the world, I would still prefer a humble hut. I guess in Mexico. Al Sublette once said what I wanted was a thatched hut in Lowell, a real wild thing to say, anyways, I was headed strait for Mex City but now that Gene has sent the 25 I can afford Frisco and will come. I look forward to talks. Also chow mein and wine. Also walks. Neal. Maybe miss greenie. Also I want to spend one week in the riverbottom at Chittenden pass. Also a week on the Santa Barbara channel coast. Also I want to visit the Buddhist Monastery at 60 Las Encinas Lane, Santa Barbara. Also I might try bhikkuing in early Salinas riverbottom near Wunpost, very wild country. I just want to find some place, where, if I feel like being in a trance all day and don't wanta move for nothin, nobody there to stop me, nothin to stop me. I *know* that the secret lies in the old Yoga secrets of India, let alone Dhyana, and that any man who does not, as you, practice Dhyana, is simply wandering in the dark. The mind has its own intrinsic brightness but it's only revealable when you stop thinking and let the body melt away. The longer you can hold this position of Cessation in Light, the greater everything (which is Nothing) gets, the diamond sound of rich shh gets louder, almost frightening;—the transcendental sensation of being able to see through the world like glass, clearer; etc. All yr. senses become purified and yr. mind returns to its primal, unborn, original state of Perfection . . . Don't you remember before you were born?

Read, as I'm doing, the Diamond Sutra every day, Sunday read the Dana Charity chapter; Monday, Sila kindness; Tuesday,

Kshanti patience; Wednesday, Virya Zeal; Thursday, Dyana tranquility; Friday, Prajna wisdom, Saturday, conclusion.

By living with this greatest of sutras you become immersed in the Truth that it is all One Undifferentiated Purity, creation and the phenomena, and become free from such conceptions as self, other selves, many selves, One Self, which is absurd, "selfhood is regarded as a personal possession only by terrestrial beings"—no difference between that star and this stone.

. . . .

A passage from a letter to Philip Whalen dated February 7, 1956.

I'd like to found a kind a monastery in the plateau country outside Mexico City, if I had the money—but I'll start this next Fall with the first of the buildings, my own dobe hut, windowless, with open outdoor fireplace, a rain shelter and nothing much else, you block up the windows, 20 miles outside Mexico City—it seems like a good location. But I cant imagine what my rules would be, what rules would conform with pure essence Buddhism, say. That would be, I spose, NO RULES. Pure Essence is what I think I want, and lay aside all the arbitrary rest of it, Hinayana, Shuinayana, etc. Mahayana, Zen, Shmen, here's what I want to do:

Only two things to do. One, train our mind on the emptiness aspect of things, and Two, take care of our body. Because all things are different appearances of the same emptiness. Just no more to it than that. And the knowing of this, that all things are different appearances of the same emptiness, this is bhikkuhood . . . the continual striving to know it continually, and the consequent earnest teaching of it, this bodhisattvahood. . . . and the perfect success in perfect and continual knowing of this so that it is no longer "knowing" but the Emptiness-hood itself, this is Buddhahood. The Path is knowing and struggling to know this. Too, I should add a Seventh Paramita, the Samadhi Paramita and devote every day of the calendar week to one Paramita: Sunday

Dana, Monday Sila, Tuesday Kshanti, Wednesday Zeal, Thursday Virya, Friday Prajna, Saturday Samadhi. . . . Philip, there's no difference between you and the tree and the fence, different appearances of the same (holy-if-you-will) empty essence. It is in the Hridaya Prajna Paramita, ie., like, the tree and the fence are emptiness, the tree and the fence are not different from emptiness, neither is emptiness different from the tree and the fence, indeed, emptiness is the tree & the fence. Because emptiness is everything and everything is emptiness. And even emptiness is a word, so, a prayer, the world, I mean the word emptiness is emptiness, the word emptiness is not different from emptiness, neither is emptiness different from the word emptiness, indeed, emptiness is the word emptiness!

. . . .

In a letter to Gary Snyder written on March 8, 1956, Kerouac discusses Snyder's translations of Han Shan (whose name translates as "Cold Mountain"), a seventh-century mountain mystic. Three hundred poems of Cold Mountain (Han Shan) survive; when Kerouac refers here to Cold Mountain as one of the great poems, rather than poets, of the world, he refers only to those poems Snyder translated. Kerouac also discusses a recent issue of the Berkeley Bussei, *the Buddhist magazine then edited by Will Petersen, and then goes on to predict that Buddhism will "keep moving east."*

I'm busy translating the Diamond Sutra from the English-of-the-Translators, to an English to be understood by ordinary people (who are not to be divided from the Buddha). For instance, I think "imaginary judgment" will be a good translation of "arbitrary conception," which is such a tough phrase, even I couldn't understand it with all my philological considerings . . . Dharma, would be, "truth law." Nirvana, "Blown-outness" . . . Tathata, "That-Which-Everything-Is" and Tathagata, "Attainer-To-That-Which-Everything-Is". . . . Bodhisattva-Manasattvas, "Beings of Great Wisdom"—Dipankara Buddha:

"Awakened One Dipankara". . . . I bought a little 5 & 10 black bindbook and on the tiny pages have typed out the Diamond Sutra using above "translations" and dividing the reading-chore into seven days, that is, Monday Sila Kindness, Sunday Dana Charity, etc. to Saturday Shamdhi Ecstasy (adding that 7th invisible paramita). . . . The Diamondcutter of Ideal Wisdom. . . . a splendid little Book of Prayers to fit right in the flap of my rucksack instead of that vast arbitrary Goddard Bible. . . . In the littlebook I've also typed out the Maha Prajna Paramita Hridaya and Han Shan's Cold Mountain but for simplicity's sake I used no punctuation whatever on your poem; see what you think of this stanza as such:

> I spur my horse through the wrecked town
> The wrecked town sinks my spirit
> High low old parapet walls
> Big small the aging tombs
> I waggle my shadow all alone
> Not even the crack of a shrinking coffin is heard
> I pity all these ordinary bones
> In the Book of the Immortals they're not named

How's it look? I think it's more Chinese that way. Easier to read & I love it. The more I read Cold Mountain the more I realize it to be one of the great poems of the world. In it (those few pitiful lines) are indeed packed 30 years of Prajna. The last stanzas, the last 2, are incomparable & immortal words. "Tears. . . ." "The long flowing like a sinking river" . . . . "moonlight on Cold Mountain is white. . . ."

[. . .] Am looking forward to meeting Alan Watts, his article in *Bussei* shows a genuine Buddhist sincerity which is saying a lot for a man I also thought was a bit of a fop (from sound of his voice on radio).

Phil [Whalen] sent me *Bussei* with my poem and haikus. I thought the Will Petersen article the most intelligent and very best thing in there, a really profound Buddhist it takes to say "where there is no emptiness there is no form" and to gauge that from staring at the rocks of Ryaonji. Dharmaware the Cambodian wrote a simple good one . . . to be understood by ordinary people. Your Piute Creek made me realize you're a better poet than I thought. "A clear, attentive mind/has no meaning but that/which is truly seen" previously all your poems I'd either read drunk in yr cabin or heard (drunk) recited in town . . . Now, in peace of woods, I read your "No one loves rock, yet we are here," and I nod. "All the junk that goes with being human/drops away"— There will be some poetry of considerable interest and Buddhist importance, comin out of you in Japan, I predict. I don't want to flatter you or make imaginary judgments, however, for you're really beyond praise or blame. Nakamura is right about religious freedom in the west was not so hot . . . Alex Wayman is a brisk forthright scholar etc. It's all coming. Buddhism keeps movin east . . . it'll end up in Russia among the mad Orthodox saints . . . the Premier of Russia will embrace the Buddhists of Mongolia.

The president of the United States will meditate in the Meditation Room. And us Hsuen Tsangs and Nagarjunas and Ashvaghoshas will smile in eternity.

Prajna Prayer:

Gary here's what I hope to see before I die. A whole bunch of bhikkus are sitting in the open, one of them holds his juju beads and recites out loud, while the others follow bead by bead, he is reciting spontaneous prayers that begin with the big Buddha bead and run through the other wooden ones and the two glass beads. He goes, say, like this: "Sitting in the open is the emptiness of the Buddha bead, sitting in the open is not different from the emptiness of the Buddha bead, neither is the emptiness of the Buddha bead different from sitting in the open, indeed, the emptiness of the Buddha bead, is sitting in the open. . . . confused as to what to pray now, is emptiness; confused as to what to pray now, is not different from emptiness, neither is emptiness different from being confused as to what to pray now, indeed, emptiness is being confused as to what to pray now". . . (this on first regular wood bead) (the others follow, fingering, listening) . . . (each has his turn) (it sometimes gets charming and amusing and yet there is that continuous Praja canceling out all attributes) . . . (The disciple comes to the first glassbead) . . . "The dust in my dream last night, is emptiness of the Ananda glassbead; the dust of my dream last night is not different from the emptiness of the Ananda glassbead, neither is the emptiness of the Ananda glassbead different from the dust of my dream last night, indeed, emptiness of the Ananda glassbead is the dust of my dream last night" . . . and so on. I know this works because it's worked for me, alone, with dogs, in my Twin Tree Grove here, every night now for the past 6 weeks . . . "The bowing weeds is emptiness, the bowing weeds is not different from emptiness, neither is emptiness different from the bowing weeds, indeed, emptiness is the bowing weeds." "That nothing ever happens, is emptiness; that nothing ever happens, is not different from emptiness; neither is emptiness different from that nothing ever happens; indeed, emptiness is that nothing ever happens . . . "

. . . .

Kerouac wrote the novel Desolation Angels *in two parts. Book One was composed in 1956 and Book Two in 1961. Both of these passages are from Book One; they are based on Kerouac's time as a fire lookout on Desolation Peak in the summer of 1956. "Irwin Garden" is Allen Ginsberg. While he had greatly anticipated his time in solitude on the mountains, by the end of his short time there he referred to it as "that hated rock-top trap" and rushed running down the mountain to "the world that awaits me!"*

My toilet is a little peaked wood outhouse on the edge of a beautiful Zen precipice with boulders and rock slate and old gnarled enlightened trees, remnants of trees, stumps, torn, tortured, hung, ready to fall, unconscious, Ta Ta Ta—the door I keep jammed open with a rock, faces vast triangular mountain walls across Lightning Gorge to the east, at 8:30 A.M. the haze is sweet and pure—and dreamy—Lightning Creek mores and mores her roar—Three Fools join in, and Shull and Cinnamon feed him, and beyond, Trouble Creek, and beyond, other forests, other primitive areas, other gnarled rock, straight east to Montana—On foggy days the view from my toilet seat is like a Chinese Zen drawing in ink on silk of gray voids, I half expect to see two giggling old dharma bums, or one in rags, by the goat-horned stump, one with a broom, the other with a pen quill, writing poems about the Giggling Lings in the Fog—saying, "Hanshan, what is the meaning of the void?"

"Shihte, did you mop your kitchen floor this morning?"

"Hanshan, what is the meaning of the void?"

"Shihte, did you mop—Shihte, did you mop?"

"He he he he."

"Why do you laugh, Shihte?"

"Because my floor is mopped."

"Then what is the meaning of the void?"

Shihte picks up his broom and sweeps empty space, like I once saw Irwin Garden do—they wander off, giggling, in the fog, and all's left are the few near rocks and gnarls I can see and above, the Void goes into the Great Truth Cloud of upper fogs, not even one black sash, it is a giant vertical drawing, showing 2 little masters and then space endlessly above them—"Hanshan, where is your mop?"

"Drying on a rock."

A thousand years ago Hanshan wrote poems on cliffs like these, on foggy days like these, and Shihte swept out the monastery kitchen with a broom and they giggled together, and King's Men came from far and wide to find them and they only ran, hiding, into crevasses and caves—Suddenly I see Hanshan now appearing before my Window pointing to the east, I look that way, it's only Three Fools Creek in the morning haze, I look back, Hanshan has vanished, I look back at what he showed me, it's only Three Fools Creek in the morning haze.

What else?

. . .

[. . .] but enough! enough of rocks and trees and yalloping y-birds! I wanta to go where there's lamps and telephones and rumpled couches with women on them, where there're rich thick rugs for toes, where the drama rages all unthinking for after all would That-Which-Passes-Through-Everything ask for one or the other? —What'm I gonna do with snow? I mean real snow, that gets like ice in September so's I can no longer crunch it in my pails—I'd rather undo the back straps of red-heads dear God and roam the redbrick walls of perfidious samsara than this rash rugged ridge full of bugs that sting in harmony and mysterious earth rumbles—Ah sweet enough the afternoon naps I took i' the grass, in Silence, listening to the radar mystery—and sweet enough the last sunsets when at last I knew they were the last, dropping like perfect red seas behind the jagged rocks—No, Mexico City on a Saturday night, yea in my room with chocolates in a box and Boswell's Johnson and a bedlamp, or Paris on a Fall afternoon watching the children and the nurses in the windblown park with the iron fence and old rimed monument—yea, Balzac's grave—In Desolation, Desolation is learned, and 't's no desolation there beneath the fury of the world where all is secretly well—

. . . .

From Heaven and Other Poems, *published in 1977.*

A TV Poem

Tathata is Essence Isness
And I see it Akshobying
like innumerable moth lights
In the lavender plaster wall
behind the television forest of wires
in my sister's cool livingroom

the radiating isness not obliterated,
transcendentally seen, by either
white plaster or wall lavender
wingboards with bridge of black
and wires of Oh dots

Meanwhile the gray lost unturned on
  screen shows its gray black
And then the reflected window
  outdoor blob squares
Like silver shining
A TV show with me deep gloomily
  invited included in the
Slow motionless background
  where you cannot see
My white sea moving shirt
  of pencil on lap page

So that the scene is real
  a show of world
But through it all still I see
Transcendental (and hear) radiations
  from some pure and tranquil
Blank and empty center Screen
  of Mind's Immortal Ecstasy
And even Reynolds' Blue Boy
  on the wall over there
Bathed in holy day light
  Has his little black fly

Permeative with Buddhamoths
    and Buddha Lands
And his pale face with the
    Black hair cut
Sways, moves, force-weaver
    Middle way
     Middle
      W
      a
      y

Like a middle void hole
    cloud be decking
Human sad hat holding
    impression of
Dance—
        Attainer to Actual Isness
        Adoration to Your No Need to Move

Do nothing & ye shall soon agree

. . . .

Collected in Pomes All Sizes, *this poem was also paraphrased in* The Dharma Bums.

Poems of the Buddhas of Old

by Jean-Louis

I

The boys were sittin
In a grove of trees
Listenin to Buddy
Explainin the keys.

"Boys, I say the keys
Cause there's lots a keys
But only one door,
One hive for the bees.

So listen to me
And I'll try to tell all
As I heard it long ago
In the Pure Land Hall.

Life is like a dream,
You only think it's real
Cause you're born a sucker
For that kind of deal;

But if the Truth was known
You ain't here nohow
And neither am I
Nor that cow and sow

You see across the field
One standing silently
The other rutting ragefully
In essence so quietly.

For you good boys
With winesoaked teeth
That can't understand
These words on a heath

I'll make it simpler
Like a bottle a wine
And a good woodfire
Under the stars divine.

Now listen to me
And when you have learned
The Dharma of the Buddhas
Of old and yearned

To sit down with the truth
Under a lonesome tree
In Yuma Arizony
Or anywhere you might be

Don't thank me for telling
What was told me,
This is the Wheel I'm turning,
This is the reason I be.

Mind is the maker
For no reason at all
Of all this creation
Created to fall."

II

"Who played this cruel joke
On bloke after bloke
Packing like a rat
Across the desert flat?"

Asked Montana Slim
Gesturing to him
The buddy of the men
In this lion's den.

"Was it God got mad
Like the Indian cad
Who was only a giver
Crooked like the river?

Gave you a garden,
Let the fruit harden,
Then comes the flood
And the loss of your blood?

Pray tell us, good buddy
And don't make it muddy
Who played this trick
On Harry and Dick

And why is so mean
The Eternal scene,
Just what's the point
Of this whole joint?"

III

Replied the good buddy:
"So now the bird's asleep
And that air plane gone
Let's all listen deep.

Everybody silent
Includin me
To catch the roar
Of eternity

That's ringin in our ears
Never-endingly.
You hear it Tom, Dick
And Harry Lee?

You hear it Slim
From Old Montan'?
You hear it Big Daddy
And Raggedy Dan?

You know what I mean
When I say eternity?
You heard it in your crib—
Shhh—Infinity."

IV

Up spoke Big Daddy
From Baltimore
An enormous Negro
Forevermore:

"You mean that shushin
And that fussin
A-slushin in my ears
For all these years?

When I was so high
Jess a little guy
I thought it was me
In the whisperin sea.

I asked my Mam
About that jam,
She didn't say nothin,
She sewed the button.

It was quiet and late
At the afternoon grate.
Her face showed no sign
Of that whisperin line

But as we sat waitin
Instead of abatin
The noise got to roar
Like an openin door

That opened my haid
Like if it was daid
And the only thing alive
Was that boomin jive

And we looked at each other
Child and mother
Like wakin from a dream
In a spirit stream."

V

"Well spoken, Big Daddy!"
Cried the buddy real glad.
"This proves that you know
And you'll never be sad.

For that was the sound
That we all hear now
And I want you to know
It's no sound nohow

But the absence of sound
Clear and pure,
The silence now heard
In heaven for sure.

What's heaven?
By Nirvana mean I?
This selfsame no-sound
Silence sigh

Eternal and empty
Of sounds and things
And all thievin rivers
Complainin brings.

For if we can sit here
In this riverbottom sand
And come to see
And understand

That we got in us
Ability to hear
Holy Emptiness
Beyond the ear

And block our ears
And hear inside
And know t'aint here
Nor there, the tide,

But everywhere, inside,
Outside, all throughout
Mind's dream, Slim?
What you gripin about?

Imaginary rivers
And gardens too,
A movie in the mind
Of me and you.

The point
Of this whole joint
Is stop, sit,
And thee anoint

With teachings such
As these, and more,
To find the key
Out this dark corridor.

The effulgent door,
The mysterious knob,
The bright room gained
Is the only job."

The boys was pleased
And rested up for more
And Jack cooked mush
In honor of the Door.

. . . .

Kerouac wrote The Dharma Bums *in November 1957, while* On the Road *was on the best-seller list. His portrait of Gary Snyder (renamed "Japhy Ryder")—which included a lengthy description of Snyder's vision of a "rucksack revolution"—inspired many young people in the counterculture of the sixties to reject a life of materialism and, instead, journey to Asia in pursuit of spiritual training. The novel goes on to chronicle the wanderings of Ray Smith (Kerouac's pseudonym for himself), his return to his sister's home in North Carolina after his meeting with the dharma bums, and his subsequent summer trip out west in 1956 to take up his position as a fire lookout on Desolation Peak.*

The little Saint Teresa bum was the first genuine Dharma Bum I'd met, and the second was the number one Dharma Bum of them all and in fact it was he, Japhy Ryder, who coined the phrase. Japhy Ryder was a kid from eastern Oregon brought up in a log cabin deep in the woods with his father and mother and sister, from the beginning a woods boy, an axman, farmer, interested in animals and Indian lore so that when he finally got to college by hook or crook he was already well equipped for his early studies in anthropology and later in Indian myth and in the actual texts of Indian mythology. Finally he learned Chinese and Japanese and became an Oriental scholar and discovered the greatest Dharma Bums of them all, the Zen Lunatics of China and Japan. At the same time, being a Northwest boy with idealistic tendencies, he got interested in oldfashioned I.W.W. anarchism and learned to play the guitar and sing old worker songs to go with his Indian songs and general folksong interests. I first saw him walking down the street in San Francisco the following week (after hitchhiking the rest of the way from Santa Barbara in one long zipping ride given me, as though anybody'll believe this, by a beautiful darling young blonde in a snow-white strapless bathing suit and barefooted with a gold bracelet on her ankle, driving a next-year's cinnamon-red Lincoln Mercury, who wanted benzedrine so she could drive all the way to the City and when I said I had some in my duffel bag yelled "Crazy!")—I saw Japhy loping along in that curious long stride of the mountainclimber, with a small knapsack on his back filled with books and toothbrushes and whatnot which was his small "goin-to-the-city" knapsack as apart from his big full rucksack complete with sleeping bag, poncho, and cookpots. He wore a little goatee, strangely Oriental-looking with his somewhat slanted green eyes, but he didn't look like a Bohemian at all, and was far from being a Bohemian (a hanger-onner around the arts). He was wiry, suntanned, vigorous, open, all howdies and glad talk and even yelling hello to bums on the street and when asked a question answered right off the bat from the top or bottom of his mind I don't know which and always in a sprightly sparkling way.

"Where did you meet Ray Smith?" they asked him when we walked into The Place, the favorite bar of the hepcats around the Beach.

"Oh I always meet my Bodhisattvas in the street!" he yelled, and ordered beers.

. . .

[. . .] Japhy was in rough workingman's clothes he'd bought secondhand in Goodwill stores to serve him on mountain climbs and hikes and for sitting in the open at night, for campfires, for hitchhiking up and down the Coast. In fact in his little knapsack he also had a funny green alpine cap that he wore when he got to the foot of a mountain, usually with a yodel, before starting to tromp up a few thousand feet. He wore mountain-climbing boots, expensive ones, his pride and joy, Italian make, in which he clomped around over the sawdust floor of the bar like an oldtime lumberjack. Japhy wasn't big, just about five foot seven, but strong and wiry and fast and muscular. His face was a mask of woeful bone, but his eyes twinkled like the eyes of old giggling sages of China, over that little goatee, to offset the rough look of his handsome face. His teeth were a little brown, from early backwoods neglect, but you never noticed that and he opened his mouth wide to guffaw at jokes. Sometimes he'd quiet down and just stare sadly at the floor, like a man whittling. He was merry at times. He showed great sympathetic interest in me and in the story about the little Saint Teresa bum and the stories I told him about my own experiences hopping freights or hitchhiking or hiking in woods. He claimed at once that I was a great "Bodhisattva," meaning "great wise being" or "great wise angel," and that I was ornamenting this world with my sincerity. We had the same favorite Buddhist saint, too: Avalokitesvara, or, in Japanese, Kwannon the Eleven-Headed. He knew all the details of Tibetan, Chinese, Mahayana, Hinayana, Japanese and even Burmese Buddhism but I warned him at once I didn't give a goddamn about the mythology and all the names and national flavors of Buddhism, but was just interested in the first of Sakyamuni's four noble truths, *All life is suffering*. And to an extent interested in the third, *The suppression of suffering can be achieved*, which I didn't quite believe was possible then. (I hadn't yet digested the Lankavatara Scripture which eventually shows you that there's nothing in the world but the mind itself, and therefore all's possible including the suppression of suffering.)

. . . .

In this passage "Warren Coughlin" (Philip Whalen) and "Alvah Goldbook" (Allen Ginsberg) discuss dharma with "Ray Smith" (Kerouac) and "Japhy Ryder" (Snyder):

Then Coughlin said "Tell 'em about Great Plum, Japh."

Instantly Japhy said "Great Plum Zen Master was asked what the great meaning of Buddhism was, and he said rush flowers, willow catkins, bamboo needles, linen thread, in other words hang on boy, the ecstasy's general, 's what he means, ecstasy of the mind, the world is nothing but mind and what is the mind? The mind is nothing but the world, goddammit. Then Horse Ancestor said 'This mind is Buddha.' He also said 'No mind is Buddha.' Then finally talking about Great Plum his boy, 'The plum is ripe.'"

"Well that's pretty interesting," said Alvah, "but Où sont les neiges d'antan?"

"Well I sort of agree with you because the trouble is these people saw the flowers like they were in a dream but dammit all the world is *real* Smith and Goldbook and everybody carries on like it was a dream, shit, like they were themselves dreams or dots. Pain or love or danger makes you real again, ain't that right Ray like when you were scared on that ledge?"

"Everything was real, okay."

"That's why frontiersmen are always heroes and were always my real heroes and will always be. They're constantly on the alert in the realness which might as well be real as unreal, what difference does it make, Diamond Sutra says 'Make no formed conceptions about the realness of existence nor about the unrealness of existence,' or words like that. Handcuffs will get soft and billy clubs will topple over, let's go on being free anyhow."

"The President of the United States suddenly grows cross-eyed and floats away!" I yell.

"And anchovies will turn to dust!" yells Coughlin.

"The Golden Gate is creaking with sunset rust," says Alvah.

"And anchovies will turn to dust," insists Coughlin.

"Give me another slug of that jug. How! Ho! Hoo!" Japhy leaping up: "I've been reading Whitman, know what he says, *Cheer up slaves, and horrify foreign despots,* he means that's the attitude for the Bard, the Zen Lunacy bard of old desert paths, see the whole thing is a world full of rucksack wanderers, Dharma Bums refusing to subscribe to the general demand that they consume production and therefore have to work for the privilege of consuming, all that crap they didn't really want anyway such as refrigerators, TV sets, cars, at least new fancy cars, certain hair oils and deodorants and general junk you finally always see a week later in the garbage anyway, all of them imprisoned in a system of work, produce, consume, work, produce, consume, I see a vision of a great rucksack revolution thousands or even millions of young Americans wandering around with rucksacks, going up to mountains to pray, making children laugh and old men glad, making young girls happy and old girls happier, all of 'em Zen Lunatics who go about writing poems that happen to appear in their heads for no reason and also by being kind and also by strange unexpected acts keep giving visions of eternal freedom to everybody and to all living creatures [. . .]"

. . . .

"Ray Smith" (Kerouac) goes to his sister's home in North Carolina, where he lived with his mother, Mémère, his sister Caroline ("Ti Nin"), his brother-in-law Paul ("Lou"), and his nephew Paul Junior ("Little Lou").

They all wanted me to sleep on the couch in the parlor by the comfortable oil-burning stove but I insisted on making my room (as before) on the back porch with its six windows looking out on the winter barren cottonfield and the pine woods beyond, leaving all the windows open and stretching my good old sleeping bag on the couch there to sleep the pure sleep of winter nights with my head buried inside the smooth nylon duck-down warmth. After they'd gone to bed I put on my jacket and my earmuff cap and railroad gloves and over all that my nylon poncho and strode out in the cottonfield moonlight like a shroudy monk. The ground was covered with moonlit frost. The old cemetery down the road gleamed in the frost. The roofs of nearby farmhouses were like white panels of snow. I went through the cottonfield rows followed by Bob, a big bird dog, and little Sandy who belonged to the Joyners down the road, and a few other stray dogs (all dogs love me) and came to the edge of the forest. In there, the previous spring, I'd worn out a little path going to meditate under a favorite baby pine. The path was still there. My official entrance to the forest was still there, this being two evenly spaced young pines making kind of gate posts. I always bowed there and clasped my hands and thanked Avalokitesvara for the privilege of the wood. Then I went in, led moonwhite Bob direct to my pine, where my old bed of straw was still at the foot of the tree. I arranged my cape and legs and sat to meditate.

The dogs meditated on their paws. We were all absolutely quiet. The entire moony countryside was frosty silent, not even the little tick of rabbits or coons anywhere. An absolute cold blessed silence. Maybe a dog barking five miles away toward Sandy Cross. Just the faintest, faintest sound of trucks rolling out the night on 301, about twelve miles away, and of course the distant occasional Diesel baugh of the Atlantic Coast Line passenger and freight trains going north and south to New York and Florida. A blessed night. I immediately fell into a blank thoughtless trance wherein it was again revealed to me "This thinking has stopped" and I sighed because I didn't have to think any more and felt my whole body sink into a blessedness surely to be believed, completely relaxed and at peace with all the ephemeral world of dream and dreamer and the dreaming itself.

. . .

But my serenity was finally disturbed by a curious argument with my brother-in-law; he began to resent my unshackling Bob the dog and taking him in the woods with me. "I've got too much money invested in that dog to untie him from his chain."

I said "How would you like to be tied to a chain and cry all day like the dog?"

He replied "It doesn't bother *me*" and my sister said "And *I* don't care."

I got so mad I stomped off into the woods, it was a Sunday afterrnoon, and resolved to sit there without food till midnight and come back and pack my things in the night and leave.

. . .

In the woods again that night, fingering the juju beads, I went through curious prayers like these: "My pride is hurt, that is emptiness; my business is with the Dharma, that is emptiness; I'm proud of my kindness to animals, that is emptiness; my conception of the chain, that is emptiness; Ananda's pity, even that is emptiness" [. . .] suddenly under the tree at night, I had the astonishing idea: "Everything is empty but awake! Things are empty in time and space and mind." I figured it all out and the next day feeling very exhilarated I felt the time had come to explain everything to my family. They laughed more than anything else. "But listen! No! Look! It's simple, let me lay it out as simple and concise as I can. All things are empty, ain't they?"

"Whattayou mean, empty, I'm holding this orange in my hand, ain't I?"

"It's empty, everythin's empty, things come but to go, all things made have to be unmade, and they'll have to be unmade simply *because* they were made!"

Nobody would buy even that.

"You and your Buddha, why don't you stick to the religion you were born with?" my mother and sister said.

"Everything's gone, already gone, already come and gone," I yelled. "Ah," stomping around, coming back, "and things are empty because they appear, don't they, you see them but they're made up of atoms that can't be measured or weighed or taken hold of, even the dumb scientists know that now, there *isn't* any finding of the farthest atom so-called, things are just empty arrangements of something that seems solid appearing in the space, they ain't either big or small, near or far, true or false, they're ghosts pure and simple."

"Ghostses!" yelled little Lou amazed. He really agreed with me but he was afraid of my insistence on "Ghostses."

"Look," said my brother-in-law, "if things were empty how could I feel this orange, in fact taste it and swallow it, answer me that one."

"Your mind makes out the orange by seeing it, hearing it, touching it, smelling it, tasting it and thinking about it but without this mind, you call it, the orange would not be seen or heard or smelled or tasted or even mentally noticed, it's actually, that orange, depending on your mind to exist! Don't you see that? By itself it's a no-thing, it's really mental, it's seen only of your mind. In other words it's empty and awake."

"Well, if that's so, I still don't care." All enthusiastic I went back to the woods that night and thought, "What does it mean that I am in this endless universe, thinking that I'm a man sitting under the stars on the terrace of the earth, but actually empty and awake throughout the emptiness and awakedness of everything? It means that I'm empty and awake, that I *know* I'm empty, awake, and that there's no difference between me and anything else. In other words it means that I've become the same as everything else."

. . . .

From "Ray Smith's" (Kerouac's) time on Desolation Peak:

Lo, in the morning I woke up and it was beautiful blue sunshine sky and I went out in my alpine yard and there it was, everything Japhy said it was, hundreds of miles of pure snow-covered rocks and virgin lakes and high timber, and below, instead of the world, I saw a sea of marshmallow clouds flat as a roof and extending miles and miles in every direction, creaming all the valleys, what they call low-level clouds, on my

6600-foot pinnacle it was all far below me. I brewed coffee on the stove and came out and warmed my mist-drenched bones in the hot sun of my little woodsteps. I said "Tee tee" to a big furry cony and he calmly enjoyed a minute with me gazing at the sea of clouds. I made bacon and eggs, dug a garbage pit a hundred yards down the trail, hauled wood and identified landmarks with my panoramic and firefinder and named all the magic rocks and clefts, names Japhy had sung to me so often: Jack Mountain, Mount Terror, Mount Fury, Mount Challenger, Mount Despair, Golden Horn, Sourdough, Crater Peak, Ruby, Mount Baker bigger than the world in the western distance, Jackass Mountain, Crooked Thumb Peak, and the fabulous names of the creeks: Three Fools, Cinnamon, Trouble, Lightning and Freezeout. And it was all mine, not another human pair of eyes in the world were looking at this immense cycloramic universe of matter. I had a tremendous sensation of its dreamlikeness which never left me all that summer and in fact grew and grew, especially when I stood on my head to circulate my blood, right on top of the mountain, using a burlap bag for a head mat, and then the mountains looked like little bubbles hanging in the void upsidedown. In fact I realized they were upsidedown and I was upsidedown! There was nothing here to hide the fact of gravity holding us all intact upsidedown against a surface globe of earth in infinite empty space. And suddenly I realized I was truly alone and had nothing to do but feed myself and rest and amuse myself, and nobody could criticize. The little flowers grew everywhere around the rocks, and no one had asked them to grow, or me to grow.

. . .

Then would come wild lyrical drizzling rain, from the south, in the wind, and I'd say "The taste of rain, why kneel?" and I'd say "Time for hot coffee and a cigarette, boys," addressing my imaginary bhikkus. The moon became full and huge and with it came Aurora Borealis over Mount Hozomeen ("Look at the void and it is even stiller," Han Shan had said in Japhy's translation); and in fact I was so still all I had to do was shift my crossed legs in the alpine grass and I could hear the hoofs of deers running away somewhere. Standing on my head before bedtime on that rock roof of the moonlight I could indeed see that the earth was truly upsidedown and man a weird vain beetle full of strange ideas walking around upsidedown and boasting, and I could realize that man remembered why this dream of planets and plants and Plantagenets was built out of the primordial essence. Sometimes I'd get mad because things didn't work out well, I'd spoil a flapjack, or slip in the snowfield while getting water, or one time my shovel went sailing down into the gorge, and I'd be so mad I'd want to bite the mountaintops and would come in the shack and kick the cupboard and hurt my toe. But let the mind beware, that though the flesh be bugged, the circumstances of existence are pretty glorious.

. . . .

An excerpt from On the Origins of a Generation, *published in* Playboy, *June 1959.*

Recently Ben Hecht said to me on TV "Why are you afraid to speak out your mind, what's wrong with this country, what is everybody afraid of?" Was he talking to me? And all he wanted me to do was speak out my mind *against* people, he sneeringly brought up Dulles, Eisenhower, the Pope, all kinds of people like that habitually he would sneer at with Drew Pearson, *against* the world he wanted, this is his idea of freedom, he calls it freedom. Who knows, my God, but that the universe is not one vast sea of compassion actually, the veritable holy honey, beneath all this show of personality and cruelty. In fact who knows but that it isn't the solitude of the oneness of the essence of everything, the solitude of the actual oneness of the unbornness of the unborn essence of everything, nay the true pure foreverhood, that big blank potential that can ray forth anything it wants from its pure store, that blazing bliss, *Mattivajrakaruna* the Transcendental Diamond Compassion!

No, I want to speak *for* things, for the crucifix I speak out, for the Star of Israel I speak out, for the divinest man who ever lived who was a German (Bach) I speak out, for sweet Mohammed I speak out, for Buddha I speak out, for Lao-tse and Chuang-tse I speak out, for D. T. Suzuki I speak out . . . why should I attack what I love out of life. This is Beat. Live your lives out? Naw, *love* your lives out. When they come and stone you at least you won't have a glass house, just your glassy flesh.

. . .

[. . .] in 1955 I published an excerpt from *Road* (melling it with parts of *Visions of Neal*) under the pseudonym "Jean-Louis," it was entitled *Jazz of the Beat Generation* and was copyrighted as being an excerpt from a novel-in-progress entitled *Beat Generation* (which I later changed to *On the Road* at the insistence of my new editor) and so then the term moved a little faster. The term and the cats. Everywhere began to appear strange hepcats and even college kids went around hep and cool and using the terms I'd heard on Times Square in the early Forties, it was growing somehow. But when the publishers finally took a dare and published *On the Road* in 1957 it burst open, it mushroomed, everybody began yelling about a Beat Generation. I was being interviewed everywhere I went for "what I meant" by such a thing. People began to call themselves beatniks, beats, jazzniks, bopniks, bugniks and finally I was called the "avatar" of all this.

Yet it was as a Catholic, it was not at the insistence of any of these "niks" and certainly not with their approval either, that I went one afternoon to the church of my childhood (one of them), Ste. Jeanne d'Arc in Lowell, Mass., and suddenly with tears in my eyes and had a vision of what I must have really meant with "Beat" anyhow when I heard the holy silence in the church (I was the only one in there, it was five p.m., dogs were barking outside, children yelling, the fall leaves, the candles were flickering alone just for me), the vision of the word Beat as being to mean beatific. . . . There's the priest preaching on Sunday morning, all of a sudden through a side door of the church comes a group of Beat Generation characters in strapped raincoats like the I.R.A. coming in silently to "dig" the religion . . . I knew it then.

But this was 1954, so then what horror I felt in 1957 and later 1958 naturally to suddenly see "Beat" being taken up by everybody, press and TV and Hollywood borscht circuit to include the "juvenile delinquency" shot and the horrors of a mad teeming billyclub New York and L.A. and they began to call *that* Beat, *that* beatific. . . . Bunch of fools marching against the San Francisco Giants protesting baseball, as if (now) in my name and I, my childhood ambition to be a big league baseball star hitter like Ted Williams so that when Bobby Thomson hit that homerun in 1951 I trembled with joy and couldn't get over it for days and wrote poems about how it is possible for the human spirit to win after all! Or, when a murder, a routine murder took place in North Beach, they labeled it a Beat Generation slaying although in my childhood I'd been famous as an eccentric in my block for stopping the younger kids from throwing rocks at the squirrels, for stopping them from frying snakes in cans or trying to blow up frogs with straws. Because my brother had died at the age of nine, his name was Gerard Kerouac, and he'd told me "Ti Jean never hurt any any living being, all living beings whether it's just a little cat or squirrel or whatever, all, are going to heaven straight into God's snowy arms so never hurt anything and if you see anybody hurt anything stop them as best you can" and when he died a file of gloomy nuns in black from St. Louis de France parish had filed (1926) to his deathbed to hear his last words about Heaven. And my father, too, Leo, had never lifted a hand to punish me, or to punish the little pets in our house, and this teaching was delivered to me by the men in my house and I have never had anything to do with violence, hatred, cruelty, and all that horrible nonsense which, nevertheless, because God is gracious beyond all human imagining, he will forgive in the long end . . . that million years I'm asking about you, America.

And so now they have beatnik routines on TV, starting with satires about girls in black and fellows in jeans with snap-knives and sweatshirts and swastikas tattooed under their armpits, it will come to respectable m.c.s of spectaculars coming out nattily attired in Brooks Brothers jean-type tailoring and sweater-type pull-ons, in other words, it's a simple change in fashion and manners, just a history crust—like from the Age of Reason, from old Voltaire in a chair to romantic Chatterton in the moonlight—from Teddy Roosevelt to Scott Fitzgerald . . . so there's nothing to get excited about. Beat comes out, actually, of old American whoopee and it will only change a few dresses and pants and make chairs useless in the livingroom and pretty soon we'll have Beat Secretaries of State and there will be instituted new tinsels, in fact new reasons for malice and new reasons for virtue and new reasons for forgiveness. . . .

But yet, but yet, woe, woe unto those who think that the Beat Generation means crime, delinquency, immorality, amorality . . . woe unto those who attack it on the grounds that they simply don't understand history and the yearnings of human souls . . . woe unto those who don't realise that America must, will, is, changing now, for the better I say. Woe unto those who believe in the atom bomb, who believe in hating mothers and fathers, who deny the most important of the Ten Commandments, woe unto those (though) who don't believe in the unbelievable sweetness of sex love, woe unto those who are the standard bearers of death, woe unto those who believe in conflict and horror and violence and fill our books and screens and livingrooms with that crap, woe in fact unto those who make evil movies about the Beat Generation where innocent housewives are raped by beatniks! Woe unto those who are the real dreary sinners that even God finds room to forgive. . . .

Woe unto those who spit on the Beat Generation, the wind'll blow it back.

. . . .

From Scattered Poems, *a collection published in 1970. These poems were written from 1956 to 1968 and published earlier in a variety of periodicals, including the* Berkeley Bussei.

The "Haiku" was invented and developed over hundreds of years in Japan to be a complete poem in seventeen syllables and to pack in a whole vision of life in three short lines. A "Western Haiku" need not concern itself with the seventeen syllables since Western languages cannot adapt themselves to the fluid syllabillic Japanese. I propose that the "Western Haiku" simply say a lot in three short lines in any Western language.

Above all, a Haiku must be very simple and free of all poetic trickery and make a little picture and yet be as airy and graceful as a Vivaldi Pastorella. Here is a great Japanese Haiku that is simpler and prettier than any Haiku I could ever write in any language: —J. K.

A day of quiet gladness,—
Mount Fuji is veiled
In misty rain.
(Basho) (1644–1694)

Here is another:

She has put the child to sleep,
And now washes the clothes;
The summer moon.
(Issa) (1763–1827)

And another, by Buson (1715–1783):

The nightingale is singing,
Its small mouth
Open.

Some Western Haikus

Jack Kerouac

Birds singing
  in the dark
—Rainy dawn.

—

Missing a kick
  at the icebox door
It closed anyway.

—

Evening coming—
  the office girl
Unloosing her scarf.

—

The rain has filled
  the birdbath
Again, almost

—

Juju beads on the
  Zen Manual:
My knees are cold.

—

In my medicine cabinet,
  the winter fly
has died of old age.

. . . .

Escapade, *a men's magazine, more well known for its pictures of scantily clad women than its essays on philosophy, was the unlikely outlet for most of Kerouac's essay writing on Buddhism. The essay excerpted here, which presents the Four Noble Truths, ran in October* 1959 *as Kerouac's regular column, "The Last Word."*

Because none of us want to think that the universe is a blank dream on account of our minds so we want *belief* and plenty names, we want lists of laws and a little bit of harrumph shouldersback separation from the faceless UGH of True Heaven, I see men now standing erect in bleaky fields waving earnest hands to explain, yet ghosts, pure naught ghosts—And even the great Chinese who've known so much for so long, will paint delicately on silk the Truth Cloud upper skies that lead off over rose-hump unbelievable mountains and crunchy trees, indefinable waterfalls of white, then the earthbound scraggle tree twisted to a rock, then, because Human Chinese, the little tiny figures of men on horseback lost in all that, usually leaving 8/10ths of the upper silk to scan th'unscannable Void—So I was wiser when I was younger after a bad love affair and sat in my lonely November room thinking: "It's all a big crrrock, I wanta die," and thinking: "The dead man's lips are pressed tasting death, as bitter as dry musk, but he might as well be tasting saccharine for all he knows," yet these thoughts didn't stand up to the Four Noble Truths as propounded by Buddha and which I memorized under a streetlamp in the cold wind of night:

(1) All Life is Sorrowful
(2) The Cause of Suffering is Ignorant Desire
(3) The Suppression of Suffering Can Be Achieved
(4) The Way is the Noble Eightfold Path
(which you might as well say is just as explicit in Bach's *Goldberg Variations.*)

Not knowing it could just as well be:

(1) All Life is Joy
(2) The Cause of Joy is Enlightened Desire
(3) The Expansion of Joy Can be Achieved
(4) The Way is the Noble Eightfold Path
since what's the difference, in supreme reality, we are neither subject to suffering nor joy—Why not?—Because who says?

But it was Asvaghosha's incomparable phrase that hooked me on the true morphine of Buddha: "REPOSE BEYOND FATE"—because since life is nothing but a short vague dream encompassed round by flesh and tears, and the ways of men are the ways of death (if not now, eventually, you'll see), the ways of beautiful women such as those pictured in this magazine are eventually the ways of old age, and since nothing we do seems to go right in the end, goes sour, but no more sour than what Nature intends in need of sour fertilizer for continuers and continuees, "repose beyond fate" meant "rest beyond what happens to you," "give it up, sit, forget it, stop thinking," YOUR OWN PRIVATE MIND IS GREATER THAN ALL—So that my first meditation was a tremendous sensation of "When did I do this last?" (it seemed so natural so right) "Why didn't I do it before?"—And all things vanished, what was left was the United Stuff out of which all things appeared to be made of without being made into anything really, all things I then saw as unsubstantial trickery of the mind, furthermore it was already long gone out of sight, the liquid waterball earth a speck in sizeless spaces [. . . .]

. . . .

The pieces in Lonesome Traveler *were written between 1958 and 1960. The following excerpt comes from a longer chapter entitled "Mexico Fellaheen," "fellaheen" being the term embraced by the Beats but which originated with Oswald Spengler in* The Decline of the West *as a word for the disenfranchised, the down-and-out, the beat.*

A FEW WEEKS LATER I go to see my first bullfight, which I must confess is a *novillera,* a novice fight, and not the real thing they show in the winter which is supposed to be so artistic. Inside it is a perfect round bowl with a neat circle of brown dirt being harrowed and raked by expert loving rakers like the man who rakes second base in Yankee Stadium only this is Bite-the-Dust Stadium.—When I sat down the bull had just come in and the orchestra was sitting down again.—Fine embroidered clothes tightly fitted to boys behind a fence.—Solemn they were, as a big beautiful shiny black bull rushed out gallumphing from a corner I hadnt looked, where he'd been apparently mooing for help, black nostrils and big white eyes and outspread horns, all chest no belly, stove polish thin legs seeking to drive the earth down with all that locomotive weight above—some people sniggered—bull galloped and flashed, you saw the riddled-up muscle holes in his perfect prize skin.—Matador stepped out and invited and the bull charged and slammed in, matador sneered his cape, let pass the horns by his loins a foot or two, got the bull revolved around by cape, and walked away like a Grandee—and stood his back to the dumb perfect bull who didnt charge like in "Blood & Sand" and lift Señor Grandee into the upper deck. Then business got underway. Out comes the old pirate horse with patch on eye, picador KNIGHT aboard with a lance, to come and dart a few slivers of steel in the bull's shoulderblade who responds by trying to lift the horse but the horse is mailed (thank God)—a historical and crazy scene except suddenly you realize the picador has started the bull on his interminable bleeding. The blinding of the poor bull in mindless vertigo is continued by the brave bowlegged little dart man carrying two darts with ribbon, here he comes head-on at the bull, the bull head-on for him, wham, no head-on crash for the dart man has stung with dart and darted away before you can say boo (& I did say boo), because a bull is hard to dodge? Good enough, but the darts now have the bull streaming with blood like Marlowe's Christ in the heavens.—An old matador comes out and tests the bull with a few capes' turn then another set of darts, a battleflag now shining down the living breathing suffering bull's side and everybody *glad.*—And now the bull's charge is just a stagger and so now the serious hero matador comes out for the kill as the orchestra goes one boom-lick on bass drum, it get quiet like a cloud passing over the sun, you hear a drunkard's bottle smash a mile away in the cruel Spanish green aromatic countryside—children pause over tortas—the bull stands in the sun head-bowed, panting for life, his sides actually *flapping* against his ribs, his shoulders barbed like San Sebastian.—The careful footed matador youth, brave enough in his own right, approaches and curses and the bull rolls around and comes stoggling on wobbly feet at the red cape, dives in with blood streaming everywhichaway and the boy just accommodates him through the imaginary hoop and circles and hangs on tiptoe, knockkneed. And Lord, I didnt want to see his smooth tight belly ranted by no horn.—He rippled his cape again at the bull who just stood there thinking "O why cant I go home?" and the matador moved closer and now the animal bunched tired legs to run but one leg slipped throwing up a cloud of dust.—But he dove in and flounced off to rest.—The matador draped his sword and called the humble bull with glazed eyes.—The bull pricked his ears and didnt move.—The matador's whole body stiffened like a board that shakes under the trample of many feet—a muscle showed in his stocking.—Bull plunged a feeble three feet and turned in dust and the matador arched his back in front of him like a man leaning over a hot stove to reach for something on the other side and flipped his sword a yard deep into the bull's shoulderblade separation.—Matador walked one way, bull the other with sword to hilt and staggered, started to run, looked up with human surprise at the sky & sun, and then gargled—O go see it folks!—He threw up ten gallons of blood into the air and it splashed all over—he fell on his knees choking on his own blood and spewed and twisted his neck around and suddenly got floppy doll and his head blammed flat.—He still wasnt dead, an extra idiot rushed out and knifed him with a wren-like dagger in the neck nerve and still the bull dug the sides of his poor mouth in the sand and chewed old blood.—His eyes! O his eyes!—Idiots sniggered because the dagger did this, as though it would not.—A team of hysterical horses were rushed out to chain and drag the bull away, they galloped off but the chain broke and the bull slid in dust like a dead fly kicked unconsciously by a foot.—Off, off with him!—He's gone, white eyes staring the last thing you see.—Next bull!— First the old boys shovel blood in a wheel-barrow and rush off with it. The quiet raker returns with his rake—"Ole!," girls throwing flowers at the animal-murder in the fine britches.— And I saw how everybody dies and nobody's going to care, I felt how awful it is to live just so you can die like a bull trapped in a screaming human ring.—

Jai Alai, Mexico, Jai Alai!

. . . .

"The Yen for Zen," an article by Alfred G. Aronowitz, ran in the October 1960 issue of Escapade. *Aronowitz interviewed Alan Watts, LeRoi Jones, and Gary Snyder for this article, but he concludes with text based on his interviews with Kerouac. (In the back of the same issue was Kerouac's ninth installment of "The Last Word," in which he continued his exposition of Buddhism.)*

Both Snyder and his deep convictions, in fact, probably are best described in *The Dharma Bums,* which, incidentally, is also a tribute to Kerouac's own deep convictions. Because, no matter what Watts may think of it, Kerouac is sincere in his belief that the book is at least a quasi-religious document.

"I'm a great Buddhist scholar," Kerouac says, with an innocent intensity. "I have a tremendous interest in all religions. But I became a Mahayana Buddhist, see, not a Zen Buddhist," and he displays a large, loose-leaf folder containing several hundred pages of typewritten sheets and entitled: "Some of the Dharma." The sheets are covered with religious aphorisms, thoughts, poetry and *haikus,* which are small poems full of both the same irrationality, simplicity and pith as the koans. Each page in the loose-leaf folder has been arranged to present almost a Mondrian effect, with pencil lines drawn in rectangles about each body of type. "This is all Mahayana Buddhism. I wrote all this myself. Just little haikus, . . . little poems . . . little children's poems. I type them up like that in that design.

"How did I become a Buddhist?" he says. "Well, after that love affair I describe in *The Subterraneans,* I didn't know what to do. I went home and I just sat in my room, hurting. I was suffering, you know, from the grief of losing a love, even though I really wanted to lose it. Well, I went to the library to read Thoreau. I said, 'I'm going to cut out from civilization and go back and live in the woods like Thoreau,' and I started to read Thoreau and he talked about Hindu philosophy. So I put Thoreau down and I took out, accidentally, *The Life of Buddha* by Ashvagosa.

"You know what Buddha did? He was married, he was the son of a maharaja. He had a harem, a son, a wife . . . But when he was thirty years old he became very melancholy. He didn't even look at the dancing girls any more. They said, 'What's the matter with you? The dancing girls are so beautiful.'

"He said, 'If these girls are so beautiful now, they'd stay beautiful. They wouldn't grow old . . . die . . . become corrupt . . . decay . . . fall apart.' He said, 'I gotta get out of here and find some way to stop all this.' He was deeply unhappy. He had to sneak out at night on a white horse. He cut all his golden hair off—he had long, blond hair—he was an aryan, you know, an aryan Indian. And he cut off his long, blond hair and he sat in the woods amid peace, and he found out that the cause of suffering was *birth!* If we hadn't been born, none of all this would have happened. Oh, yes, that the cause of suffering, of grief, of decay and of death is simply birth. So, he also discovered that the world didn't really exist, and it doesn't exist, except in some relationship to the form of being, which fits me perfectly. I have some eighteen-year-old writings which are pure Buddhism!

"You know, D. T. Suzuki sent out a message that he wanted to see me. He had just read, you know, *The Dharma Bums,* so I got on the phone and the secretary was there and I said, 'Okay, I'd like to see him.' And she said, 'Well, when do you want to make the appointment?' I said, '*Right now!*' You know, like Buddhism. 'Sure enough,' he said, 'come over right now,' so we went over. I don't know what he thinks of us. Well, like

I told him a koan: 'When the Buddha was about to speak, a horse spoke instead.' You see, that was a koan I invented. He said, 'Oh, the Western mind is too complicated.' So I wrote to Phil Whalen and I told him that. And he wrote back and said, 'Tell Mr. Suzuki that I had no idea that there was such a thing as a Western mind. In Buddhism, there's only a universal mind.' So Whalen cut Suzuki there.

"We talked about millions of things. He made us some green tea—thick green tea that's like thick pea soup, in little bowls. And you drink it and you get high. He said, 'That's the weak ones, you want some strong ones?' He said"—and Kerouac speaks in a high-pitched voice, imitating Suzuki—"he said, 'You boys sit here, write haiku, I go in kitchen, make more green tea.' You boys, that's me, Allen Ginsberg, and Peter Orlovsky. He comes back and Peter said: 'You have an interesting crack in your wall. That looks like The Void.' He says, 'Oh, yes, I never noticed it before.' Then he starts showing us pictures of Han Shan and another Chinese poet.

"But as we left—it was a delightful thing, the whole thing. As we left, I said, 'Dr. Suzuki, I'd like to spend the rest of my life with you.' He said, 'Sometime,' and then he started pushing us out the door. Very funny. And then we went out the door and he wouldn't let us go from the sidewalk. He kept waving his finger at us, saying, 'Remember the green tea! Remember, green tea!'

"He's a little short man, with big hairs growing out of his eyebrows, enormous, two-inch-long eyebrows. Which I told him reminded me of the Bush of the Dharma. You know, the young and tender bush in the spring. One that when it really gets growing five or six years later, you can't uproot such a bush? That's why I think he let his eyebrows grow.

"You know, the first thing I said to him when we first walked in? He said, 'You sit in this chair, you sit in this chair, and you sit in this chair.' He had all the chairs. And we all sat down and in the silence of the opening statement, I suddenly yelled out: 'Why did Bodhidharma come from the West?' Then I went on talking and he didn't answer me. So I don't think he liked that. But I think he likes us . . . "

Although Kerouac is not exactly a Zen Buddhist, he has had his share of satori, enough, in fact, to share with others.

His spontaneous prose, for example, is a form of enlightenment, or at least he intends it as such.

"Buddha," he says, "told his young cousin, Ananda, 'I'm going to ask you a question, Al, and I want you to answer me spontaneously, without presuppositions in your mind. Because,' he said, 'all the Buddhas of the past, present and future have arrived at enlightenment by this very same method. The spontaneity of their radiance,' and all that kind of stuff. There is that in Buddhism. Sudden enlightenment. And Zen. Bang! [. . . .]"

It is with the same spontaneity, apparently, that Kerouac has left Buddhism. Born a Roman Catholic, Kerouac says he always has remained a Roman Catholic after all. And if Buddhism has enlightened him, it has been to other truths. For him, Kerouac says, it was a choice between love as Buddha preached it or love as Kerouac practiced it.

"Buddhism is just words," he explains. "Also wisdom is heartless. I quit Buddhism because Buddhism—or Mahayana Buddhism—preaches against entanglement with women. To me, the most important thing in life is love."

. . . .

Big Sur *was written in October of 1961 and describes a brief period that Kerouac spent at Lawrence Ferlinghetti's Bixby Canyon cabin in northern California. Kerouac sought anonymity and an opportunity to recover from his alcohol indulgences, while simultaneously looking over the text for the* Book of Dreams *that Ferlinghetti wanted to publish. But the solitude was too much for Kerouac. He sought out friends, who ended up accompanying him on an alcoholic binge. The trip proved to be Kerouac's last West Coast sojourn and the beginning of his retreat into a solitary life back east.*

At high noon the sun always coming out at last, strong, beating down on my nice high porch where I sit with books and coffee and the noon I thought about the ancient Indians who must have inhabited this canyon for thousands of years, how even as far back as the 10th Century this valley must have looked the same, just different trees: these ancient Indians simply the ancestors of the Indians of only recently say 1860—How they've all died and quietly buried their grievances and excitements—How the creek may have been an inch deeper since logging operations of the last 60 years have removed some of the watershed in the hills back there—How the women pounded the local acorns, acorns or shmacorns, I finally found the natural nuts of the valley and they were sweet tasting—And men hunted deer—In fact God knows what they did because I wasnt here—But the same valley, a thousand years of dust more or less over their footsteps of 960 A.D.—And as far as I can see the world is too old for us to talk about it with our new words—We will pass just as quietly through life (passing through, passing through) as the 10th century people of this valley only with a little more noise and a few bridges and dams and bombs that wont even last a million years—The world being just what it is, moving and passing through, actually alright in the long view and nothing to complain about—Even the rocks of the valley had earlier rock ancestors, a billion billion years ago, have left no howl of complaint—Neither the bee, or the first sea urchins, or the clam, or the severed paw—All sad So-Is sight of the world, right there in front of my nose as I look,—And looking at that valley in fact I also realize I have to make lunch and it wont be any different than the lunch of those olden men and besides it'll taste good—Everything is the same, the fog says "We are fog and we fly by dissolving like ephemera," and the leaves say "We are leaves and we jiggle in the wind, that's all, we come and go, grow and fall"—Even the paper bags in my garbage pit say "We are man-transformed paper bags made out of wood pulp, we are kinda proud of being paper bags as long as that will be possible, but we'll be mush again with our sisters the leaves come rainy season"—The tree stumps say "We are tree stumps torn out of the ground by men, sometimes by wind, we have big tendrils full of earth that drink out of the earth"—Men say "We are men, we pull out tree stumps, we make paper bags, we think wise thoughts, we make lunch, we look around, we make a great effort to realize everything is the same"—While the sand says "We are sand, we already know," and the sea says "We are always come and go, fall and plosh"—The empty blue sky of space says "All this comes back to me, then goes again, and comes back again, then goes again, and I dont care, it still belongs to me"—The blue sky adds "Dont call me eternity, call me God if you like, all of you talkers are in paradise: the leaf is paradise, the tree stump is paradise, the paper bag is paradise, the man is paradise, the sand is paradise, the sea is paradise, the man is paradise, the fog is paradise"—Can you imagine a man with marvelous insights like these can go mad within a month? (because you must admit all those talking paper bags and sands were telling the truth)—But I remember seeing a mess of leaves suddenly go skittering in the wind and into the creek, then floating rapidly down the creek towards the sea, making me feel a nameless horror even then of "Oh my God, we're all being swept away to sea no matter what we know or say or do"—And a bird who was on a crooked branch is suddenly gone without my even hearing him.

. . . .

Later in the novel "Jack Duluoz" (Kerouac) and "Dave Wain" (Lew Welch) go to visit "George Baso" (Albert Saijo), who is recovering from tuberculosis.

He sits there on the lawn bench looking down and when Dave asks him "well you gonna be alright soon George" he says simply "I dont know"—He really means "I dont care"—And always warm and courteous with me he now hardly pays any attention to me [. . .] His answers come like an old man's (he's only 30)—"I guess all the Dharma talk about everything is nothing is just sorta sinking in my bones," he concedes, which makes me shudder—(On the way Dave's been telling us to be ready because George's changed so) [. . . .] But ah, as we're leaving and waving back at him and he's turned around tentatively to go into the hospital I linger behind the others and turn around several times to wave again—Finally I start to make a joke of it by ducking around a corner and peeking out and waving again—He ducks behind a bush and waves back—I dart to a bush and peek out—Suddenly we're two crazy hopeless sages goofing on a lawn—Finally as we part further and further and he comes closer to the door we are making elaborate gestures and down to the most infinitesimal like when he steps inside the door I wait till I see him sticking a finger out—So from around my corner I stick out a shoe—So from his door he sticks out an eye—So from my corner I stick out nothing but just yell "Wu!" [. . .] He goes into the hospital but a moment later he's peeking out this time from the ward window!—I'm behind a tree trunk thumbing my nose at him—There's no end to it, in fact—The other kids are all back at the car wondering what's keeping me—What's keeping me is that I know George will get better and live and teach the joyful truth and George knows I know this, that's why he's playing the game with me, the magic game of glad freedom which is what Zen or for that matter the Japanese soul ultimately means, I say, "And someday I will go to Japan with George" I tell myself after we've made our last little wave because I've heard the supper bell ring and seen the other patients rush for the chow line and knowing George's fantastic appetite wrapped in that little frail body I dont wanta hang him up tho he nevertheless does one last trick: He throws a glass of water out the window in a big froosh of water and I dont see him anymore.

"Wotze mean by that?" I'm scratching my head going back to the car.

. . . .

The following is an excerpt from "The First Word," Kerouac's January 1967 version of the first column he wrote for Escapade, *in June 1959.*

If you don't stick to what you first thought, and to the words the thought brought, what's the sense of bothering with it anyway, what's the sense of foisting your little lies on others, or, that is, hiding your little truths from others? What I find to be really "stupefying in its unreadability" is this laborious and dreary lying called craft and revision by writers, and certainly recognized by the sharpest psychologists as sheer blockage of the mental spontaneous process known 2,500 years ago as "The Seven Streams of Swiftness."

In the *Surangama Sutra,* Gotama Buddha says, "If you are now desirous of more perfectly understanding Supreme Enlightenment, you must learn to answer questions spontaneously with no recourse to discriminative thinking. For the Tathagatas (the Passers-Through) in the ten quarters of the universes, because of the straight-forwardness of their minds and the spontaneity of their mentations, have ever remained, from beginningless time to endless time, of one pure Suchness with the enlightening nature of pure Mind Essence."

Which is pretty strange old news. You can also find pretty much the same thing in Mark 13:11. "Take no thought beforehand what ye shall speak, neither do ye premeditate: but whatsoever shall be given you in that hour, that speak ye: for it is not ye that speak, but the Holy Ghost." Mozart and Blake often felt they weren't pushing their own pens, 'twas the "Muse" singing and pushing.

But I would also like to compare spontaneous composition of prose and verse to the incomparable, heartbreaking discipline of the fire ordeal. You had to get through the fire "to prove your innocence" or just die in it "guilty"—there was certainly no chance to stop and think it over, to chew on the end of your pencil and erase something. O maybe you could pause a second or two for another direction but the trick was to act now (or speak now, as in writing) or forever hold your tongue.

In another sense spontaneous, or ad lib, artistic writing imitates as best it can the flow of the mind as it moves in its spacetime continuum, in this sense it may really be called Space Age Prose someday because when astronauts are flowing through space and time they too have no chance to stop and reconsider and go back. It may be they won't be reading anything else but spontaneous writing when they do get out there, the science of the language to fit their science of movement.

But I'd gone so far to the edges of language where the babble of the subconscious begins, because words "come from the Holy Ghost" first in the form of a babble which suddenly by its sound indicates the word truly intended (in describing the story sea in *Desolation Angels* I heard the sound "Peligroso" for "Peligroso Roar" without knowing what it meant, wrote it down involuntarily, later found out it means "dangerous" in Spanish)—I began to rely too much on babble in my nervous race away from cantish cliches, chased the proton too close with my microscope, ended up ravingly enslaved to sounds, became unclear and dull as in my ultimate lit'ry experiment *Old Angel Midnight (Evergreen Review* and *Lui* in Paris in French). There's a delicate balancing point between bombast and babble.

And now my hand doesn't move as fast as it used to, and so many critics have laughed at me for those 16 originally-styled volumes of mine published in 16 languages in 42 countries, never for one moment calling me "sensitive" or artistically dignified but an unlettered literary hoodlum with diarrhea of the mouth, I'm having to retreat closer back to the bombast (empty abstraction) of this world and make my meaning plainer, i.e., dimmer, but the Space Age of the future won't bother with my "later" works if any, or with any of these millions of other things written today that sound alike.

To break through the barrier of language with WORDS, you have to be in orbit around your mind, and I may go up again if I regain my strength. It may sound vain but I've been wrestling with this angelic problem with at least as much discipline as Jacob.

Allen Ginsberg
(1926-   )

"Sooner or later let go what you loved hated or shrugged off, you walk in the park
You look at the sky, sit on a pillow, count up the stars in your head, get up and eat."
—ALLEN GINSBERG

Allen Ginsberg was just seventeen when, while traveling on the ferry to New York, he got down on his knees and made his first vow: to devote his life to the working oppressed. Thirty years later, with his Tibetan Buddhist teacher Chogyam Trungpa Rinpoche, Ginsberg would make a similar vow: the Bodhisattva Vow to save all sentient beings. Between these two pledges, however, Ginsberg was to forever change the voice of American poetry and become a central figure in the counter-culture.

In 1943, when Ginsberg made his first declaration, he was soon to enroll at Columbia University, where he went to pursue a secret crush and a career as a labor lawyer. But Ginsberg's interests and ambitions shifted; by his sophomore year, he had, along with William Burroughs, Lucien Carr, and Jack Kerouac, become a charter member of what would become known as the Beat Generation. Kerouac and Carr had already talked about trying to formulate a "New Vision" for literature when Ginsberg joined their ranks. Rather than addressing conventional themes in an established style, the "New Vision" held truthful self-expression of one's own experience—one's own mind—to be paramount. Ten years later Ginsberg composed a poem that proved to be a perfect fulfillment of that vision.

On October 13, 1955, Ginsberg read "Howl" at the Six Gallery in San Francisco to an electrified audience. Later that night Lawrence Ferlinghetti, a poet and the owner of City Lights Bookstore, composed a telegram for Ginsberg, which echoed Emerson's words to Whitman: "I greet you at the beginning of a great career." He also offered to publish "Howl," a move which later resulted in obscenity charges, a trial, and a whirlwind of publicity. That the Beat Generation had made its way into public consciousness was largely a result of Ginsberg's efforts. By borrowing mailing lists and sending out a hundred postcards, Ginsberg was responsible for the huge turnout at the Six Gallery. He was also the person to introduce Kerouac to Gary Snyder, further bridging the gap between the East Coast Beats and the writers of the San Francisco Literary Renaissance. And a decade or so later Ginsberg proved to be yet another bridge, as he went through a transformation from a Beat poet to a political activist and psychedelia pioneer, thereby helping to usher in the countercultural revolution of the sixties and seventies.

Although Ginsberg became acquainted with Buddhist thought before Kerouac, he did not begin serious study for many years. His initial interest was sparked by leafing through a book of reproductions of Chinese paintings at the New York Public Library, and while he sought out texts and encouraged his friend Neal Cassady to explore Buddhism, his own interest faded rapidly. Through his friendship with Kerouac and Snyder, Ginsberg became familiar with some aspects of Buddhist thought, but it was only years later, while traveling in India, that he found personal relevance in the teachings. There he met a Tibetan lama, Dudjom Rinpoche, and Ginsberg asked him about drug-induced visions. Dudjom Rinpoche counseled him not to cling to any vision, whether it was good or bad. This advice helped to release Ginsberg from an obsessive attachment to a mystical vision he'd had in 1948: he had heard William Blake's voice reciting "Ah, Sunflower" and felt that Blake was speaking to him through eternity; he experienced a sense of freedom and felt himself a part of a timeless universe. But, he says, he "doomed himself" for the next fifteen years to trying to repeat the original vision through various means, from LSD to the obscure South American drug yage.

On a visit Ginsberg made to Gary Snyder and Joanne Kyger in Japan, Dudjom Rinpoche's words began to take hold and he finally accepted that he would never recover his original vision; in the act of relinquishing it, however, he found what he'd been seeking. That moment began a period of spiritual exploration during which he practiced Hindu mantra chanting and sitting meditation. In 1971, after about a year of steady sitting, Ginsberg met Chogyam Trungpa Rinpoche. He studied with him closely and, at his request, cofounded the Jack Kerouac School of Disembodied Poetics at Naropa Institute in Boulder, Colorado, the Buddhist-inspired university founded by the Tibetan teacher. Ginsberg now studies with Gelek Rinpoche, whose center, Jewel Heart, is in Ann Arbor, Michigan. Recent collections include *White Shroud: Poems 1980–85* and *Cosmopolitan Greetings: Poems 1986–1992*.

Ginsberg's poems are autobiographical and arranged in chronological order according to the date of the events they describe (rather than by the time of their writing), an order Ginsberg designated in his *Collected Poems* to construct a kind of autobiography. Names of the periods Ginsberg ascribes to each poem, "roughly indicating time, geography, and motif or 'season' of experience," are listed before each work, along with dates. Interviews, lectures, and letters are interspersed chronologically.

. . . .

This letter to Neal Cassady, written on May 14, 1953, expresses Ginsberg's raw initial reaction to coming across Buddhist paintings and Zen texts. This naive but strong first response to the teachings of Buddhism prefigures Ginsberg's later interest and serious study. Ginsberg's unfamiliarity with Buddhist terminology is clear in his solecism "Zenzen," which he refers to as meaning conversations between Zen masters and disciples. The term he may have been thinking of is sanzen, *a general term for a formal appearance before a roshi (teacher). The conversations Ginsberg writes about are koans, a formulation in baffling language that points to ultimate truth. In his letter, Ginsberg also includes an early draft of his first Buddhist-inspired poem, "Sakyamuni Buddha Coming Out from the Mountain," the finished version of which appears in the section entitled* The Green Automobile, *poems written from 1953–54, in* Collected Poems 1947–80.

Now, I am on a new kick 2 weeks old, a very beautiful kick which I invite you to share, as you are in a city where you have access to this kick. A prelude: I was working in a literary agency for 2 weeks and got fired for poor typing (tho you'll notice that thru the experience my typing in this letter is mistakeless and neater—I go over and correct instead of being a slob). So after making preliminary financial arrangements (all taken care of: I work for Gene during unemployed periods, do little work, live easily $$-wise, maybe will continue this way awhile tho I have old market research jobs to go back to if I desire—nice security at last) I rushed over (3 blocks) to the Public Library Vast branch 42 St and went to the fine arts room and took out a dozen volumes of Chink painting, which I never hardly laid eyes on before in m'life. True, I had attended the Met Museum of Art show of Jap paintings, which opened my eyes to the sublimity and sophistication (meaning learning and experience, not snideness) of East. But as far as Chinaland went, I had only the faintest idea that there was so much of a kulcheral heritage, so easy to get at thru book upon book of reproduction—coolie made volumes sewn together on fine linen paper by laundrymen in Shang-hai or Kyoto (Jap.) decades ago before the first world War even. That is to say, tho China is a bleak great blank in our intimate knowledge, there is actually at hand a veritable feast, a free treasury, a plethora, a cornucopia of pix—pictures, like children love to see—in good libraries and museums. So this gets me on a project and I am now spending all my free time in Columbia Fine Arts library and NY Public leafing through immense albums of asiatic imagery. I'm also reading a little about their mystique and religions which I never did from a realistic standpoint before. Most of that Buddhist writing you see is not interesting, vague, etc because it has no context to us—but if you begin to get a clear idea of the various religions, the various dynasties and epochs of art and messianism and spiritual waves of hipness, so speak, you begin to see the vastitude and intelligence of the yellow men, and you understand a lot of new mind and eyeball kicks. I am working eastward from Japan and have begun to familiarize myself with Zen Buddhism thru a book (Philosophical Library Pub.) by one D. T. Suzuki (outstanding 89 yr. old authority now at columbia who I will I suppose to go see for interesting talk) "Introduction to Zen Buddhism." Zen is a special funny late form, with no real canon or formal theology, except for a mass of several hundred anecdotes of conversations between masters and disciples. These conversations (called Zenzen I believe) are all irrational and beguiling: such as "I clap my hands, o pupil, you hear the sound. Now, answer me this what is the sound of my right hand clapping alone in space?" Or anecdotes of actions such as: "Two groups of monks arguing over which wing of monastery should have possession of a kitten. So head man says: Anybody can give me a real good reason they can have the cat, but if no one advances a convincing argument I chop cat in half and give each side half. So everybody comes up with big loudmouthed arguments and he chops cat in half. Next day into monastery comes young novice who spent week wandering in forest looking for his soul. Master say; This what happened, what would you have said to get cat? Novice look at him, take off shoes, put them on his head and walk out of room without further word. Master say:

had young novice been here yesterday that cat would have been saved." This is incidentally all very Carl Solomonish. Also story of great monk who never spoke but just held up his forefinger and everybody got the idea, no matter what they asked him. So there was a little boy running around the court seeing this, and soon the boy began running around, and whenever anybody spoke to him, he'd hold up his forefinger and lay his point across just like that as cool as you please. Well one day the monk saw him do that in the court, and he reached to his backside for his machete and WHOP! off went the kid's finger. The kid grabs his hand with a look of astoundment and surprise and opens his mouth to let out an agony-howl and the master suddenly lunges forward in front of him, zonk, stick up his finger in the air, and stares right at the kid. End of joke, except that the kid grew up to be a famous and holy monk on the basis of this lesson.

Well anyway, to continue, all these Zenzen, or conversations or anecdotes are given to the Zen novitiates, and made up as they go along sometimes, until the novitiate is completely beflabbered intellectually and stops thinking. Meanwhile all along while he's been shooting his mouth off like anyone else trying to explain the sound of one hand in the air, and other rediculous questions metaphysical and otherwise, till now. Then he gets the point. He begins to look about him. If he says "What is the Eternal?" the Zen master answers "That bird over there", or "my left foot." If he says, "Tell me, master, Why did Gautama Buddha walk all the way from India to China in the year 0450 BC?" the answer he gets is likely to be "Buddha never made no such trip, what you talking about boy hah?" So now he begins to look at the water fall. If he keeps asking silly questions, he also is often insulted like Cannastra insulted girls, or slapped around, or pushed off the monastery porch.

Then finally one day he gets the Big point and has what is known as SATORI, or illumination. This is a specific flash of vision which totally changes his ken. Then he's graduated, goes off to hiding or into the world, does whatever he wants in the earth.

Zen also says "There is no god," and "god is big toe" and "I am god" and "don't presume to think you are god." That is their idea of God is very interesting: they refuse to have a theology or admit that one exists, or anything verbal at all. That's the point of these anecdotes; to exhaust words. Then the man sees anew the universe. The kid in the story had satori after losing finger, at that moment. Satori also comes oft by accident or after monk gets slapped or nose-tweaked.

Interesting is that this is not a small sect but the great formal final religion of the last 1000 years in China & Japan—the basis of all later great post 500 AD Jap-Chink art.

Here followeth poem based on a famous painting, with notes:

*Sakyamuni*1 Coming Out From the Mountain*

Liang Kai fecit *2
Southern Sung *3

In robes of rag, eyebrows grown long with weeping
and hooknosed woe,
dragging himself out of the cave
barefoot by the shrubs
wearing a fine beard
unhappy hands clasped to his naked breast
humility is beatness
humility is beatness
stands upright there tho' trembling:
4*Arhat who sought heaven
underneath the mountain of stone
reentering the world a bitter
wreck of a sage the flash come
earth before him his only path.
Sat thinking till he realized
how painful to
be born again

wearing a fine beard
                we can see his soul
he knows nothing, like a god
shaken:
        meek wretch:
                humility
                is beatness
before the absolute World.

*1. A name for one of the later forms of Buddha, I think
*2. Liang Kai made it, painted it—latin, Pound identifies things thus.
*3. the period—don't know when—about 1150 AD it was painted
*4. asiatic name for Sage or Mage or Saint or Holyman.
Apparently this man immured himself under a mountain till he should be wise.

. . . .

From Howl, Before and After: San Francisco Bay Area (1955–1956).

Sunflower Sutra

I walked on the banks of the tincan banana dock and sat down under the huge shade of a Southern Pacific locomotive to look at the sunset over the box house hills and cry.
Jack Kerouac sat beside me on a busted rusty iron pole, companion, we thought the same thoughts of the soul, bleak and blue and sad-eyed, surrounded by the gnarled steel roots of trees of machinery.
The oily water on the river mirrored the red sky, sun sank on top of final Frisco peaks, no fish in that stream, no hermit in those mounts, just ourselves rheumy-eyed and hung-over like old bums on the riverbank, tired and wily.

Look at the Sunflower, he said, there was a dead gray shadow
against the sky, big as a man, sitting dry on top of a pile
of ancient sawdust—
—I rushed up enchanted—it was my first sunflower,
memories of Blake—my visions—Harlem
and Hells of the Eastern rivers, bridges clanking Joes Greasy
Sandwiches, dead baby carriages, black treadless tires
forgotten and unretreaded, the poem of the riverbank,
condoms & pots, steel knives, nothing stainless, only the
dank muck and the razor-sharp artifacts passing into the
past—
and the gray Sunflower poised against the sunset, crackly
bleak and dusty with the smut and smog and smoke of
olden locomotives in its eye—
corolla of bleary spikes pushed down and broken like a
battered crown, seeds fallen out of its face, soon-to-be-
toothless mouth of sunny air, sunrays obliterated on its
hairy head like a dried wire spiderweb,
leaves stuck out like arms of the stem, gestures from the
sawdust root, broke pieces of plaster fallen out of the
black twigs, a dead fly in its ear,
Unholy battered old thing you were, my sunflower O my
soul, I loved you then!
The grime was no man's grime but death and human
locomotives,
all that dress of dust, that veil of darkened railroad skin, that
smog of cheek, that eyelid of black mis'ry, that sooty hand
or phallus or protuberance of artificial worse-than-dirt—
industrial—modern—all that civilization spotting your
crazy golden crown—
and those blear thoughts of death and dusty loveless eyes and
ends and withered roots below, in the home-pile of sand
and sawdust, rubber dollar bills, skin of machinery, the guts
and innards of the weeping coughing car, the empty lonely
tincans with their rusty tongues alack, what more could I
name, the smoked ashes of some cock cigar, the cunts of
wheelbarrows and the milky breasts of cars, wornout asses
out of chairs & sphincters of dynamos—all these

entangled in your mummied roots—and you there standing
before me in the sunset, all your glory in your form!
A perfect beauty of a sunflower! a perfect excellent lovely
sunflower existence! a sweet natural eye to the new hip
moon, woke up alive and excited grasping in the sunset
shadow sunrise golden monthly breeze!
How many flies buzzed round you innocent of your grime,
while you cursed the heavens of the railroad and your
flower soul?
Poor dead flower? when did you forget you were a flower?
when did you look at your skin and decide you were an
impotent dirty old locomotive? the ghost of a locomotive?
the specter and shade of a once powerful mad American
locomotive?
You were never no locomotive, Sunflower, you were a sunflower!
And you Locomotive, you are a locomotive, forget me not!
So I grabbed up the skeleton thick sunflower and stuck it at
my side like a scepter,
and deliver my sermon to my soul, and Jack's soul too, and
anyone who'll listen,
—We're not our skin of grime, we're not our dread bleak
dusty imageless locomotive, we're all golden sunflowers
inside, blessed by our own seed & hairy naked
accomplishment-bodies growing into mad black formal
sunflowers in the sunset, spied on by our eyes under the
shadow of the mad locomotive riverbank sunset Frisco
hilly tincan evening sitdown vision.

Berkeley, 1955

. . . .

From Sad Dust Glories (1972–1974). *Among the notes that Ginsberg provides to accompany this poem are definitions for: Dharmakaya: "body of truth" (absolute Buddha nature); Nirmanakaya: "body of creation" (earthly or grounded Buddha form); and Sambhogakaya: "body of bliss" (visionary communicative aspect of Buddha speech).*

"What would you do if you lost it?"

said Rinpoche Chogyam Trungpa Tulku in the marble glittering apartment lobby
looking at my black hand-box full of Art, "Better prepare for Death". . .
The harmonium that's Peter's
the scarf that's Krishna's the bell and brass lightningbolt Phil Whalen selected in Japan
a tattered copy of Blake, with chord notations, black books from City Lights,
Australian Aborigine song sticks, green temple incense, Tibetan precious-metal finger cymbals—
A broken leg a week later enough reminder, lay in bed and after few days' pain began to weep
no reason, thinking a little of Rabbi Schacter, a little of father Louis, a little
of everything that must be abandoned,
snow abandoned,
empty dog barks after the dogs have disappeared
meals eaten passed thru the body to nourish tomatoes and corn,
The wooden bowl from Haiti too huge for my salad,
Teachings, Tantras, Haggadahs, Zohar, Revelations, poetries, Koans
forgotten with the snowy world, forgotten
with generations of icicles crashing to white gullies by roadside,
Dharmakaya forgot, Nirmanakaya shoved in coffin, Sambhogakaya eclipsed in candle-light snuffed by the playful cat—
Goodbye my own treasures, bodies adored to the nipple,
old souls worshipped flower-eye or imaginary auditory panoramic skull—
goodbye old socks washed over & over, blue boxer shorts, subzero longies,
new Ball Boots black hiplength for snowdrifts near the farm mailbox,

goodbye to my room full of books, all wisdoms I never studied,
all the Campion, Creeley, Anacreon Blake I never read through,
blankets farewell, orange diamonded trunk from Mexico
Himalayan sheepwool lugged down from Almora days with Lama Govinda and Peter trying to eat tough stubborn half-cooked chicken.
Paintings on wall, Maitreya, Sakyamuni & Padmasambhava,
Dr. Samedi with Haitian spats & cane whiskey,
Bhaktivedanta Swami at desk staring sad eye Krishna at my hopeless selfconsciousness,
Attic full of toys, desk full of old checks, files on NY police & C.I.A. peddling Heroin,
Files on laughing Leary, files on Police State, files on ecosystems all faded & brown,
notebooks untranscribed, hundreds of little poems & prose my own hand,
newspaper interviews, assemblaged archives, useless paperworks surrounding me imperfectly chronologic, humorous later in eternity, reflective of Cities' particular streets studios and boudoirs—
goodbye poetry books, I don't have to take you along anymore on a chain to Deux Magots like a red lobster
thru Paris, Moscow, Prague, Milan, New York, Calcutta, Bangkok, holy Benares, yea Rishikesh & Brindaban may yr prana lift ye over the roof of the world—
my own breath slower now, silent waiting & watching—
Downstairs pump-organs, musics, rags and blues, home made Blake hymns, mantras to raise the skull of America,
goodbye C chord, F chord, G chord, goodbye all the chords of The House of the Rising Sun
Goodbye farmhouse, city apartment, garbage subways Empire State, Museum of Modern Art where I wandered thru puberty dazzled by Van Gogh's raw-brained star-systems pasted on blue thick skyey Suchness—

Goodbye again Naomi, goodbye old painful legged poet Louis,
 goodbye Paterson the 69 between Joe Bozzo & Harry
 Haines that out-lasted childhood & poisoned the air o'er
 Passaic Valley,
goodbye Broadway, give my regards to the great falls & boys
 staring marijuana'd in wonder hearing the quiet roar of
 Godfather Williams' speech
Goodbye old poets of Century that taught fixed eye & sharp
 tongue from Pound with silent Mouni heart to Tom Veitch
 weeping in Stinson Beach,
goodbye to my brothers who write poetry & play fiddle, my
 nephews who blow tuba & stroke bass viol, whistle flute or
 smile & sing in blue rhythm,
goodbye shades of dead living loves, bodies weeping bodies
 broken bodies aging, bodies turned to wax doll or cinder
Goodbye America you hope you prayer you tenderness, you
 IBM 135-35 Electronic Automated Battlefield Igloo White
 Dragon-tooth Fuel-Air Bomb over Indochina
Goodbye Heaven, farewell Nirvana, sad Paradise adieu, adios
 all angels and archangels, devas & devakis, Bodhisattvas,
 Buddhas, rings of Seraphim, Constellations of elect souls
 weeping singing in the golden Bhumi Rungs, goodbye
 High Throne, High Central Place, Alleluiah Light
 beyond Light, a wave of the hand to Thee Central Golden
 Rose,
Om Ah Hūm A La La Ho Sophia, Soham Tara Ma, Om Phat
 Svaha Padmasambhava Marpa Mila sGam.po.pa Karmapa
 Trungpaye! Namastaji Brahma, Ave atque vale Eros,
 Jupiter, Zeus, Apollo, Surya, Indra
Bom Bom! Shivaye! Ram Nam Satyahey! Om Ganipatti, Om
 Saraswati Hrih Sowha! Ardinarishvara Radha Harekrishna
 faretheewell forevermore!
None left standing! No tears left for eyes, no eyes for weeping,
 no mouth for singing, no song for the hearer, no more
 words for any mind.

Cherry Valley, February 1, 1973

. . . .

This excerpt comes from the largely unedited transcript of a lecture entitled "First Thought, Best Thought," given in Ginsberg's Spiritual Poetics class at the Jack Kerouac School of Disembodied Poetics, Naropa Institute, July 29, 1974. Ginsberg discusses Chogyam Trungpa Rinpoche's teachings on shamatha, meditation, and breath.

The title of this course is Spiritual Poetics, which was just a spontaneous title arrived at when we had to have a title, but might as well be used. We're beginning with considerations of breath, considerations of vowel, and relation between vowel and intelligence, vowel and soul,—and how these are connected to the breath. As here, say with Chogyam's teaching, "Ah" is a basic mantra—"Ah" as the exhalation of the breath, as appreciation of the breath also. Appreciation of the empty space into which breath flows. The *open* space, into which breath flows.

So if we're talking poetics, and beginning with breath, the vowel road is connected then with the title of the course, Spiritual Poetics. And the mantric aspect is a lot more important than has been understood in western poetry—as pure breath, as exhalation of breath, as articulation of breath, as manifestation of breath, as animation, as expression in really the easiest and most natural way of your own nature, which is by breathing, and making a sound while breathing. Just like the wind makes a sound in the leaves. No more presumptuous than the wind in the leaves. Of course, no more honorable either. But at any rate, not guilty. No more guilty than the wind in the leaves. So if you take that approach, that your singing or your chanting or your poetics is as neutral, impersonal, and objective as the wind through the black oak leaves, then you wouldn't have to be ashamed of expressing yourself, because it's not yourself, it's just the wind, it's just wind, it's just breath going through you. Then you might take the trouble to fit it to whatever your subjective intellect is thinking about at the moment, and you might take the trouble to link that breath up with whatever is going on in your mind at the moment, or to what you remember is going on in your mind or your body at the moment. But that can be done as spontaneously as breathing, in the sense that the mind is always working—it's hard to stop, as those of you who have been meditating know.

How many here sit? So, nearly everybody. So we all know the experience of observing our minds moving and listening to chatter and gossip, "discursive thought," not being able to stop, and maybe not even needing to attempt to stop it, simply observing it. I've lately come to think of poetry as the possibility of simply articulating that movement, in other words, observing your mind, remembering maybe one or two thoughts back and laying it out. So in that sense it's as easy as breathing because all you're doing is listening to particulars, those particulars of what you were just thinking about. And in that respect, it's very close to meditation. Meditation is good practice for poetry. In other words, it's not the opposite, it's not an enemy of poetry. It was formerly seen to be, occasionally, by various hung-up intellectuals, who were afraid that they'd be silent, and they wouldn't be able to be poets then. But actually all it does is give you lots of space and place in time to recollect what's going on in your mind, so providing lots of material, lots of ammunition, lots of material to work with.

So if you're practicing in the line of Gertrude Stein and Kerouac, spontaneous transcription, transmission of your thought, how do you choose then what thoughts to put down? The answer is that you don't get a chance to choose because everything's going so fast. So it's like driving on a road; you just have to follow the road. And take turns, "eyeball it," as a carpenter would say. You don't have any scientific measuring rod, except your own mind, really. I don't know of any scientific measuring rod that's usable. So you just have to chance whatever you can and pick whatever you can. So there's also a process of automatic selection. Whatever you can draw in your net is it, is what you got—whatever you can remember, and whatever you can manage physically to write down is your poem, or is your material. And you've got to trust that, as the principle of selection, so you have to be a little athletic about that, in the sense of developing *means* of transcription, ease of transcription, overcoming resistance to transcription.

Student: Does that also have to do with what you choose to use, either typing, or writing, or tape recorder?

Ginsberg: Yeah, very much so in questions of form especially. I want to go into that anyway, in just a minute. First I want to get to the nub of selection, because there used to be a big academic argument about "the principle of selectivity" and of "'Beatnik' writers being unselective," and that "selection was absolutely important," that you really had to make fine distinctions between different kinds of thoughts and only choose the loftiest thoughts, or the most poetic thoughts, and you had to intercede or intervene in your mind with another mind from somewhere else, someone else's mind really, Lionel Trilling's mind or Allen Tate's mind, or Brooks and Warren's mind, the critics' minds. You had to use somebody else's mind or some objective mind to choose among the thoughts, but I think that's too hard, I think that's too much work. It'll only get you tangled up in a feedback loop of some sort, because you forget what you were thinking, and you'll think what you were supposed to be thinking. So the problem is to stay with what you were really thinking instead of what you think you're supposed to be thinking.

So from that point of view, I would say that the only thing you can get down is what you can remember and what you can write down: in other words, the actual process of writing, the physical process of writing or vocalizing or tape-recording or babbling spontaneously—that physical activity determines what gets laid out on the paper or on the air. It's a pretty good critic, because the mind, somehow or other, if you leave it alone a little bit and accept it, tends to select its own society, tends to cling to its proper own obsessions and preoccupations. Recurrent thoughts finally do get writ out, things that are really recurrent do come up and are rememberable. And one really difficult part is that there's a tendency toward censorship—

that some thoughts seem too embarrassing, too raw, too naked, too irrelevant, too goofy, too personal, too revealing, too damaging to one's own self-image, too cranky, too individualistic, too specialized, or too much copulating with your mother or something, so that you don't want to put them down. That's a real problem with everybody, including myself. The *pudeur,* modesty, shyness—like I failed to write down a dream the other day. Fortunately, I remembered it—I saw Peter Orlovsky catch me smoking, and he's very much antismoking. We were living together, and in the dream he was so dismayed that he vomited up his liver, and I realized that I was really violating something sacrosanct and rooted, physiologically rooted in him, in something real. And I got so scared of the domestic situation that I didn't write the dream down. But it was actually one of the more interesting dream-poem possibilities that I'd had in the last month.

But in the moment of writing, there'll be all sorts of images that rise, "thinks," separate "thinks" that will be unappetizing, and I think that's the most important part. The parts that embarrass you the most are usually the most interesting poetically, are usually the most naked of all, the rawest, the goofiest, and strangest and most eccentric and at the same time, most representative, most universal, because most individual, most particular, most specific, vomiting out a piece of liver, specific situation, smoking. Actually, I thought that was really just my scene, but really it's universal, it's an archetype, as much as anything's an archetype. And that was something I learned from Kerouac, which was that spontaneous writing could be embarrassing, or could *seem* to be embarrassing. So the cure for that is to write things down which you'll not publish and which you won't show people. To write secretly, to write for nobody's eye, nobody's ear but your own, so you can actually be free to say what you want. In other words, it means abandoning being a poet, abandoning any careerism, abandoning even the idea of writing any poetry, really abandoning, giving up as hopeless—abandoning the possibility of really expressing yourself to the nations of the world. Abandoning the idea of being a prophet with honor and dignity, and abandoning the glory of poetry and just settling down in the muck of your own mind. And the way that's practiced is that you take the writing out a week later and look at it. It's no longer embarrassing, by that time it seems funny. The blood has dried, sort of. So you really have to make a resolution just to write for yourself, in the sense of no bullshit to impress others, not writing poetry to impress yourself, but just writing what your self is saying.

. . .

Chogyam Trungpa told me something about two years ago which extended something that Kerouac had also said. Kerouac and I were worrying about this problem, trying to formulate it, and he said that if the mind is shapely, the art will be shapely. Or, "Mind is shapely, art is shapely." It's a question of knowing your mind. So the discipline, in a sense, would be having a mind and knowing it. And then when you're writing, that writing will be interesting according to that actual mind[. . . .] I was writing a spontaneous chain poem with Chogyam and he said, and we finally agreed, "First thought is best thought." That was sort of the formula: first thought, best thought. That is to say, the first thought you had on your mind, the first thought you thought before you thought, yes, you'd have a better thought, before you thought you should have a more formal thought—first thought, best thought. If you stick with first flashes, then you're all right. But the problem is, how do you *get* to that first thought—that's always the problem. The first thought is always the great elevated, cosmic, noncosmic, *shunyata* thought. And then, at least according to the Buddhist formulation, after that you begin imposing names and forms and all that. So it's a question of catching yourself at your first open thought.

. . . .

From Ego Confessions *(1974–1977). In a note accompanying this poem, Ginsberg identifies the Gyalwa Karmapa as "the 16th lama head of Milarepa lineage, Kagyu order of Tibetan Buddhism."*

Ego Confession

I want to be known as the most brilliant man in America
Introduced to Gyalwa Karmapa heir of the Whispered
    Transmission Crazy Wisdom Practice Lineage
as the secret young wise man who visited him and winked
    anonymously decade ago in Gangtok
Prepared the way for Dharma in America without mention-
    ing Dharma—scribbled laughter
Who saw Blake and abandoned God
To whom the Messianic Fink sent messages darkest hour
    sleeping on steel sheets "somewhere in the Federal Prison
    system" Weathermen got no Moscow Gold
who went backstage to Cecil Taylor serious chat chord struc-
    ture & Time in a nightclub
who fucked a rose-lipped rock star in a tiny bedroom slum
    watched by a statue of Vajrasattva—
and overthrew the CIA with a silent thought—
Old Bohemians many years hence in Viennese beergardens'll
    recall
his many young lovers with astonishing faces and iron breasts
gnostic apparatus and magical observation of rainbow-lit
    spiderwebs
extraordinary cooking, lung stew & Spaghetti a la Vongole
    and recipe for salad dressing 3 parts oil one part vinegar
    much garlic and honey a spoonful
his extraordinary ego, at service of Dharma and completely
    empty
unafraid of its own self's spectre

parroting gossip of gurus and geniuses famous for their reti-
  cence—
Who sang a blues made rock stars weep and moved an old
  black guitarist to laughter in Memphis—
I want to be the spectacle of Poesy triumphant over trickery
  of the world
Omniscient breathing its own breath thru War tear gas spy
  hallucination
whose common sense astonished gaga Gurus and rich
  Artistes—
who called the Justice department & threaten'd to Blow the
  Whistle
Stopt Wars, turned back petrochemical Industries' Captains
  to grieve & groan in bed
Chopped wood, built forest houses & established farms
distributed monies to poor poets & nourished imaginative
  genius of the land
Sat silent in jazz roar writing poetry with an ink pen—
wasn't afraid of God or Death after his 48th year—
let his brains turn to water under Laughing Gas his gold
  molar pulled by futuristic dentists
Seaman knew ocean's surface a year
carpenter late learned bevel and mattock
son, conversed with elder Pound & treated his father gently
—All empty all for show, all for the sake of Poesy
to set surpassing example of sanity as measure for late
  generations
Exemplify Muse Power to the young avert future suicide
accepting his own lie & the gaps between lies with equal
  good humor
Solitary in worlds full of insects & singing birds all solitary
—who had no subject but himself in many disguises
some outside his own body including empty air-filled space
  forests & cities—
Even climbed mountains to create his mountain, with ice ax
  & crampons & ropes, over Glaciers—

San Francisco, October 1974

Thoughts on a Breath

Cars slide minute down asphalt lanes in front of
        Dallas Hilton Inn
Trees brown bare in December's smog-mist roll up
        to the city's squared towers
beneath electric wire grids trestled toward country water
        tanks
distanced under cloud streak crossed with fading
        vapor trails.
Majestic in a skirt of human fog, building blocks
        rise at sky edge,
Branches and house roofs march to horizon.

I sat again to complete the cycle, eyes open seeing
        dust motes in the eye screen
like birds over telephone wires, curve of the eyeball
        where Dallas and I meet—
white motel wall of the senses—ear roar
        oil exhaust, snuffle and bone growl
        motors rolling North Central freeway
Energy playing over Concrete, energy
        hymning itself in emptiness—
What've I learned since I sat here four years ago?
In the halls of the head or out thru the halls of the senses,
        same space
Trucks rolling toward Dallas skyscrapers
        or mind thoughts floating thru my head
vanish on a breath—What was it I began
        my meditation on?
Police state, Students, Poetry open tongue,
        anger and fear of Cops,
oil Cops, Rockefeller Cops, Oswald Cops,
        Johnson Cops Nixon Cops
        president Cops
SMU Cops Trustee Cops CIA Cops
        FBI Cops Goon Squads of Dope
Cops busted Stony Burns and sent him to
        Jail 10 years and a day

for less than a joint of Grass, a Citizen
        under republic, under Constitution, of Texas?
We sit here in a police state and sigh, knowing
        we're trapped in our bodies,
our fear of No meat, no oil, no money, airplanes
        sex love kisses jobs no
        work
Massive metal bars about, monster machines
        eat us, Controlled by army
        Cops, the Secret Police, our own thoughts!
Punishment! Punish me! Punish me! we scream
        in our hearts, cocks spurting alone
        in our fists!
What thoughts more flowed thru our hearts alone
        in Dallas? Flowed thru our hearts like oil
        thru Hilton's faucets?
Where shall we house our minds, pay
        rent for Selves, how
        protect our bodies
from inflation, starvation, old age, smoking
        Cancer, Coughing Death?
Where get money to buy off the
        skeleton? If we work with Kissinger
Can we buy time, get off on parole? Does
        Rockfeller want Underground
Newspapers printing his subconscious mind's
        nuclear oil wars?
Will 92nd Armored Division be sent to seize
        Arabia oilfields
as threatened December's *US News &*
        World Report?
What'd we remember that destroyed these armies
        with a breath?
How pay rent & stay in our bodies
        if we don't sell our minds to Samsara?
If we don't join the illusion—that Gas is life—
        How can we in Dallas SMU
look forward to our futures?
        work with our hands

like niggers growing Crops in the field,
  & plow and harvest our own corny
  fate?
Oh Walt Whitman salutations you knew the laborer,
  the sexual intelligent horny handed
  man who lived in Dirt
and fixed the axles of Capitalism, dumbed and
  laughing at hallucinated Secretaries
  Of State!
Oh intellect of body back & Cock whose red neck
supports the S&M freaks of Government
  police & Fascist Monopolies—
Kissinger bare assed & big buttocked
  with a whip, in leather boots
scrawling on a memo to Chile "No more
  civics lectures please"
When the ambassador complained about Torture
  methods used in the Detention Stadium!
And I ride the planes that Rockefeller gassed
  when he paid off Kissinger!
Stony Burns sits in jail, in a stone cell in
  Huntsville
and breathes his news to solitude.
        Homage
to the Gurus, Guru om! Thanks to the teachers
  who taught us to breathe,
to watch our minds revolve in emptiness,
  to follow the rise & fall of thoughts,
Illusions big as empires flowering &
  Vanishing on a breath!
Thanks to aged teachers whose wrinkles
  read our minds' newspapers &
  taught us not to Cling to yesterday's
  thoughts,
nor thoughts split seconds ago, but
  let cities vanish on a breath—
Thanks to teachers who showed us behold
  Dust motes in our own eye,
  anger our own hearts,

emptiness of Dallases where we
    sit thinking knitted brows—
Sentient beings are numberless I vow
    to liberate all
Passions unfathomable I vow to
    release them all
Thought forms limitless I vow to
    master all
Awakened space is endless I vow to
    enter it forever.

Dallas, December 4, 1974

Mugging

1.

Tonite I walked out of my red apartment door on East tenth
  street's dusk—
Walked out of my home ten years, walked out in my honking
  neighborhood
Tonite at seven walked out past garbage cans chained to concrete anchors
Walked under black painted fire escapes, giant castiron plate
  covering a hole in ground
—Crossed the street, traffic lite red, thirteen bus roaring by
  liquor store,
past corner pharmacy iron grated, past Coca Cola & Mylai
  posters fading scraped on brick
Past Chinese Laundry wood door'd, & broken cement stoop
  steps For Rent hall painted green & purple Puerto Rican
  style
Along E. 10th's glass splattered pavement, kid blacks &
  Spanish oiled hair adolescents' crowded house fronts—
Ah, tonite I walked out on my block NY City under humid
  summer sky Halloween,
thinking what happened Timothy Leary joining brain police
  for a season?

thinking what's all this Weathermen, secrecy & selfrighteousness beyond reason—F.B.I. plots?
Walked past a taxicab controlling the bottle strewn curb—
past young fellows with their umbrella handles & canes leaning against a ravaged Buick
—and as I looked at the crowd of kids on the stoop—a boy stepped up, put his arm around my neck
tenderly I thought for a moment, squeezed harder, his umbrella handle against my skull,
and his friends took my arm, a young brown companion tripped his foot 'gainst my ankle—
as I went down shouting Om Ah Hūm to gangs of lovers on the stoop watching
slowly appreciating, why this is a raid, these strangers mean strange business
with what—my pockets, bald head, broken-healed-bone leg, my softshoes, my heart—
Have they knives? Om Ah Hūm—Have they sharp metal wood to shove in eye ear ass? Om Ah Hūm
& slowly reclined on the pavement, struggling to keep my woolen bag of poetry address calendar & Leary-lawyer notes hung from my shoulder
dragged in my neat orlon shirt over the crossbar of a broken metal door
dragged slowly onto the fire-soiled floor an abandoned store, laundry candy counter 1929—
now a mess of papers & pillows & plastic car seat covers cracked cockroach-corpsed ground—
my wallet back pocket passed over the iron foot step guard
and fell out, stole by God Muggers' lost fingers, Strange—
Couldn't tell—snakeskin wallet actually plastic, 70 dollars my bank money for a week,
old broken wallet—and dreary plastic contents—Amex card & Manf. Hanover Trust Credit too—business card from Mr. Spears British Home Minister Drug Squad—my draft card—membership ACLU & Naropa Institute Instructor's identification
Om Ah Hūm I continued chanting Om Ah Hūm

Putting my palm on the neck of an 18 year old boy fingering
my back pocket crying "Where's the money"
"Om Ah Hūm there isn't any"
My card Chief Boo-Hoo Neo American Church New Jersey &
Lower East Side
Om Ah Hūm—what not forgotten crowded wallet—Mobil
Credit, Shell? old lovers addresses on cardboard pieces,
booksellers calling cards—
—"Shut up or we'll murder you"—"Om Ah Hūm take it
easy"
Lying on the floor shall I shout more loud?—the metal door
closed on blackness
one boy felt my broken healed ankle, looking for hundred
dollar bills behind my stocking weren't even there—a
third boy untied my Seiko Hong Kong watch rough from
right wrist leaving a clasp-prick skin tiny bruise
"Shut up and we'll get out of here"—and so they left,
as I rose from the cardboard mattress thinking Om Ah Hūm
didn't stop em enough,
the tone of voice too loud—my shoulder bag with 10,000
dollars full of poetry left on the broken floor—

November 2, 1974

II

Went out the door dim eyed, bent down & picked up my
glasses from step edge I place them while dragged in the
store—looked out—
Whole street a bombed-out face, building rows' eyes & teeth
missing
burned apartments half the long block, gutted cellars, hall-
ways' charred beams
hanging over trash plaster mounded entrances, couches &
bedsprings rusty after sunset
Nobody home, but scattered stoopfuls of scared kids frozen in
black hair
chatted giggling at house doors in black shoes, families

cooked For Rent some six story houses mid the street's wreckage
Nextdoor Bodega, a phone, the police? "I just got mugged" I said
to the man's face under fluorescent grocery light tin ceiling—
puffy, eyes blank & watery, sickness of beer kidney and language tongue
thick lips stunned as my own eyes, poor drunken Uncle minding the store!
O hopeless city of idiots empty eyed staring afraid, red beam top'd car at street curb arrived—
"Hey maybe my wallet's still on the ground got a flashlight?"
Back into the burnt-doored cave, & the policeman's gray flashlight broken no eyebeam—
"My partner all he wants is sit in the car never gets out Hey Joe bring your flashlight—"
a tiny throway beam, dim as a match in the criminal dark
"No I can't see anything here" . . . "Fill out this form"
Neighborhood street crowd behind a car "We didn't see nothing"
Stoop young girls, kids laughing "Listen man last time I messed with them see this—"
rolled up his skinny arm shirt, a white knife scar on his brown shoulder
"Besides we help you the cops come don't know anybody we all get arrested
go to jail I never help no more mind my business everytime"
"Agh!" upstreet think "Gee I don't know anybody here ten years lived half block crost Avenue C
and who knows who?"—passing empty apartments, old lady with frayed paper bags
sitting in the tin-boarded doorframe of a dead house.

December 10, 1974

Gospel Noble Truths

Born in this world
You got to suffer
Everything changes
You got   no soul

Try to be gay
Ignorant   happy
You get the blues
You eat jellyroll

There is one Way
You take the high road
In your Big Wheel
8 steps you fly

Look at the View
Right to horizon
Talk to the sky
Act like you talk

Work like the sun
Shine in your heaven
See what you done
Come down & walk

Sit   you sit down
Breathe when you breathe
Lie down   you lie down
Walk where you walk

Talk when you talk
Cry when you cry
Lie down   you lie down
Die when you die

Look when you look
Hear what you hear
Taste what you taste   here
Smell what you smell

Touch what you touch
Think what you think
Let go Let it go   Slow
Earth Heaven & Hell

Die when you die
Die when you die
Lie down   you lie down
Die when you die

New York Subway, October 17, 1975

. . . .

From Plutonian Ode (1977–1980).

Reflections at Lake Louise

I

At midnight the teacher lectures on his throne
Gongs, bells, wooden fish, tingling brass
Transcendent Doctrines, non-meditation, old dog barks
Past present future burn in Candleflame

incense fills intellects—
Mornings I wake, forgetting my dreams,
dreary hearted, lift my body out of bed
shave, wash, sit, bow down to the ground for hours.

II

Which country is real, mine or the teacher's?
Going back & forth I cross the Canada border, unguarded,
guilty, smuggling 10,000 thoughts.

III

Sometimes my guru seems a Hell King, sometimes a King in
Eternity,
sometimes a newspaper story, sometimes familiar eyed
father, lonely mother, hard working—
Poor man! to give me birth who may never grow up
and earn my own living.

May 7, 1980

IV

Now the sky's clearer, clouds lifted, a patch of blue
shows above Mt. Victoria. I should go walking to the Plain of
the Six Glaciers
but I have to eat Oryoki style, prostrate hours in the basement, study for Vajrayana Exams—
If I had a heart attack on the path around the lake would I be
ready to face my mother?

Noon

V

Scandal in the Buddhafields
The lake's covered with soft ice inches thick.
Naked, he insulted me under the glacier!
He raped my mind on the wet granite cliffs!

He misquoted me in the white mists all over the *Nation.*
Hurrah! the Clouds drift apart!
        Big chunks of blue sky fall down!
Mount Victoria stands with a mouth full of snow.

VI

I wander this path along little Lake Louise, the teacher's too
        busy to see me,
my dharma friends think I'm crazy, or worse, a lonely neu-
        rotic, maybe I am—
Alone in the mountains, same as in snowy streets of New
        York.

VII

Trapped in the Guru's Chateau surrounded by 300 disciples
I could go home to Cherry Valley, Manhattan, Nevada City
to be a farmer forever, die in Lower East Side slums, sit with
        no lightbulbs in the forest,
Return to my daily mail Secretary, *Hard Times,* Junk mail and
        love letters, get wrinkled old in Manhattan
Fly out and sing poetry, bring home windmills, grow toma-
        toes and Marijuana
chop wood, do Zazen, obey my friends, muse in Gary's Maidu
        Territory, study acorn mush,
Here I'm destined to study the Higher Tantras and be a slave
        of Enlightenment.
Where can I go, how choose? Either way my life stands before
        me,
mountains rising over the white lake 6 A.M., mist drifting
        between water and sky.

May 7–9, 1980

From White Shroud: Poems (1980–1985).

Why I Meditate

I sit because the Dadaists screamed on Mirror Street
I sit because the Surrealists ate angry pillows
I sit because the Imagists breathed calmly in Rutherford and
Manhattan
I sit because 2400 years
I sit in America because Buddha saw a Corpse in Lumbini
I sit because the Yippies whooped up Chicago's teargas skies
once
I sit because No because
I sit because I was unable to trace the Unborn back to the
womb
I sit because it's easy
I sit because I get angry if I don't
I sit because they told me to
I sit because I read about it in the Funny Papers
I sit because I had a vision also dropped LSD
I sit because I don't know what else to do like Peter Orlovsky
I sit because after Lunacharsky got fired & Stalin gave
Zhdanov a special tennis court I became a rootless
cosmopolitan
I sit inside the shell of the old Me
I sit for world revolution

July 19, 1981

Thoughts Sitting Breathing II

When I sat in my bedroom for devotions, meditations &
prayers
my Gomden on a sheepskin rug beside the mirrored closet,
white curtains morning sunlit, Friday *Rocky Mountain News*
"Market Retreats in Busiest Day"
lying on the table by Nuclear Nightmare issue of *Newsweek,*
Katherine Mansfield's thick bio & Addington Symonds' *The
Greek Poets*

lifting a white lamp above my headboard pillow illuminating
Living Country Blues' small print 1 A.M. last night,
with B complex bottled, green mint massage oil, High Blood
Pressure nightly Clonadine Hydrochloric pills,
athlete's foot Tolnaftate cream, newsclip scissors and a rusty
shoe-last bookweight standing on xeroxed Flying Saucer
papers,
new ballpoint pens, watch, wallet, loose coins keys Swiss
army knife
toothpicks, pencil sharpener & filefolder of Buddhist Analytic
Psyche papers
scattered random across this bedstead desk—
As I breathed between white walls, Front Range cliffs resting
in the sky outside south windows
I remembered last night's television suitcoat tie debate, the
neat Jewish right wing student outwitted a nervous
Dartmouth pimply liberal editor
knowing that boy who swears to "get the Government off our
backs" would give my tax money to Army brass bands
FBI rather than St. Mark's Poetry Project—
He can't read verse with any sense of humor sharp eyed
but then some poets can't either, did Ed Dorn find me fatu-
ous, can I breathe in hot black anger & breathe out white
cool bliss?
Doomed guilty layman all my life! these pills causing
impotency?
Could I move bookcases & clothes out of my bedroom, 8 foot
desk file cabinets & typewriter
to the small apartment next door N.Y., would that end my
hideous Public Karma,
Telephones tingling down my spine, pederast paranoid hyp-
notic burnt out teenage fruitcake poets
banging the door for protection from Brain Damaged Electric
Guitar Police in New Wave Blue Vibration Uniforms?
Be that as it may as blue empty Buddha floats through blue
bodied sky,
should I settle down & practice meditation, care for my nervous Self, do nothing,

arrange paper manuscripts, die in Lower East Side peace
instead of heart attack in Ethiopia,
What way out of this Ego? let it appear disappear, mental
images
Nothing but thoughts, how solve World Problems by worrying in my bedroom?—
Still one clear word-mighty poem might reveal what Duncan
named Grief in America
that one hundred million folk malnourish the globe while
Civic Powers inflate $200 billion War Machines this
year—
and who gets rich on that, don't all of us get poor heart?—
but what do I know of Military Worlds?
Airfields and Aircraft Carriers, bugle Corps, ice cream conces-
sions,
million dollar Computer rockets—yes I glimpse CIA's spooky
dope deal vanity—but nothing of Camp Pendleton's
brainy Thoughts
Norfolk officers' vast housing tracts, messes and helicopters,
food resource
logistics Pentagon committees've amassed—NORAD's
Rapture Mountain
Maybe get rid of Cold War, give Russian Empire warm
weather access,
inaugurate trillion dollar Solar Power factories on every
Continent—
Yes access to sunny blue ocean, not Cold Murmansk &
Vladivostok Ports they need a vast hot harbor
International Agreement big warships forbidden, no battle-
ships from Russia or America in the azure Greek pond—
What about pirates, storms at sea or kamikaze Hell's Angel
North Africans shooting Jews?
Well a few small Police boats, no Cruiser or Nuclear Subs—
Yes a warm weather port for Russian access South I thought
sitting on my bedroom floor cushion 10:30 A.M. getting
hungry breathing thru shades & curtains on transparent
windows, morning sun shining on white painted walls
and gray rug—
So remembering the old story of Russia's claim to a warm

weather harbor I came back to myself, blue clouded Colorado sky adrift above the Bluff Street Boulder house.

November 8, 1982

. . . .

From a largely unedited conversation with James MacKenzie conducted in 1982. Others present include Dan Eades ("DE") and Peter Orlovsky ("PO"). In the interview, Ginsberg has just mentioned the dramatic and historical responsibility that he feels, as one of the Beats, for his role in opening up the "American consciousness."

JM: Is that something you've come to think about recently?

AG: No, we knew that back in 1948–49. You see Gary [Snyder] and I and others, by '48 had had some kind of psychedelic breakthrough without drugs—that is psychedelic mind manifestation—which I've talked about at great length in other places [. . .] and by '58, around the time when the media began coming around really heavily, exploring what we were having to say and distorting it and projecting a Frankenstein vision of it all over America, by that time—I remember there was one night I lay in my bed, in the middle of the night, realizing that if all those people were coming around, we must have touched some nerve, and if what we were saying had any truth to it . . . and then I shuddered in bed, realizing that America was going to take some awful fall and go through some great transmogrification and change because if other people's minds were going to be opened as ours were, or they were going to glimpse some of the nightmare of Moloch, of the money-bank capitalist earth-eating monster realization that we had already had, that everybody was going to go through a funny change. Like it took me to go through a bughouse to get adjusted to it, so I realized that in a sense we had an awesome responsibility that we had sort of intuited but hadn't asked for, but which I took very seriously, and realized it as a sort of national shiver around 1958—that it was really serious—that what we were talking about, though it seemed light and funny and, you know, beatnik humor and angels in the valleys and "High on the peak top, bats! and down in the valley the lamb," though it was all poetical, that there was strange penitrant awareness that we had been gifted with or latched on to.

JM: Can you say what made you see that then?

AG: We'd already had, by '48, some sort of alteration of our own private consciousness; by '55 we made some kind of public articulation of it; by '58 it had spread sufficiently so that the mass media were coming around for information, and by that time I realized that if our private fancies, our private poetries, were so serious that they absorbed the attention of the big, serious military generals who write for *Time* magazine, there must be something strange going on.

JM: You're speaking of the discovery of the Beats, and that made you know that it was . . .

AG: No, I'm speaking of the *exploitation* of the Beats—the Beat discovery is '52 or something. I'm talking about the mass media spread and exploitation, actually, in the stereotype characterization, the Frankenstein image that they put down. See, and as I saw the Frankenstein image being laid down by everything from Congress for Cultural Freedom, *Encounter* magazine, through *Partisan Review,* through *Time* magazine, through the *New York Daily News,* you know, sort of like a yellow press image of what was originally a sort of ethereal and angelic perception of America, and the world, and the nature of the mind, I realized early that if they were going to do that to us who were relatively innocent—just a bunch of poets—if they were going to make *us* out to be the monsters, then they must have been making the whole universe out to be a monster all along, like from the Communists to the radicals to anarchists to the Human Being in America; so then I began reflecting back that what we were doing had some kinship with what Whitman was doing in announcing large magnanimous full-consciousness of American person. Then I began digging Whitman's use of the word "Person" and linking our own struggle back to the tradition that was immediately contactable in the Populist good heart of William Carlos Williams, with whom we were in direct contact; and that linked us up, both by study and personal contact and letter, with Pound and his struggle with America; and through Williams to a great extent with Alfred Steiglitz and the Bohemians of the '20s and An American Place Gallery; and forgotten figures like John Herrmann of 1932 who won a literary prize with Thomas Wolfe for a proletarian novel; and Sherwood Anderson for his examination of the beating heart of lonely souls in Winesburg, Ohio; and the strange, cranky privacy of Melville in his old age writing love stories to Billy Budd, the handsome sailor; and Thoreau pondering in the woods about the overgrowth of competitive materialism in his own time as distinct from solitary study of minute particular detail of nature of which he accomplished by himself; and Thoreau going to jail not to pay war taxes for the Mexican War. So when the mass media began creating a hallucinatory image of the poetry activity that we were involved with and took that as sort of like something to mock and make an enemy of, then I realized that the whole country had a false mentality built up which was almost on the scale of mass hallucination. And so in 1958, Independence Day, I wrote an essay ("Poetry, Violence, and the Trembling Lambs," see *A Casebook on the Beat,* Thomas Parkinson, Ed., 1961) saying that America was going to have a nervous breakdown, and that part of the cause of it could be located in that year's 30 billion dollar military budget and the growth of the military police state; that one aspect of it was the persecution of the junkies and the drug people who were basically sensitives who may or may not have been fucked up but needed compassion and medical care rather than Swastika-like police agencies chasing them down with guns, calling them "fiends," which is a terrible violation of the human spirit to create a class of people in America called "fiends"—I mean it's diabolical. . . once you realize that you've got a class of armed police calling another group "fiends," you've really got a situation so surrealistic and hallucinatory and violent that there could be no outcome but some massive nervous breakdown in America when people find out that they've not only been lied to but drawn into a dream of reality which is not only false but painful and bitter and murderous. So I began seeing very clearly a line of transmission, gnostic insight—I think I picked up the gnostic aspect of it very early from [Professor] Raymond Weaver at Columbia, who was a friend of Kerouac's and mine, who suggested Kerouac read the Egyptian gnostics. I never explored it until maybe '67, and picked up on the actual tradition, except through Blake as of '48 and Blake was also a gnostic, and I had some direct transmission there. But I was seeing the transmission, in America, as a transmission of Person, the concept of Person, the feeling of Person, as a breakthrough, a *reasonable* breakthrough, beyond the purely conceptual mind that had gone mad with fake conceptions of thinking, head cut off from the body and cut off from affective feeling. So when I was lying in bed one night in 1958 I shuddered, realizing that America was taking a fall, was going to have to take a big fall.

Later, the conversation turns to Ginsberg's method of spontaneous composition.

AG: The point of "Howl" that Rexroth made at one time or another, that was historically interesting, was that it was a return to the vocalization of the poem, a return from the page to the voice in which everybody was interested—Olson, Creeley, Williams, all the Black Mountain Poets, Snyder, Whalen—actual voice. With "Howl" it was from voice, to spoken conversation voice, to chant, or to long breath chant, tending to the bardic-chanting direction, the ecstatic direction, and then from chanting it actually moves to song with Dylan in the next generation: and so returns to us as song. [. . .] now I am in an interesting situation where a lot of material I do, write, compose, the only *exact* extant manuscripts are chance tape recordings of poetry readings I improvise. So at almost every poetry reading I do some improvisation, you know, at one point or another—sometimes extended, sometimes generally rhymed blues form or ballad form, and I'm just slowly verging toward trying to improvise without music, you know, and do my regular forms like "Howl" or "Sunflower" or something like that, but without the crutch of music, or rhyme. Haven't gotten to that yet. Almost did the other day, though, because I went to a lecture of Chogyam Trungpa, and he said, "When we finish with the Refuge Ceremony, would you improvise a poem?" And I figured out, let's see now (semi-chanting) "Krishna has left the light bulbs, but the illumination shines by itself. Allah is gone out of the Holland Tunnel . . ." And I figured out four or five lines to begin with—then he forgot to call me up (laughing) after the ceremony. But it made me think of how to do it without music, you know, just thinking fast: I had to—for that situation, to improvise sensible Buddhist imagery, on the subject of there being no god but our own empty mind. [. . .]

Later, Ginsberg returns to the role of the Beats:

I don't think it's a question of being too conscious of our roles, in fame or history, because that's just part of the general reverberations of eternal consciousness which is much larger; it's part of the understanding of life as a dream or an illusion or a play, and it's not quite a corny matter of making a good act. It's more involved with Bodhisattva's vow in Buddhism, which is "sentient beings are numberless, vow to illuminate all; attachments are inexhaustible, vow to liberate all; nature gates, Dharma gates are countless, vow to enter every one; Buddha path limitless, endless, vow to follow through." And there's a certain natural impulse toward that, which then becomes more conscious as you study Dharma and meditate, but that Bodhisattvic compassion aspect was something that was very clear very early in Kerouac, and was really the basis of my feeling of love for him; and his tenderness to me was the realization that we were going to die, that we're here a very brief time, and that the body, the situation we were in, the houses we were in were all full of tears of mortality. And with Kerouac, the realization of the existence of suffering was very strong; and the briefness of it, the mortal clouds over it, the skies brooding over the pitiful lonely short brief man-vanity puppet-doll sense in his prose, that was really clear in his person and his prose. That perception in Kerouac, which he awakened in me, is very similar to the substance of the Bodhisattva vow.

From White Shroud (1980–1985).

In My Kitchen in New York

For Bataan Faigao

Bend knees, shift weight—
Picasso's blue deathhead self portrait
    tacked on refrigerator door—
This is the only space in the apartment
    big enough to do T'ai chi—
Straighten right foot & rise—I wonder
    if I should have set aside that garbage
    pail—
Raise up my hands & bring them back to
    shoulders—The towels and pajama
    laundry's hanging on a rope in the hall—
Push down & grasp the sparrow's tail—
    Those paper boxes of grocery bags are
    blocking the closed door—
Turn north—I should hang up all
    those pots on the stovetop—
Am I holding the world right?—That
    Hopi picture on the wall shows
    rain & lightning bolt—
Turn right again—thru the door, God
    my office space, a mess of
    pictures & unanswered letters—
Left on my hips—Thank God Arthur Rimbaud's
    watching me from over the sink—

Single whip—piano's in the room, well
        Steven & Maria finally'll move to their
        own apartment next week! His pants're
        still here & Julius in his bed—
This gesture's the opposite of St. Francis
        in Ecstasy by Bellini—hands
        down for me—
I better concentrate on what I'm doing—
        weight in belly, move from hips—
No, that was the single whip—that apron's
        hanging on the North wall a year
        I haven't used it once
Except to wipe my hands—the Crane
        spreads its wings—have I paid
        the electric bill?
Playing the guitar—do I have enough $
        to leave the rent paid while I'm
        in China?
Brush knee—that was good
        halvah, pounded sesame seed,
        in the icebox a week—
Withdraw & push—I should
        get a loft or giant living room—
The land speculators bought up all
        the square feet in Manhattan,
        beginning with the Indians—
Cross hands—I should write
        a letter to the *Times* saying
        it's unethical.

Come to rest hands down knees
        straight—I wonder how
        my liver's doing. O.K. I guess
        tonite, I quit smoking last
        week. I wonder if they'll blow
        up an H Bomb? Probably not.

Manhattan Midnight, September 5, 1984

. . . .

From Cosmopolitan Greetings: Poems 1986–1992.

On Cremation of Chogyam Trungpa, Vidyadhara

I noticed the grass, I noticed the hills, I noticed the highways,
I noticed the dirt road, I noticed car rows in the parking lot
I noticed ticket takers, I noticed the cash and checks & credit cards,
I noticed buses, noticed mourners, I noticed their children in red dresses,
I noticed the entrance sign, noticed retreat houses, noticed blue & yellow Flags—
noticed the devotees, their trucks & buses, guards in Khaki uniforms
I noticed crowds, noticed misty skies, noticed the all-pervading smiles & empty eyes—
I noticed pillows, colored red & yellow, square pillows and round—
I noticed the Tori Gate, passers-through bowing, a parade of men & women in formal dress—
noticed the procession, noticed the bagpipe, drum, horns, noticed high silk head crowns & saffron robes, noticed the three piece suits,
I noticed the palanquin, an umbrella, the stupa painted with jewels the colors of the four directions—
amber for generosity, green for karmic works, noticed the white for Buddha, red for the heart—
thirteen worlds on the stupa hat, noticed the bell handle and umbrella, the empty head of the cement bell—
noticed the corpse to be set in the head of the bell—
noticed the monks chanting, horn plaint in our ears, smoke rising from atop the firebrick empty bell—
noticed the crowds quiet, noticed the Chilean poet, noticed a Rainbow,

I noticed the Guru was dead, I noticed his teacher bare
breasted watching the corpse burn in the stupa,
noticed mourning students sat crosslegged before their books,
chanting devotional mantras,
gesturing mysterious fingers, bells & brass thunderbolts in
their hands
I noticed flame rising above flags & wires & umbrellas &
painted orange poles
I noticed the sky, noticed the sun, a rainbow round the sun,
light misty clouds drifting over the Sun—
I noticed my own heart beating, breath passing thru my nostrils
my feet walking, eyes seeing, noticing smoke above the
corpse-fir'd monument
I noticed the path downhill, noticed the crowd moving
toward buses
I noticed food, lettuce salad, I noticed the Teacher was absent,
I noticed my friends, noticed our car the blue Volvo, a young
boy held my hand
our key in the motel door, noticed a dark room, noticed a
dream
and forgot, noticed oranges lemons & caviar at breakfast,
I noticed the highway, sleepiness, homework thoughts, the
boy's nippled chest in the breeze
as the car rolled down the hillsides past green woods to the
water,
I noticed the houses, balconies overlooking a misted horizon,
shore & old worn rocks in the sand
I noticed the sea, I noticed the music, I wanted to dance.

May 28, 1987, 2:30–3:15 A.M.

. . . .

Ginsberg notes that "Big Eats" was a Mahamudra poetics exercise suggested by the Tibetan teacher Khenpo Tsultrim Gyamtso in 1991. The first of five verses, twenty-one syllables each, begins in "neurotic confusion" (Samsara) and the last concludes grounded in "ordinary mind" (Dharmakaya). From Cosmopolitan Greetings: Poems 1986–1992.

Big Eats

Big deal bargains TV meat stock market news paper headlines love life Metropolis
Float thru air like thought forms float thru the skull, check
the headlines catch the boyish ass that walks
Before you fall in bed blood sugar high blood pressure lower,
lower, your lips grow cold.
Sooner or later let go what you loved hated or shrugged off,
you walk in the park
You look at the sky, sit on a pillow, count up the stars in your
head, get up and eat.

August 20, 1991

. . . .

An excerpt from Ginsberg's introduction to Pomes All Sizes *by Jack Kerouac.*

My own poetry's always been modeled on Kerouac's practice of tracing his mind's thoughts and sounds directly on the page. Poetry can be "writing the mind," the Ven. Chogyam Trungpa phrased it, corollary to his slogan "First thought, best thought," itself parallel to Kerouac's formulation "Mind is shapely, Art is shapely." Reading *Mexico City Blues* to that great Buddhist teacher from the front carseat on a long drive Karme Choling Retreat Center (1972 called Tail of the Tiger) to New York, Trungpa laughed all the way as he listened: "Anger doesn't like to be reminded of fits. . . . The wheel of the quivering meat conception. . . . The doll-like way she stands / bowlegged in my dreams waiting to serve me. . . . Don't ignore other parts of the mind. . . ." As we got out of the car he stood on the pavement and said, *It's a perfect exposition of mind.*

The next day he told me, *I kept hearing Kerouac's voice all night, or yours and Anne Waldman's. . . .* It'd given him a new idea of American poetry, for his own poetry—thus Trungpa

Rinpoche's last decade's open-form international spontaneous style *First Thought Best Thought* poetry collection. Thus two years later "Jack Kerouac School of Disembodied Poetics" was founded with Naropa Institute, certainly a center for meeting of classical Eastern wisdom meditative practice with Western alert spontaneous candid thought, healthy synthesis of Eastern and Western Mind, at last these twain've met forever Hallelujah Svaha! [. . .]

PART II

Retrospect on Beat Generation

Meditating, still thinking of Kerouac's role as Dharma Bodhisattva Bringer or Messenger in *Mexico City Blues,* and after conversation with Wm. Burroughs at 4:00 P.M., inquiring Jack's catalytic effect in encouraging Bill to write—also having inspected Ann Charters' Viking Portable Library 1992 *Beat Reader*, ruminated:—

That the quality most pure in Kerouac was his grasp that life is really a dream ("a dream already ended," he wrote) as well as being real, both real and dream, both at the same time—a deep insight that cut through knots of artificial intellect, extremism, totalitarian rationality, "new reasons for spitefulness," cut through all the basic vanity, resentment, & wrongheadedness that cursed most XX-Century political and literary movements—or weakened them with impermanent grounding or stained them with the fog of misdirection. That realization of dream as the suchness of this universe pervaded the spiritual intelligence of all Beat writers on differing levels, whether Burroughs' suspicion of all "apparent sensory phenomena"; Herbert Huncke's *Evening Sun Turned Crimson;* Corso's paradoxical wit (viz., "Death hiding beneath the kitchen sink: 'I'm not real' it cried, 'I'm just a rumor spread by Life,'" a late paradox, or his earlier "Dirty Ears aims a knife at me/I pump him full of lost watches"); or Orlovsky's compassionate view of Minnerbia. "Her teeth-brush dream is the one she loves best"; or Snyder's meditations in mind wilderness; or Sensei Whalen's pithy aphorisms, "Poetry is a graph of the mind moving"; or McClure's insight into the gnat, "Nature abhors a vacuum"; or Lamantia's *Ecstasis* prophecy, "I long for the/it is nameless that I long for"; even John Wieners' heavy woe's the work of conscious dreamer, "Particles of light/worshipped in the pitches of the night."

But the doctrine of consciousness of Sunyatā, emptiness, with all its transcendental wisdom including panoramic awareness, oceanic city vastness, a humoresque appreciation of minute details of the big dream, especially "character in the bleak inhuman aloneness" in "Memorial Cello Time" is most clearly and consistently set forth in the body of Kerouac's prose, poetry, and essays.

This basic metaphysical understanding of the eternal nature of dream, more or less clearly perceived by the various "Beat" authors according to their individual temperaments, served as common ground and saved their essential work from the decay of time—because the "message" was permanent, as "change" and "emptiness" are a permanent gnosis from Heraclitus' time to now. As Beauty itself is the realization of simultaneous "emptiness" & "form," the co-emergent wisdom of Buddhadharma.

"Come back and tell me in a hundred years," Kerouac commanded—his koan.

"What was the face you had before you were born?"—that question was always at the heart of Beat poetry. It could be called the "Golden Ash" school, as Kerouac qualified existence. Thus Beat: "a dream already ended. . . ." Thus beatific, "the Golden Ash" of dream. One could call this Heart Failure a big success.

1/8/92

. . . .

A portion of the unedited transcript of a lecture given in Vienna in 1994.

Meditation and Poetics

What I've set out to do was to write a "gradum ad parnassus" a "graded road to Parnassus" by means of using slogans in the Maoist style or Tibetan form. Eastern thought teaches by slogans that seem to link logically, one after another, to some conclusion of compassion which is the ultimate result of sitting with yourself, suffering the fact of being in a body, knowing you're going to die and that everybody else is, that your intestines are rumbling, your feet hurt, your bones ache and that you're getting old or you're growing into puberty—one or another.

The situation is that we have the mind constantly producing thoughts, memories, future projections, prophecies.

So how do you work with a chaos, that complication, or continuous stream of undifferentiated thoughts, different thoughts?

Shakespeare suggests that, as Buddha does, the interesting thing to discover is that consciousness is discontinuous. It's not a continuous stream of consciousness where one thought follows another thought. There's a gap in between and we really don't know where the thoughts come from or how they link.

In that sense there's a kind of chaos. In that one minute, we might be thinking about frankfurters and the next minute we might be thinking about *Renaldo and Clara* and the next minute we might have to think about going to pee-pee.

So in writing then, rather than attempting to impose your fixed Marxist or Catholic or Hegelian idea on your thoughts, perhaps you might just take them as they come and write them down as they come in the order in which they come.

So the first slogan is: First thought, best thought! This is from Chogyam Trungpa Rinpoche, a Tibetan lama and he also says, as I've said, in meditation: "Take a friendly attitude toward your thought." Even if it involves sleeping with your mother. Just observe it! You don't have to do it, you just have to observe it.

One of the Presidents of the United States (John Adams) once said: "The mind must be loose," rather than fixated or solidified. So Charles Olson, the American poet, in his essay *Projective Verse* said: "One perception must immediately and directly lead to a further perception." One thought does lead to another thought. And as Shakespeare said: "Every third thought shall be my grave." Shakespeare was aware of "Thought number one, thought number two, thought number three." That's in one of the last plays of Shakespeare, a speech by Prospero in *The Tempest.*

Philip Whalen, an American poet, who is now a Zen Master in San Francisco, said: "My writing is a picture of the mind moving."

So we have the notion of "Surprise Mind," because we never know what we'll be thinking in one minute. It will rise on its own so the mind is a complete surprise. So Chogyam Trungpa Rinpoche, the founder of Naropa Institute, therefore said: "Magic is the total appreciation of chance." Magic is the total delight in accident, the total pleasure in surprise mind, the appreciation of the fact that the mind changes, that one perception leads to another, and that in itself is a great play of mind. You don't have to go further in order to create a work of art.

But then there's the problem that the mind may be very contradictory. One minute perhaps you want to sleep with your mother and the next minute you might want to sleep with your brother. So Walt Whitman said that that was allowable: "Do I contradict myself? Very well, I contradict myself. I am large, I contain multitudes."—because he had a democratic mind!

And John Keats said a very similar thing in a letter to his brother quoting a phrase which is well known to many English poets: "Negative capability."

He was dining with a group of boring academic poets and thought: What was it that made a man a genius like Shakespeare? And he wrote, "What quality went to form a man of achievement, especially in literature? 'Negative capability,' That is: When a man is capable of being in uncertainties, mysteries, doubts, without any irritable reaching after fact and reason." Not insisting on either black or white but having both: Black *and* white! Or as the poet Gregory Corso says: "If you have a choice between two different things, take both."

Since the mind is discontinuous and one thought follows another, if the form of your poem follows the form of your mind then you have a "formal" poetry. Something like Ezra Pound's *Cantos* or Kerouac's prose. Certain poems, like *The Waste Land,* are in a sense collage or tapestry of different thoughts.

One thought moving on another, you have a sort of modern form. The poet Robert Creeley said to Charles Olson in a letter: "Form is never more than an extension of content." If the content or subject matter of a poem—if the plot or theme of the poem—is the nature of the mind and the movement of the mind, then you have an open field for poetry in which any thought will be appropriate following another. Something like spontaneous speech or something like collage.

Frank Lloyd Wright, the architect, said: "Form follows function."

Here, I'm defining the content and the function—or the theme of a certain kind of modern poetry and film—as a mirror of the activity of the actual mind during the time of writing. Which was Kerouac's idea. So that the prose or the poetry should include everything that goes on in the mind of the writer during the time his pen is touching the paper until it picks up from the paper.

How can you include all those thoughts? Well, you can't include everything. You can only include what you can get down on paper. So then the process is self-selecting!

Maybe these notions might be too "ephemeral" or transitory, but there is an interesting motto by Louis Zukofsky—two verses that say: "Nothing is better for being eternal, / or so white as the white that dies of a day." It's also a kind of a Yiddish saying—he was a Jewish poet: "Nothing is *besser* for being eternal, / or so white as the white that dies of a day."

Ah . . . from that point of view you might also notice that "Ordinary mind includes eternal perceptions." The most vivid perceptions may come, not by searching for perception, but simply by observing your own mind.

So the process then for poetry would be, "To notice what you notice!," just as you are noticing your breath—that extra awareness of noticing what you see hear smell and feel. And the English phrase that is equivalent to that is: "Catch yourself thinking!" It's an idiomatic phrase. I don't think there's an equivalent idiom in German for: "Catch yourself thinking," like "Wake up to your mind and catch (or notice) yourself thinking."

Next, for the poet to "Observe what is vivid." Then the question rises: "How do we know what is vivid?" And the answer is: "If it's vivid, it's vivid. If it's not vivid, it's not vivid!" . . . So the slogan there is, "Vividness is self-selecting." It's like falling off a log! You don't have to work so hard to find something vivid. If it's vivid, it's there. If it's not vivid, you wouldn't remember it anyway.

So we have from William Wordsworth the notion of: "Spots of time." Luminous moments or moments of "Epiphany," moments which are memorable and which recur over and over in memory. And from another Tibetan lama, Gelek Rinpoche (my present teacher), the very interesting phrase: "My mind is open to itself."

So there is no problem of dredging up some great symbols from your unconscious, we are all constantly thinking and talking to ourselves. (Especially when we go to bed at night in the dark. Lying there with our eyes closed in the thick black fog of silence. "Each on his bed spoke to himself alone, making no sound.") This is the ground.

Diane di Prima
(1934-   )

"Whether we are aware of it or not, something of Buddhism pervades American consciousness. When Bodhidharma came from India to China with the Buddhism that was to become Ch'an and later Zen, his answer to the Chinese emperor's request for "the holy teachings" was "VASTNESS, NO HOLINESS!" *This seems to me to be at the very core of who we are, what we are doing in the world at this time, as a nation and as a species, as we move out of time into space. . . ."* —DIANE DI PRIMA

Diane di Prima's interest in poetry and meditation converged when at age twenty-two she began to explore Zen and meditative composition with writing teacher James Waring. A year later, in 1957, di Prima met Allen Ginsberg, Jack Kerouac, and Gregory Corso. Her first book of poetry, *This Kind of Bird Flies Backwards,* was published in 1958 and was followed in 1960 by *Dinners and Nightmares.* With coeditor LeRoi Jones (Amiri Baraka) she began *The Floating Bear,* a mimeographed newsletter, which became a vital voice in the community of Beat writers.

In 1962, di Prima met Shunryu Suzuki Roshi in San Francisco. She then packed up a zafu, a meditation cushion, and brought it back to New York and started sitting by herself. In Buddhist practice, she has written, she found the perfect complement to her work as a poet: "My work, my life, is images. This is what I do. When I first began sitting zazen I realized I was clearing my mind. By practicing deeply, the images start to flow. My teacher never contradicted this. Dharma practice and art are two sides of the same coin. Meditation is a rest from the art work." In 1968, she moved to the West Coast in order to "participate in the revolution" and to have more time to study with Suzuki Roshi at the Zen Center, where poets Philip Whalen and Gary Snyder were also practicing. While handing out free food with the Diggers, teaching writing workshops, and founding the Poets Press, di Prima continued to produce many volumes of poetry, much of her writing reflecting her strong political commitments and activism. After Suzuki Roshi's death, she became disaffiliated from the San Francisco center and studied for periods with Katagiri Roshi, Kwong Roshi, and Kobun Chino Roshi, as well as Chogyam Trungpa Rinpoche, whom she had met in 1970.

Di Prima taught at the 1974 opening session of the Poetics Program at Naropa Institute in Boulder, Colorado. In 1983, di Prima decided that eleven years without a teacher and a practice community was too much, and took up formal study with Chogyam Trungpa. The same year she cofounded the San Francisco Institute of Magical and Healing Arts. At present she continues to write poetry as well as to study Tibetan Buddhism, magic, alchemy, and healing.

The poems are arranged in the order in which they appear in di Prima's collection *Selected Poems 1956–75,* followed by some from *Pieces of a Song.*

. . . .

From Selected Poems 1956–1975.

The Master

oblong drippings on the tabletop.
steelwool.
ambulatory pieces of myself
                    making it around town
dust on my sandals
the green leaves still press the window
which doesnt mean we have another chance
means nothing
one way or the other
like a sax player, looking for the tune
no one behind him.

steel wool.
the green leaves. and I wonder who pulls the strings
they are pulled.
my arms ache.
instead of which, I wouldn't really mind
like in the "old days"   a bruise or two on my shoulder.

dust & more dust
rising too, the horses, making it into distances
will it all settle.
to say I have not lied, I will not lie, I do not lie?
It is the mind
moving.
take me along.

Buddhist New Year Song

I saw you in green velvet, wide full sleeves
seated in front of a fireplace, our house
made somehow more gracious, and you said
"There are stars in your hair"— it was truth I
brought down with me

to this sullen and dingy place that we must make golden
make precious and mythical somehow, it is our nature,
and it is truth, that we came here, I told you,
from other planets
where we were lords, we were sent here,
for some purpose

the golden mask I had seen before, that fitted
so beautifully over your face, did not return
nor did that face of a bull you had acquired
amid northern peoples, nomads, the Gobi desert

I did not see those tents again, nor the wagons
infinitely slow on the infinitely windy plains,
so cold, every star in the sky was a different color
the sky itself a tangled tapestry, glowing
but almost, I could see the planet from which we had come

I could not remember (then) what our purpose was
but remembered the name Mahakala, in the dawn

in the dawn confronted Shiva, the cold light
revealed the "mindborn" worlds, as simply that,
I watched them propagated, flowing out,
or, more simply, one mirror reflecting another.
then broke the mirrors, you were no longer in sight
nor any purpose, stared at this new blackness
the mindborn worlds fled, and the mind turned off:

a madness, or a beginning?

Prajapati

O Lord of Beasts
Herder of stars across the heavens
Hill god
Rudra
Who walks at dusk
We are all your beasts, who walk on these blue hills
Drawn by the sound of your bells
We hear your dance
Lord of the mountain
Young man with matted hair
There, in your bracelets—
Look, he raises his foot, the universe
Dissolves. He raises his hand
His hand says, have no fear.
Rush to see this, you maidens and young men
The king of the mountain is dancing
Draw closer
Look in his eyes

. . . .

From Revolutionary Letters, *published in 1968.*

Rant, From a Cool Place

'I see no end of it, but the turning upside down
of the entire world' —ERASMUS

We are in the middle of a bloody, heartrending revolution
Called America, called the Protestant reformation, called
Western man,

Called individual consciousness, meaning I need a refrigerator
and a car
And milk and meat for the kids so I can discover that I don't
need a car
Or a refrigerator, or meat, or even milk, just rice and a place
with no wind to sleep next to someone
Two someones keeping warm in the winter learning to weave
To pot and to putter, learning to steal honey from bees, wearing the bedclothes by day, sleeping under
(or in) them at night; hording bits of glass, colored stones,
and stringing beads
How long before we come to that blessed definable state
Known as buddhahood, primitive man, people in a landscape
together like trees, the second childhood of man

I don't know if I will make it somehow nearer by saying all
this
out loud, for christs sake, that Stevenson was killed, that
Shastri was killed
both having dined with Marietta Tree
the wife of a higher-up in the CIA
both out of their own countries mysteriously dead, as how
many others
as Marilyn Monroe, wept over in so many tabloids
done in for sleeping with Jack Kennedy—this isn't a poem—
full of cold prosaic fact
thirteen done in in the Oswald plot : Jack Ruby's cancer that
disappeared in autopsy
the last of a long line—and they're waiting to get Tim Leary
Bob Dylan
Allen Ginsberg
LeRoi Jones—as, who killed Malcolm X? They give themselves away
with TV programs on the Third Reich, and I wonder if I'll
live to sit in Peking or Hanoi
see TV programs of LBJ's Reich : our great SS analysed, our
money exposed, the plot to keep Africa

genocide in Southeast Asia now in progress Laos Vietnam
                    Thailand Cambodia O soft-spoken
                    Sukarno
O great stone Buddhas with sad negroid lips torn down by us
                    by the red guard all one force
one levelling mad mechanism, grinding it down to earth and
                    swamp to sea to powder
till Mozart is something a few men can whistle
or play on a homemade flute and we bow to each other
telling old tales half remembered gathering shells
learning again 'all beings are from the very beginning
                    Buddhas'
or glowing and dying radiation and plague we come to that
                    final great love illumination
'FROM THE VERY FIRST NOTHING IS.'

Jan. 1967

. . . .

From Selected Poems 1956–75.

Alba, for a Dark Year

the star, the child, the light
returns
the darkness will not win completely
nor will the green dragon
entirely devour the sun

what is this softness that will not take no
for an answer
that penetrates and masses
like love
in an empty heart?

Buddha has seen
the morning star
dawns purple
and then gold
in the snowy mountains

your hands
flicker like sunlight
among candles

children
sit down in the streets
they buy
peace with their blood
it shines
on the gloomy pavement

our prayers
envelope us like a crystal sphere
in which we are all moving

. . . .

From Revolutionary Letters. *There are forty-three revolutionary letters in all.*

Revolutionary Letter #7

there are those who can tell you
how to make molotov cocktails, flamethrowers,
bombs whatever
you might be needing
find them and learn, define
your aim clearly, choose your ammo
with that in mind

it is not a good idea to tote a gun
or knife
unless you are proficient in its use
all swords are two-edged, can be used against you
by anyone who can get 'em away from you

it is
possible even on the east coast
to find an isolated place for target practice
success
will depend mostly on your state of mind :
meditate, pray, make love, be prepared
at any time, to die

Revolutionary Letter #13

now let me tell you
what is a Brahmasastra
Brahmasastra, hindu weapon of war
near as I can make out
a flying wedge of mind energy
hurled at the foe   by god or hero
or many heroes
hurled at a problem or enemy
cracking it

Brahmasastra can be made
by any or all
can be made by all of us
straight or tripping, thinking together
like : all of us stop the war
at nine o'clock tomorrow, each take one soldier
see him clearly, love him, take the gun
out of his hand, lead him to a quiet spot
sit him down, sit with him as he takes a joint
of viet cong grass from his pocket . . .

Brahmasastra can be made
by all of us, tripping together
winter solstice
at home, or in park, or wandering
sitting with friends
blinds closed, or on porch, no be-in
no need
to gather publicly
just gather spirit, see the forest growing
put back the big trees
put back the buffalo
the grasslands of the midwest with their herds
        of elk and deer
put fish in clean Great Lakes
desire that all surface water on the planet
be clean again. Kneel down and drink
from whatever brook or lake you conjure up.

Revolutionary Letter #33

how far back
are we willing to go? that seems to be
the question. the more we give up
the more we will be blessed, the more
we give up, the further back we go, can we
make it under the sky again, in moving tribes
that settle, build, move on and build again
owning only what we carry, do we need
the village, division of labor, a friendly potlatch
a couple of times a year, or must it be
merely a 'cybernetic civilization'
which may or may not save the water, but will not
show us our root, or our original face, return
us to the source, how far
(forward is back) are we willing to go
after all?

. . . .

From Selected Poems 1956–1975.

Trajectory

suffering, sd the Lama, is the greatest blessing
because it reminds us
to seek the disciplines, like :
I don't drink coffee 'cause I once
had an ulcer; and of the four
"continents" of humans, this, the South
Continent (planet Earth) he says
is best because hardest. So this
1970 must be
an excellent time
when even the telephone poles scream in agony
when the streets are fire beneath
all our windows,
when even the Bodhisattvas stop their ears.

as if they could.
as if we could, we sit
zazen, retreat to the woods
fast, pray, remember bardos
unwritten, even in Tibet.
they come again.
they have us by the throat.

we break before the image of the future
now no more blood runs
from the wounded Earth. our hope
lies in the giant squid that Melville saw, that was
acres across. our hope
lies in the insect world, that the rustling
Buddha of locusts, of ants, tarantulas

of scorpions & spiders
teaching crustacean compassion might extend it
to our species
(the Hopi say that it's been done before
and plant their last corn before coal mines
destroy the water table)   a child of mine
waits to be born in this.   *Tristesse.*   *Tristesse.*

Dolor. Now is no star seen
as it was seen by our fathers
now is no color on the hills, no brightness
in the bay. Now do sea creatures rot
with oily fur
with oily feathers choke on black sand.
the hungry ghosts like a wind
descend on us.

Sixth Notebook Incantation

Ping-ponging back & forth across America
starting small grass fires where I land
in Minnesota jail, Wyoming
community college, high schools of South Tucson
may I always remember the Bodhisattvas
sitting down in BIA cafeteria, may I
cut hamburger with the sword of Manjusri
pluck lotuses on windy Nebraska hills
set jewels of Lokeshvara round my neck
after I brush my teeth in steam-heated
dormitory bathroom.
Pure light of ancient wisdom, stay w/me
like a follow spot, pierce my
                    armored heart, clean
cobwebs of plastic food & deadened
                    eternal sorrow.
"How do you like it here?" "I like it
very much."

Brief Wyoming Meditation

I read
Sand Creek massacre: White Antelope's scrotum
                                        became tobacco pouch
for Colorado Volunteer;
I see
destitute prairie: short spiny grass & dusty wind
& all for beef too expensive to eat;
I remember
at least two thirds of you voted for madman Nixon
were glad to bomb the "gooks" in their steamy jungle
& I seek
  I seek
  I seek
the place where your nature meets mine,
          the place where we touch

nothing lasts long
nothing
but earth
& the mountains

No Problem Party Poem

first glass broken on patio no problem
forgotten sour cream for vegetables no problem
Lewis MacAdam's tough lower jaw no problem
cops arriving to watch bellydancer no problem
plastic bags of melted ice no problem
wine on antique tablecloth no problem
scratchy stereo no problem
neighbor's dog no problem
interviewer from Berkeley Barb no problem
absence of more beer no problem
too little dope no problem

leering Naropans no problem
cigarette butts on the altars no problem
Marilyn vomiting in planter no problem
Phoebe renouncing love no problem
Lewis renouncing Phoebe no problem
hungry ghosts no problem
absence of children no problem
heat no problem
dark no problem
arnica scattered in nylon rug no problem
ashes in bowl of bleached bones & juniper berries no problem
lost Satie tape no problem
loss of temper no problem
arrogance no problem
boxes of empty beer cans & wine bottles no problem
thousands of styrofoam cups no problem
Gregory Corso no problem
Allen Ginsberg no problem
Diane di Prima no problem
Anne Waldman's veins no problem
Dick Gallup's birthday no problem
Joanne Kyger's peyote no problem
wine no problem
rum no problem
coca-cola no problem
getting it on in the wet grass no problem
running out of toilet paper no problem
decimation of pennyroyal no problem
destruction of hair clasp no problem
paranoia no problem
claustrophobia no problem
growing up on Brooklyn streets no problem
growing up in Tibet no problem
growing up in Chicano Texas no problem
bellydancing certainly no problem
figuring it all out no problem
giving it all up no problem
giving it all away no problem

devouring everything in sight no problem
        what else in Allen's refrigerator?
        what else in Anne's cupboard?
        what do you know that you
                haven't told me yet?
no problem.   no problem.   no problem.

staying another day no problem
getting out of town no problem
telling the truth, almost no problem
        easy to stay awake
        easy to go to sleep
        easy to sing the blues
        easy to chant sutras
what's all the fuss about?

it decomposes—no problem
we pack it in boxes—no problem
we swallow it with water, lock it in the trunk,
    make a quick getaway.   NO PROBLEM.

. . . .

The following passages are based on a lecture di Prima gave at Naropa Institute on June 24, 1975. In the talk, entitled "Light/and Keats," di Prima explores the connections between Keats's idea of "negative capability" and Buddhist practice. Di Prima includes passages from Keats's letters in her talk.

[. . .] there is a growing system of thought that Keats is evolving, but systematizing it would be simplistic—it would do him an injustice. As he said, "I have never yet been able to perceive how anything can be known for truth by consecutive reasoning." I want to just take the quotes and look at them—follow him chronologically through the process.

> *December 22, 1817.*—[*The winter solstice, by the way.*] The excellence of every art is its intensity, capable of making all disagreeables evaporate from their being in close relationship with Beauty and Truth . . . several things dove-tailed in my mind, and at once it struck me what quality went to form a Man of Achievement, especially in Literature, and which Shakespeare possessed so enormously—I mean *Negative Capability,* that is, when a man is capable of being in uncertainties, mysteries, doubts, without any irritable reaching after fact and reason. Coleridge, for instance, would let go by a fine isolated verisimilitude caught from the Penetralium of mystery, from being incapable of remaining content with half-knowledge. This pursued through volumes would perhaps take us no further than this, that with a great poet the sense of Beauty overcomes every other consideration, or rather obliterates all consideration.

So, at this point what he's calling a sense of beauty, what obliterates all consideration or all thinking process, is that same experience that we have *whenever* it all drops away. A kind of satori. My friend Katagiri Roshi, who's a Zen master in Minneapolis, gave six lectures once on the word WOW. WOW, as the complete American Zen experience. When it all drops away, when the sense of beauty obliterates all consideration, or the sense of the overwhelmingness of it. Wow, that's all we said for the last three days, me and my two friends, as we drove here from California, through all this incredible country, and we kept saying. . . . They were asleep one night and I'm driving, and saying Wow, Wow.

Negative capability. Now you see how that idea, first of the man of genius not partaking of any individual character, becomes a bigger or more universal idea, which is that idea of negative capability of *not pursuing any viewpoint.* It's kind of a real Eastern idea. Except that it happened fresh from nothing at this point in this kid in some dumpy English suburb. "When a man is capable of being in uncertainties, mysteries, doubts, without any irritable reaching after fact and reason." And to get that state, clearly enough focused to make it the matter of poetry, so that you don't try to "make sense," but become this receiving tube, become this focusing point [. . . .]

> *May 3, 1818.* An extensive knowledge is needful to thinking people—it takes away the heat and fever; and helps, by widening speculation, to ease the Burden of the Mystery. . . . The difference of high Sensations with and without knowledge appears to me this: the latter case we are falling continually ten thousand fathoms deep and being blown up again, without wings, and with all the horror of a bare shouldered Creature—in the former case, our shoulders are fledged, and we go through the same air and space without fear.

The way he talks about knowledge there is almost a Buddhist sense of knowledge. Without knowledge high sensations give us just that sense of falling, and there's no way to simply allow it, allow them to occur. Unless you can allow what Keats calls Sensation with that negative capability, you'll never get out of where you were in the first place, never pierce the veils. A Buddhist statement, really, or a gnostic one—in the full sense of gnosis: knowledge eases the Burden of the Mystery.

> *October 9, 1818.* Poetry must work out its own salvation in a man: It cannot be matured by law and precept, but by sensation and watchfulness in itself—That which is creative must create itself—

"That which is creative must create itself." This is an attempt to describe the workings of the creative imagination—that thing which spins itself out of itself. Experienced also in meditation. "Sensation and *watchfulness.*" I think you can see here that poetry was for Keats—can be for us—a complete practice, a form of what Suzuki Roshi called "Way-seeking Mind," leading us to knowledge. The creative creates itself.

> *October 27, 1818.* As to the poetical Character itself (I mean that sort, of which, if I am anything, I am a member; that sort distinguished from the Wordsworthian, or

> egotistical Sublime; which is a thing per se and stands alone), it is not itself—it has no self—It is everything and nothing—It has no character—it enjoys light and shade; it lives in gusto, be it foul or fair, high or low, rich or poor, mean or elevated—It has as much delight in conceiving an Iago as an Imogen. What shocks the virtuous philosopher delights the chameleon poet. . . . A poet is the most unpoetical of anything in existence, because he has no Identity—he is continually informing and filling some other body. The Sun,—the Moon,—the Sea, and men and women, who are creatures of impulse, are poetical, and have about them an unchangeable attribute; the poet has none, no identity—he is certainly the most unpoetical of all God's creatures. . . . It is a wretched thing to confess; but it is a very fact, that not one word I ever utter can be taken for granted as an opinion growing out of my identical Nature—how can it, when I have no Nature? When I am in a room with people, if I ever am free from speculating on creations of my own brain, then not myself goes home to myself, but the identity of every one in the room begins to press upon me, so that I am in a very little time annihilated—not only among men; it would be the same in a nursery of Children . . .

This is, I believe, where he most insistently tries to come to terms with *having no Nature.* The open space in which the poem occurs. That theme, "not myself goes home to myself," you know, but the identity of every creature . . . harks back to that earlier passage I read about the man of genius having no individual character, as opposed to what Keats calls "the egotistical Sublime." Only now—a year later—he much more urgently tries to get in there and explore, talk about, that open space. Maybe it would have been better if Buddhism *had* come to England, because he would have had some mechanisms for dealing with that loss of self. He might have had techniques for being that man of genius and remaining centered, so that maybe he wouldn't have gotten sick. [. . .]

. . . .

From Selected Poems 1956–1975.

Visit to Katagiri Roshi

A pleasure.
We talk of here & there
gossip about the folks in San Francisco
laugh a lot. I try
to tell him (to tell someone)
what my life is like:
the hungry people, the trying
    to sit zazen in motels;
the need in America like a sponge
    sucking up
whatever prana & courage
"Pray to the Bodhisattvas" sez
    Katagiri Roshi.

I tell him
that sometimes, traveling, I am
too restless to sit still, wiggle &
    itch. "Sit
only ten minutes, five minutes
at a time" he sez—first time
it has occurred to me that this
wd be OK.

As I talk, it becomes OK
there becomes some continuity
in my life; I even understand
    (or remember)
why I'm on the road.

As we talk a continuity, a
    transfer of energy
takes place.
It is *darshan,* a blessing,
transmission of some basic joy
some way of seeing.
LIKE A TANGIBLE GIFT IN THE HAND
    In the heart.
It stays with me.

. . . .

From Pieces of a Song, *1990.*

Life Chant

may it come that all the radiance
will be known as our own radiance
—TIBETAN BOOK OF THE DEAD

cacophony of small birds at dawn
        may it continue
sticky monkey flowers on bare brown hills
        may it continue
bitter taste of early miner's lettuce
        may it continue
music on city streets in the summer nights
        may it continue
kids laughing on roofs on stoops on the beach in the snow
        may it continue
triumphal shout of the newborn
        may it continue
deep silence of great rainforests
        may it continue

fine austerity of jungle peoples
        may it continue
rolling fuck of great whales in turquoise ocean
        may it continue
clumsy splash of pelican in smooth bays
        may it continue
astonished human eyeball squinting thru aeons at astonished
                                        nebulae who squint back
        may it continue
clean snow on the mountain
        may it continue
fierce eyes, clear light of the aged
        may it continue
rite of birth & of naming
        may it continue
rite of instruction
        may it continue
rite of passage
        may it continue
love in the morning, love in the noon sun
love in the evening among crickets
        may it continue
long tales by fire, by window, in fog, in dusk on the mesa
        may it continue
love in thick midnight, fierce joy of old ones loving
        may it continue
the night music
        may it continue
grunt of mating hippo, giraffe, foreplay of snow leopard
                    screeching of cats on the backyard fence
        may it continue
without police
        may it continue
without prisons
        may it continue
without hospitals, death medicine: flu & flu vaccine
        may it continue
without madhouses, marriage, highschools that are prisons
        may it continue

without empire
            may it continue
in sisterhood
            may it continue
thru the wars to come
            may it continue
in brotherhood
            may it continue
tho the earth seem lost
            may it continue
thru exile & silence
            may it continue
with cunning & love
            may it continue
as woman continues
            may it continue
as breath continues
            may it continue
as stars continue
            may it continue

may the wind deal kindly w/us
may the fire remember our names
may springs flow, rain fall again
may the land grow green, may it swallow our mistakes

we begin the work
        may it continue
the great transmutation
        may it continue
a new heaven & a new earth
        may it continue
        may it continue

Harold Norse
(1916–   )

Harold Norse began his literary career at the age of twenty-two when, after attending W. H. Auden's first U.S. reading, Norse befriended the eminent poet and took up a post as his secretary. Norse's literary friends included such established writers as Tennessee Williams and James Baldwin and a very young Allen Ginsberg. Although Norse's poetry had been published in journals since 1934, it was not until the early fifties that his career began to take off; William Carlos Williams singled him out for his reading at New York's Museum of Modern Art in a discovery program presenting new poets. The following year Norse left for Europe to pursue writing and translation.

Norse began to learn about Buddhism in Florence in 1956 through a book given to him by a friend. Shortly thereafter the poet became ill with viral pneumonia and went to convalesce in Spain; he brought his newfound meditative practices with him.

When Norse received a letter from William Carlos Williams, he was stunned to read that poets back home had started to pursue the same interest. On February 14, 1957, Williams had written to urge him to return to the States to take part in a new literary movement: "They are headed by Allen Ginsberg, Jack Kerouac . . . A feature of the united front that these men present is that they are all Zen Buddhists, one of their most influential members [Gary Snyder] is at the present time living in a monastery in Japan. . . ." Norse recorded his reaction in his memoirs: "I was astonished, for I too was practicing Buddhist meditation. My friend Edgar had given me a book published in Ceylon called *The Way of Mindfulness* by Bhikku Soma. He also sent me the name of a German Buddhist monk in his eighties to whom I wrote for advice while practicing meditation. The effect on me of learning that Allen Ginsberg was doing this in New York was electric, not to mention that he had become a leader in a literary movement."

While Norse did not take Williams's advice to return to the U.S., he nevertheless came into close contact with other Beat writers. In Paris in 1959, Gregory Corso introduced Norse to William Burroughs, who urged Norse to move into the two-dollar-a-day "Beat Hotel," so-called for its clientele, which included, at various times, Burroughs, Brion Gysin, Allen Ginsberg, and others. Norse lived there for three years, sharing ideas and collaborating with Burroughs on a catalogue for an exhibition of Norse's "cosmographs," a series of ink drawings. Norse returned to the U.S. in the seventies and became a leading proponent of gay liberation. He has authored thirteen volumes of poetry; a cut-up novel, *Beat Hotel*; an autobiography, *Memoirs of a Bastard Angel;* and *The American Idiom,* a ten-year correspondence with William Carlos Williams.

. . . .

Published in Big Table 3, *1960.*

The Fire Sermon

Those monks with matted hair
Those ancient priests half-nude
Who followed the Great One in his wanderings
They knew what childish passions keep from us
Who flex our fleshly intellect
Those monks   those ancient priests
Chanting in forests   disciplined in wastes
By roots of trees   by lakes
Calm in the dust storm   under the tiger's glow
Smiling at the long tooth   unmoved by the dancing girl
By raging thug   by elements
At the river bank   in the desert   on the mountain peak
Following wisdom   And at Gaya Head
The Blessed One gathering the monks around him said
"All things   O priests   are on fire"   And the world blazed
Eyes   lips   sex   blood   taste   birth   death
Liver   idea   pain   beautiful   blue
A huge bonfire of time and we in the center
"And the free man knows he is no more for this world"
O ancient priests   O countrymen

. . . .

From Karma Circuit: 20 Poems and a Preface, *1966.*

Kali Yug

            it's Kali Yug &
        the planet's expanding
    like a rotten orange ready to burst
the sun hasn't long to burn
& the asteroid
earthwards with deadly aim
                hurries to keep

its apocalyptic rendezvous
the atlantic thrusts up
an undersea mountain
pushing south america
& africa further apart
& bombs in the grip
of lunatics
keep me awake
nights

what poem can influence
a munitions manufacturer?

poems can't deflect bullets
can't alter pain
or suffering
or make me for one instant forget
that i will die

this is absurd i am not afraid
of death but the void i have not yet
filled with poems or
understanding

go
tell it on the
mountain
that the priest who mumbles a prayer
with soft waving hands
& jewelled crucifix
or the
proud grayhaired surgeon
indifferent
to desperation
has more dignity
or that you barely
alive & overworked
with your thermometers & bedpans

& practical air
in your white
nursecap
have less validity

man man

is this a fantasy of ether
on a lifelong operating table?

Athens 1965

. . . .

From Hotel Nirvana: Selected Poems 1953–1973.

The House Is on Fire!

Flowerchildren I'm with you Diggers I'm with you too
I'm with your frame of reference I'm with your Dharma
I want to share this Love that is pushing my Nerves out of my Skin
beating my head against the noise of London & the boys of London
I want beautiful Personal Cities
no put-downs rules or regulations throw the City wide open to Love
Compassion not Walls of Fire
not Philistine Hells
no crooks fuzz sadistic Games
love communes need no moneygame to score Bread
make lips available down on each other in final Twentieth
Century gasp of Delight forget the Manufacturer's Label
keep clear of the Gates of the Midland Bank
let's journey to Space beyond the London Planetarium
travel on Astral feet

beyond Evil environment o love commune o god
Freedom
will we ever make it? Freedom from Things & Persons
Freedom from Thought if only to let Mind stop stop Time
go naked freeflowing
slip off our clothes
act out our fantasies
live out our dreams
but no
oh terrible lives spent in banks & offices & shops & soulless brick
buildings!
Dickensian solitudes of jails & basement kitchens!
commercials of tube & poster!
monstrous iniquities of a fucked-up century!
heads of boys cut off from bleeding trunks in Viet Nam War!
charred limbs of continuous war within ourselves
fedback to War fedback to Ourselves!
O CHRIST!
WAR IN EVERY TONGUE! IN EVERY WORD!
I'M SICK OF WAR OF WORDS
OUR OWN DOUBLETHINK MINDS
NOT KNOWING NOT KNOWING
EVEN THE POEM A LIE!
MAD UNDERTONES FORM JURASSIC SLIME IN OUR BONES!

impossible Ultimata O Lao Tse!
have I alternatives under the Law
of Reciprocal Action?
stuck under stars
in Voids
in this nowhere Universe
I call my Self?

flaming naphtha & napalm soak the earth
as I sit here writing poems in London

about the nastiness of Man
THE HOUSE IS ON FIRE!
& we go on
talking

London 1967

PART TWO

The San Francisco Poets

Gary Snyder
(1930-   )

"I perceived that there was a kind of freedom and mobility that one gained in the world, somewhat analogous to the wandering Buddhist monk of ancient times, that was permitted you by having a proper pack and sleeping bag, so that you could go out on the road and through the mountains into the countryside. The word for Zen monk in Chinese, yun shui, *means literally "clouds and water," and it's taken from a line in Chinese poetry, "To float like clouds, to flow like water . . ."*

—GARY SNYDER

Gary Snyder grew up in Washington State, where he developed a powerful awareness of nature. As a boy of nine or ten, he saw Chinese landscape paintings that struck an immediate chord: To him they looked like "real mountains," like the Cascades. At Reed College in Portland, Oregon, Snyder was able to share his interest in Chinese poetry, haiku, and Buddhism with his friends Philip Whalen and Lew Welch. After a year of graduate school in anthropology, Snyder enrolled at the University of California at Berkeley to study Asian languages.

In the summers, Snyder worked as a mountain lookout, where according to the journal from one summer, 1953, he passed the time with a volume of the collected Blake, sumi painting, and *Walden.* Members of his family had been homesteaders and Wobblies, and there was much in Thoreau's anarchic politics and connection to nature that had a resonance for Snyder. In 1955 Snyder participated in the Six Poets at the Six Gallery reading, and made fast friends with Jack Kerouac. Kerouac sensed in Snyder a coming together of different strands of American myths and created a character based on Snyder, Japhy Ryder, who was to galvanize a generation and touch off a "rucksack revolution" across the country. As Snyder has said: "If my life and work is in some sense a kind of an odd extension, in its own way, of what Thoreau, Whitman, John Muir, etc. are doing, then Jack hooked into that and he saw that as valuable to him for his purposes in this century." In the same interview with Barry Gifford and Lawrence Lee, Snyder added: "In a way the Beat Generation is a gathering together of all the available models and myths of freedom in America that had existed before, namely: Whitman, John Muir, Thoreau, and the American bum. We put them together and opened them out again, and it becomes like a literary motif, and then we added some Buddhism to it."

The year following the Six Gallery reading, Snyder left for Japan to engage in formal Zen practice. While he was there, studying with Oda Sesso Roshi, his first two books of poetry, *Riprap* and *Myths & Texts,* were published. Despite his physical remove from the Beat Generation, Snyder continued to wield a powerful influence on the movement both through his own work and through his friendships with many Beat writers. Joanne Kyger, Philip Whalen, and Allen Ginsberg were all drawn to Japan by Snyder's presence. He also introduced many to sitting practice, through personal example and through writings such as "Spring Sesshin at Sokoku-ji," a detailed description of monastery life published in the *Chicago Review*'s 1958 Zen issue.

In 1969, Snyder returned to the United States, where he continued his prodigious output of essays and poems. He was awarded the Pulitzer Prize for *Turtle Island,* his 1975 collection. He now lives at the bottom of the Sierra Nevada foothills, where he writes and also practices at the Ring of Bone Zendo. *No Nature*, a collection of new and selected poems, was published in 1992.

. . . .

From Riprap, *Snyder's first collection of poems, written from 1953 to 1958.*

Piute Creek

One granite ridge
A tree, would be enough
Or even a rock, a small creek,
A bark shred in a pool.
Hill beyond hill, folded and twisted
Tough trees crammed
In thin stone fractures
A huge moon on it all, is too much.
The mind wanders. A million
Summers, night air still and the rocks
Warm.   Sky over endless mountains.
All the junk that goes with being human
Drops away, hard rock wavers
Even the heavy present seems to fail
This bubble of a heart.
Words and books
Like a small creek off a high ledge
Gone in the dry air.

A clear, attentive mind
Has no meaning but that
Which sees is truly seen.
No one loves rock, yet we are here.
Night chills. A flick
In the moonlight
Slips into Juniper shadow:
Back there unseen
Cold proud eyes
Of Cougar or Coyote
Watch me rise and go.

. . . .

Snyder defines riprap *as: "a cobble of stone laid on steep, slick rock to make a trail for horses in the mountains."*

Riprap

Lay down these words
Before your mind like rocks.
            placed solid, by hands
In choice of place, set
Before the body of the mind
            in space and time:
Solidity of bark, leaf, or wall
            riprap of things:
Cobble of milky way,
            straying planets,
These poems, people,
            lost ponies with
Dragging saddles
            and rocky sure-foot trails.
The worlds like an endless
            four-dimensional

Game of *Go*.
    ants and pebbles
In the thin loam, each rock a word
    a creek-washed stone
Granite: ingrained
    with torment of fire and weight
Crystal and sediment linked hot
    all change, in thoughts,
As well as things.

. . . .

This excerpt from Myths & Texts, *the first long poem that Snyder published, comes from the section entitled "Burning," which concludes the poem. The last line seems to allude not only to the morning star that Shakyamuni Buddha saw upon his enlightenment, but also to Henry David Thoreau's* Walden, *which ends with the same sentence.*

the text

Sourdough mountain called a fire in:
Up Thunder Creek, high on a ridge.
Hiked eighteen hours, finally found
A snag and a hundred feet around on fire:
All afternoon and into night
Digging the fire line
Falling the burning snag
It fanned sparks down like shooting stars
Over the dry woods, starting spot-fires
Flaring in wind up Skagit valley
From the Sound.
Toward morning it rained.
We slept in mud and ashes,
Woke at dawn, the fire was out,
The sky was clear, we saw
The last glimmer of the morning star.

the myth

Fire up Thunder Creek and the mountain—
                    Troy's burning!
The cloud mutters
The mountains are your mind.
The woods bristle there,
Dogs barking and children shrieking
Rise from below.
Rain falls for centuries
Soaking the loose rocks in space
Sweet rain, the fire's out
The black snag glistens in the rain
& the last wisp of smoke floats up
Into the absolute cold
Into the spiral whorls of fire
The storms of the Milky Way
"Buddha incense in an empty world"
Black pit cold and light-year
Flame tongue of the dragon
Licks the sun

The sun is but a morning star

Crater Mt. L.O. 1952—Marin-an 1956

. . . .

This essay first appeared under the title "Buddhist Anarchism" in 1961 and was revised for inclusion in Earth House Hold: Technical Notes & Queries to Fellow Dharma Revolutionaries.

Buddhism and the Coming Revolution

Buddhism holds that the universe and all creatures in it are intrinsically in a state of complete wisdom, love and compassion; acting in natural response and mutual interdependence. The personal realization of this from-the-beginning state cannot be had for and by one-"self"—because it is not fully realized unless one has given the self up; and away.

In the Buddhist view, that which obstructs the effortless manifestation of this is Ignorance, which projects into fear and needless craving. Historically, Buddhist philosophers have failed to analyze out the degree to which ignorance and suffering are caused or encouraged by social factors, considering fear-and-desire to be given facts of the human condition. Consequently the major concern of Buddhist philosophy is epistemology and "psychology" with no attention paid to historical or sociological problems. Although Mahayana Buddhism has a grand vision of universal salvation, the *actual* achievement of Buddhism has been the development of practical systems of meditation toward the end of liberating a few dedicated individuals from psychological hangups and cultural conditionings. Institutional Buddhism has been conspicuously ready to accept or ignore the inequalities and tyrannies of whatever political system it found itself under. This can be death to Buddhism, because it is death to any meaningful function of compassion. Wisdom without compassion feels no pain.

No one today can afford to be innocent, or indulge himself in ignorance of the nature of contemporary governments, politics and social orders. The national polities of the modern world maintain their existence by deliberately fostered craving and fear: monstrous protection rackets. The "free world" has become economically dependent on a fantastic system of stimulation of greed which cannot be fulfilled, sexual desire which cannot be satiated and hatred which has no outlet except against oneself, the persons one is supposed to love, or the revolutionary aspirations of pitiful, poverty-stricken marginal societies like Cuba or Vietnam. The conditions of the Cold War have turned all modern societies—Communist included—into vicious distorters of man's true potential. They create populations of "preta"—hungry ghosts, with giant appetites and throats no bigger than needles. The soil, the forests and all animal life are being consumed by these cancerous collectivities; the air and water of the planet is being fouled by them.

There is nothing in human nature or the requirements of human social organization which intrinsically requires that a culture be contradictory, repressive and productive of violent and frustrated personalities. Recent findings in anthropology and psychology make this more and more evident. One can prove it for himself by taking a good look at his own nature through meditation. Once a person has this much faith and insight, he must be led to a deep concern with the need for radical social change through a variety of hopefully non-violent means.

The joyous and voluntary poverty of Buddhism becomes a positive force. The traditional harmlessness and refusal to take life in any form has nation-shaking implications. The practice of meditation, for which one needs only "the ground beneath one's feet," wipes out mountains of junk being pumped into the mind by the mass media and supermarket universities. The belief in a serene and generous fulfillment of natural loving desires destroys ideologies which blind, maim and repress—and points the way to a kind of community which would amaze "moralists" and transform armies of men who are fighters because they cannot be lovers.

Avatamsaka (Kegon) Buddhist philosophy sees the world as a vast interrelated network in which all objects and creatures are necessary and illuminated. From one standpoint, governments, wars, or all that we consider "evil" are uncompromisingly contained in this totalistic realm. The hawk, the swoop and the hare are one. From the "human" standpoint we cannot live in those terms unless all beings see with the same enlightened eye. The Bodhisattva lives by the sufferer's standard, and he must be effective in aiding those who suffer.

The mercy of the West has been social revolution; the mercy of the East has been individual insight into the basic self/void. We need both. They are both contained in the traditional three aspects of the Dharma path: wisdom (prajña), meditation (dhyāna), and morality (śīla). Wisdom is intuitive knowledge of the mind of love and clarity that lies beneath one's ego-driven anxieties and aggressions. Meditation is going into the mind to see this for yourself—over and over again, until it becomes the mind you live in. Morality is bringing it back out in the way you live, through personal example and responsible action, ultimately toward the true community (sangha) of "all beings." This last aspect means, for me, supporting any cultural and economic revolution that moves clearly toward a free, international, classless world. It means using such means as civil disobedience, outspoken criticism, protest, pacifism, voluntary poverty and even gentle violence if it comes to a matter of restraining some impetuous redneck. It means affirming the widest possible spectrum of non-harmful individual behavior—defending the right of individuals to smoke hemp, eat peyote, be polygynous, polyandrous or homosexual. Worlds of behavior and custom long banned by the Judaeo-Capitalist-Christian-Marxist West. It means respecting intelligence and learning, but not as greed or means to personal power. Working on one's own responsibility, but willing to work with a group. "Forming the new society within the shell of the old"—the I.W.W. slogan of fifty years ago.

The traditional cultures are in any case doomed, and rather than cling to their good aspects hopelessly it should be remembered that whatever is or ever was in any other culture can be reconstructed from the unconscious, through meditation. In fact, it is my own view that the coming revolution will close the circle and link us in many ways with the most creative aspects of our archaic past. If we are lucky we may eventually arrive at a totally integrated world culture with matrilineal descent, free-form marriage, natural-credit communist economy, less industry, far less population and lots more national parks.

. . . .

From Turtle Island, *1975.*

LMFBR

Death himself,
      (Liquid Metal Fast Breeder Reactor)
      stands grinning, beckoning.
Plutonium tooth-glow.
Eyebrows buzzing.
Strip-mining scythe.

Kālī dances on the dead stiff cock.

      Aluminum beer cans, plastic spoons,
plywood veneer, PVC pipe, vinyl seat covers.
                  don't exactly burn, don't quite rot,
                  flood over us,

                  robes and garbs
                  if the Kālī-yūgā

                        end of days.

Dusty Braces

O you ancestors
lumber schooners
            big moustache
long-handled underwear
sticks out under the cuffs

Jack Kerouac photographed standing before a storefront near Tompkins Square Park, New York, in the fall of 1953 by Allen Ginsberg.

© GORDON BALL

Philip Whalen (left) and Allen Ginsberg photographed by Gordon Ball in San Francisco, 1971.

© ALLEN GINSBERG

Jack Kerouac photographed in Tompkins Square Park, New York, in the fall of 1953 by Allen Ginsberg.

© ALLEN GINSBERG

Gary Snyder photographed by Allen Ginsberg in the Sierra Nevadas in 1965.

Joanne Kyger photographed by Allen Ginsberg in India in January 1962.

A photograph taken by Allen Ginsberg in Almora, India: Joanne Kyger (with mirror), Gary Snyder (with notebook), Peter Orlovsky (far right), and two guides.

Philip Whalen photographed by John Doss in Bolinas, California, 1969.

© FRED McDARRAH

Jack Kerouac and Albert Saijo spontaneously composing poetry in New York City, 1957. Photograph by Fred McDarrah.

© ALLEN GINSBERG

Joanne Kyger, Gary Snyder, and guide photographed by Allen Ginsberg on the Japan Sea in July 1963.

Diane di Prima reading from *Revolutionary Letters* at a Diggers' function held in San Francisco in December 1968. Photograph by John Doss.

© JOHN DOSS

Lenore Kandel at Muir Beach near Wobbly Rock in August 1968. Photograph by John Doss.

© JOHN DOSS

© JOHN DOSS

Lew Welch photographed by John Doss in Marin City, California, 1970.

COURTESY OF CYNTHIA ARCHER

Will Petersen practicing calligraphy in Japan, 1956.

© FRED McDARRAH

Bob Kaufman at the Living Theater, New York, 1960. Photograph by Fred McDarrah.

Lew Welch in front of City Lights Bookstore. Photograph by John Doss.

Will Petersen photographed by G. N. Katona.

William Burroughs photographed outside his home in Lawrence, Kansas, May 1991. Photograph by Allen Ginsberg.

Philip Whalen photographed by Allen Ginsberg in New York, March 1984.

Anne Waldman and William Burroughs in Boulder, Colorado, July 1984. Photograph by Allen Ginsberg.

Michael McClure photographed by Chris Felver.

Kenneth Rexroth photographed by Margo Moore.

Allen Ginsberg photographed in front of a portrait of Walt Whitman. Photograph by Misao Mizuno.

Line drawing in ink of Buddha by Allen Ginsberg.

Lawrence Ferlinghetti on the porch of his Bixby Canyon cabin, May 1993. Photograph by Chris Felver.

Harold Norse in San Francisco, photographed by Allen Ginsberg, May 1988.

© ALLEN GINSBERG

Bob Kaufman photographed by Ira Nowinski.

COURTESY OF NEW DIRECTIONS PUBLISHING CORP.

© MISAO MIZUNO

Philip Whalen photographed in Zen robes by Misao Mizuno, 1991.

tan stripes on each shoulder,
dusty braces—
    nine bows
    nine bows
you bastards
my fathers
and grandfathers, stiff-necked
punchers, miners, dirt farmers, railroad-men

killd off the cougar and grizzly

nine bows. Your itch
in my boots too,

—your sea roving
tree hearted son.

. . . .

Peter Barry Chowka interviewed Snyder for East West Journal *in New York City in 1977.*

CHOWKA: In a 1975 interview you said, "The danger *and* hope politically is that Western civilization has reached the end of its ecological rope. Right now there is the potential for the growth of a real people's consciousness." In *Turtle Island* you identify the "nub of the problem" as "how to flip over, as in jujitsu, the magnificent growth-energy of modern civilization into a nonacquisitive search for deeper knowledge of self and nature." You hint that "the 'revolution of consciousness' [can] be won not by guns but by seizing key images, myths, archetypes . . . so that life won't seem worth living unless one is on the transforming energy's side." What specific suggestions and encouragement can you offer today so that this "jujitsu flip" can be hastened, practically, by individuals?

SNYDER: It cannot even be begun without the first of the steps on the Eightfold Path, namely Right View. I'll tell you how I came to hold Right View in this regard, in a really useful way. I'm a fairly practical and handy person; I was brought up on a farm where we learned how to figure things out and fix them. During the first year or two that I was at Daitoku-ji Sodo, out back working in the garden, helping put in a little firewood, or firing up the bath, I noticed a number of times little improvements that could be made. Ultimately I ventured to suggest to the head monks some labor- and time-saving techniques. They were tolerant of me for a while. Finally, one day one of them took me aside and said, "We don't want to do things any better or any faster, because that's not the point—the point is that you live the whole life. If we speed up the work in the garden, you'll just have to spend that much more time sitting in the zendo, and your legs will hurt more." It's all one meditation. The importance is in the right balance, and not how to save time in one place or another. I've turned that insight over and over ever since.

What it comes down to simply is this: If what the Hindus, the Buddhists, the Shoshone, the Hopi, the Christians are suggesting is true, then all of industrial/technological civilization is really on the wrong track, because its drive and energy are purely mechanical and self-serving—*real* values are someplace else. The real values are within nature, family, mind, and into liberation. Implicit are the possibilities of a way of living and being which is dialectically harmonious and complexly simple, because that's the Way. Right Practice, then, is doing the details. And how do we make the choices in our national economic policy that take into account *that* kind of cost accounting—that ask, "What is the natural-spiritual price we pay for this particular piece of affluence, comfort, pleasure, or labor saving?" "Spiritual price" means the time at home, time with your family, time that you can meditate, the difference between what comes to your body and mind by walking a mile as against driving (plus the cost of the gas). There's an accounting that no one has figured out how to do.

The only hope for a society ultimately hell-bent on self-destructive growth is not to deny growth as a mode of being, but to translate it to another level, another dimension. The literalness of that other dimension is indeed going to have to be taught to us by some of these other ways. There are these wonderfully pure, straightforward, simple, Amish, won't-have-anything-to-do-with-the-government, plain folk schools of spiritual practice that are already in our own background.

The change can be hastened, but there are preconditions to doing that which I recognize more clearly now. Nobody can move from Right View to Right Occupation in a vacuum as a solitary individual with any ease at all. The three treasures are Buddha, Dharma, and Sangha. In a way the one that we pay least attention to and have least understanding of is Sangha—community. What have to be built are community networks—not necessarily communes or anything fancy. When people, in a very modest way, are able to define a certain unity of being together, a commitment to staying together for a while, they can begin to correct their use of energy and find a way to be mutually employed. And this, of course, brings a commitment to the place, which means right relation to nature [. . . .]

I would take this all the way back down to what it means to get inside your belly and cross your legs and sit—to sit down on the ground of your mind, of your original nature, your place, your people's history. Right Action, then, means sweeping the garden. To quote my teacher, Oda Sesso: "In Zen there are only two things: you sit, and you sweep the garden. It doesn't matter how big the garden is." That is not a new discovery; it's what people have been trying to do for a long time. That's why there are such beautiful little farms in the hills of Italy, people did that.

. . . .

From Left Out in the Rain, *this poem appears in the "Shasta Nation 1968–1985" section.*

We Make Our Vows Together with All Beings

Eating a sandwich
At work in the woods,

As a doe nibbles buckbrush in snow
Watching each other,
chewing together.

A Bomber from Beale
over the clouds,
Fills the sky with a roar.

She lifts head, listens,
Waits til the sound has gone by.

So do I.

. . . .

The following excerpt comes from The Practice of the Wild, *1990.*

Blue Mountains Constantly Walking

FUDŌ AND KANNON

The mountains and rivers of this moment are the actualization of the way of the ancient Buddhas. Each, abiding in its own phenomenal expression, realizes completeness. Because mountains and waters have been

> active since before the eon of emptiness, they are alive at this moment. Because they have been the self since before form arose, they are liberated and realized.

This is the opening paragraph of Dōgen Kigen's astonishing essay *Sansuikyo*, "Mountains and Waters Sutra," written in the autumn of 1240, thirteen years after he returned from his visit to Song-dynasty China. At the age of twelve he had left home in Kyoto to climb the well-worn trails through the dark hinoki and sugi (cedar-and-sequoia-like) forests of Mt. Hiei. This three-thousand-foot range at the northeast corner of the Kamo River basin, the broad valley now occupied by the huge city of Kyoto, was the Japanese headquarters mountain of the Tendai sect of Buddhism. He became a novice monk in one of the red-painted shadowy wooden temples along the ridges.

> "The blue mountains are constantly walking."

In those days travelers walked. The head monk at the Daitoku-ji Zen monks' hall in Kyoto once showed me the monastery's handwritten "Yearly Tasks" book from the nineteenth century. (It had been replaced by another handwritten volume with a few minor updates for the twentieth century.) These are the records that the leaders refer to through the year in keeping track of ceremonies, meditation sessions, and recipes. It listed the temples that were affiliated with this training school in order of the traveling time it took to get to them: from one day to four weeks' walk. Student monks from even those distant temples usually made a round trip home at least once a year.

Virtually all of Japan is steep hills and mountains dissected by fast shallow streams that open into shoestring valleys and a few wider river plains toward the sea. The hills are generally covered with small conifers and shrubs. Once they were densely forested with a cover of large hardwoods as well as the irregular pines and the tall straight hinoki and sugi. Traces of a vast network of well-marked trails are still found throughout the land. They were tramped down by musicians, monks, merchants, porters, pilgrims, and periodic armies.

We learn a place and how to visualize spatial relationships, as children, on foot and with imagination. Place and the scale of space must be measured against our bodies and their capabilities. A "mile" was originally a Roman measure of one thousand paces. Automobile and airplane travel teaches us little that we can easily translate into a perception of space. To know that it takes six months to walk across Turtle Island/North America walking steadily but comfortably all day every day is to get some grasp of the distance. The Chinese spoke of the "four dignities"—Standing, Lying, Sitting, and Walking. They are "dignities" in that they are ways of being fully ourselves, at home in our bodies, in their fundamental modes. I think many of us would consider it quite marvelous if we could set out on foot again, with a little inn or a clean camp available every ten or so miles and no threat from traffic, to travel across a large landscape—all of China, all of Europe. That's the way to see the world: in our own bodies.

Sacred mountains and pilgrimage to them is a deeply established feature of the popular religions of Asia. When Dōgen speaks of mountains he is well aware of these prior traditions. There are hundreds of famous Daoist and Buddhist peaks in China and similar Buddhist and Shinto-associated mountains in Japan. There are several sorts of sacred mountains in Asia: a "sacred site" that is the residence of a spirit or deity is the simplest and possibly oldest. Then there are "sacred areas"—perhaps many dozens of square miles—that are special to the mythology and practice of a sect with its own set of Daoist or Buddhist deities—miles of paths—and dozens or hundreds of little temples and shrines. Pilgrims might climb thousands of feet, sleep in the plain board guesthouses, eat rice gruel and a few pickles, and circumambulate set routes burning incense and bowing at site after site.

Finally there are a few highly formalized sacred areas that have been deliberately modeled on a symbolic diagram (mandala) or a holy text. They too can be quite large. It is thought that to walk within the designated landscape is to enact specific moves on the spiritual plane (Grapard, 1972). Some friends and I once walked the ancient pilgrimage route of the Ōmine Yamabushi (mountain ascetics) in Nara prefecture from

Yoshino to Kumano. In doing so we crossed the traditional center of the "Diamond-Realm Mandala" at the summit of Mt. Ōmine (close to six thousand feet) and four hiking days later descended to the center of the "Womb-Realm Mandala" at the Kumano ("Bear Field") Shrine, deep in a valley. It was the late-June rainy season, flowery and misty. There were little stone shrines the whole distance—miles of ridges—to which we sincerely bowed each time we came on them. This projection of complex teaching diagrams onto the landscape comes from the Japanese variety of Vajrayana Buddhism, the Shingon sect, in its interaction with the shamanistic tradition of the mountain brotherhood.

The regular pilgrimage up Mt. Ōmine from the Yoshino side is flourishing—hundreds of colorful Yamabushi in medieval mountain-gear scale cliffs, climb the peak, and blow conches while others chant sutras in the smoky dirt-floored temple on the summit. The long-distance practice has been abandoned in recent years, so the trail was so overgrown it was almost impossible to find. This four-thousand-foot-high direct ridge route makes excellent sense, and I suspect it was the regular way of traveling from the coast to the interior in paleolithic and neolithic times. It was the only place I ever came on wild deer and monkeys in Japan.

In East Asia "mountains" are often synonymous with wilderness. The agrarian states have long since drained, irrigated, and terraced the lowlands. Forest and wild habitat start at the very place the farming stops. The lowlands, with their villages, markets, cities, palaces, and wineshops, are thought of as the place of greed, lust, competition, commerce, and intoxication—the "dusty world." Those who would flee such a world and seek purity find caves or build hermitages in the hills—and take up the practices which will bring realization or at least a long healthy life. These hermitages in time became the centers of temple complexes and ultimately religious sects. Dōgen says:

> Many rulers have visited mountains to pay homage to wise people or ask for instructions from great sages. . . . At such time these rulers treat the sages as teachers, dis-

> regarding the protocol of the usual world. The imperial power has no authority over the wise people in the mountains.

So "mountains" are not only spiritually deepening but also (it is hoped) independent of the control of the central government. Joining the hermits and priests in the hills are people fleeing jail, taxes, or conscription. (Deeper into the ranges of southwestern China are the surviving hill tribes who worship dogs and tigers and have much equality between the sexes, but that belongs to another story.) Mountains (or wilderness) have served as a haven of spiritual and political freedom all over.

Mountains also have mythic associations of verticality, spirit, height, transcendence, hardness, resistance, and masculinity. For the Chinese they are exemplars of the "yang": dry, hard, male, and bright. Waters are feminine: wet, soft, dark "yin" with associations of fluid-but-strong, seeking (and carving) the lowest, soulful, life-giving, shape-shifting. Folk (and Vajrayana) Buddhist iconography personifies "mountains and waters" in the *rupas*—"images" of Fudō Myō-ō (Immovable Wisdom King) and Kannon Bosatsu (The Bodhisattva Who Watches the Waves). Fudō is almost comically ferocious-looking with a blind eye and a fang, seated or standing on a slab of rock and enveloped in flames. He is known as an ally of mountain ascetics. Kannon (Kuan-yin, Avalokitesvara) gracefully leans forward with her lotus and vase of water, a figure of compassion. The two are seen as buddha-work partners; ascetic discipline and relentless spirituality balanced by compassionate tolerance and detached forgiveness. Mountains and Waters are a dyad that together make wholeness possible: wisdom and compassion are the two components of realization. Dōgen says:

> Wenzi said, "The path of water is such that when it rises to the sky, it becomes raindrops; when it falls to the ground, it becomes rivers." . . . The path of water is not noticed by water, but is realized by water.

There is the obvious fact of the water-cycle and the fact that mountains and rivers indeed form each other: waters are precipitated by heights, carve or deposit landforms in their flowing descent, and weight the offshore continental shelves with sediment to ultimately tilt more uplifts. In common usage the compound "mountains and waters"—*shan-shui* in Chinese—is the straightforward term for landscape. Landscape painting is "mountains and waters pictures." (A mountain range is sometimes also termed *mai*, a "pulse" or "vein"—as a network of veins on the back of a hand.) One does not need to be a specialist to observe that landforms are a play of stream-cutting and ridge-resistance and that waters and hills interpenetrate in endlessly branching rhythms. The Chinese feel for land has always incorporated this sense of a dialectic of rock and water, of downward flow and rocky uplift, and of the dynamism and "slow flowing" of earth-forms. There are several surviving large Chinese horizontal handscrolls from premodern eras titled something like "Mountains and Rivers Without End." Some of them move through the four seasons and seem to picture the whole world.

"Mountains and waters" is a way to refer to the totality of the process of nature. As such it goes well beyond dichotomies of purity and pollution, natural and artificial. The whole, with its rivers and valleys, obviously includes farms, fields, villages, cities, and the (once comparatively small) dusty world of human affairs.

This

"The blue mountains are constantly walking."

Dōgen is quoting the Chan master Furong. Dōgen was probably envisioning those mountains of Asia whose trails he had walked over the years—peaks in the three to nine-thousand-foot range, hazy blue or blue-green, mostly tree-covered, maybe the steep jumbled mountains of coastal South China where he had lived and practiced thirteen years earlier. (Timberline at these latitudes is close to nine thousand feet—none of these are alpine mountains.) He had walked thousands of miles. ("The Mind studies the way running barefoot.")

> If you doubt mountains walking you do not know your own walking.

Dōgen is not concerned with "sacred mountains"—or pilgrimages, or spirit allies, or wilderness as some special quality. His mountains and streams are the processes of this earth, all of existence, process, essence, action, absence; they roll being and nonbeing together. They are what we are, we are what they are. For those who would see directly into essential nature, the idea of the sacred is a delusion and an obstruction: it diverts us from seeing what is before our eyes: plain thusness. Roots, stems, and branches are all equally scratchy. No hierarchy, no equality. No occult and exoteric, no gifted kids and slow achievers. No wild and tame, no bound or free, no natural and artificial. Each totally its own frail self. Even though connected all which ways; even *because* connected all which ways.

This, *thusness,* is the nature of the nature of nature. The wild in wild.

So the blue mountains walk to the kitchen and back to the shop, to the desk, to the stove. We sit on the park bench and let the wind and rain drench us. The blue mountains walk out to put another coin in the parking meter, and go on down to the 7-Eleven. The blue mountains march out of the sea, shoulder the sky for a while, and slip back into the waters.

. . . .

From No Nature, *1992.*

Ripples on the Surface

"Ripples on the surface of the water—
were silver salmon passing under—different
from the ripples caused by breezes"

A scudding plume on the wave—
a humpback whale is
breaking out in air up
gulping herring
          —Nature not a book, but a *performance,* a
high old culture

Ever-fresh events
scraped out, rubbed out, and used, used, again—
the braided channels of the rivers
hidden under fields of grass—

The vast wild
          the house, alone.
The little house in the wild,
          the wild in the house.
Both forgotten.

No nature

Both together, one big empty house.

Philip Whalen
(1923-   )

"This poetry is a picture or graph of a mind moving, which is a world body being here and now which is history . . . and you."

—PHILIP WHALEN

Philip Whalen's first exposure to Buddhism was as a high school student at his hometown library in Portland, Oregon. Curious about religions, Whalen sought out alternatives to Christianity in books on theosophy, Buddhism, and Asian thought. After being drafted and serving in the military, Whalen planned to study Oriental languages at the University of California at Berkeley but, when his money ran short, returned instead to Portland, where he attended Reed College. At Reed, he became friends with Lew Welch and Gary Snyder and eventually moved in with them. The three of them shared in Snyder's discovery of the haiku translations by R. H. Blyth and, later, the writings of D. T. Suzuki, and encouraged in each other a mutual interest in Asian thought.

After college, Whalen made his way to San Francisco, where he worked odd jobs and continued writing. In 1952, he moved into an apartment with Gary Snyder. He had followed Snyder's lead in finding employment as a fire lookout in Washington State and was still up in his watchtower in 1955 when he received an invitation from Snyder to read at the Six Poets at the Six Gallery reading. Whalen accepted and soon met Allen Ginsberg and Jack Kerouac.

In 1960, Whalen's first two books, *Like I Say* and *Memoirs of an Interglacial Age,* were published. Whalen also became friends with a number of other San Francisco poets who shared his interest in Buddhism: Joanne Kyger, Will Petersen, and Albert Saijo. In the mid-sixties, Whalen joined Snyder in Kyoto, eventually returning to the States in order to proofread his forthcoming collection, *On Bear's Head.* In 1969 Whalen returned to Kyoto for several years. In 1971, Whalen, back in the States, went to live at the San Francisco Zen Center on the invitation of the abbot, Richard Baker Roshi. One year later Whalen requested ordination as a monk, and three years later he became head monk at the Zen Mountain Center in Tassajara Springs, California. He also taught periodically at Naropa Institute as a visiting poet. During these years he published many volumes of poetry as well as a novel. In 1987, Whalen left his teacher, Baker Roshi, at his urging, and in 1991 Whalen was installed as the abbot of the Hartford Street Zen Center in San Francisco.

Whalen's productivity as a writer has slowed in proportion to the time he devotes to his Buddhist practice. For that reason, many of the poems in this selection are early works.

. . . .

From Like I Say.

from *Three Variations, All About Love*

I

So much to tell you
Not just that I love
There is so much more
You must hear and see

If I came to explain
It would do no good
Wordlessly nibbling your ear
Burying my face in your belly

All I would tell is you
And love; I must tell
Me, that I am a world
Containing more than love

Holding you and all your other
Lovers wherein you
And I are free from each other
A world that anyone can walk alone
Music, coathangers, the sea
Mountains, ink, trashy novels
Trees, pancakes, *The Tokaido Road*
The desert—it is yours

Refuse to see me!
Don't answer the door or the telephone
Fly off in a dragon-chariot
Forget you ever knew me

But wherever you are
Is a corner of me, San Juan Letrán
Or Montreal, Brooklyn
Or the Lion Gate

Under my skin at the Potala
Behind my eyes at Benares
Far in my shoulder at Port-au-Prince
Lifted in my palm among stars

Anywhere you must be you
Drugged, drunk or mad
As old, as young, whatever you are
Living or dying the place will be me

And I alone the car that carries you away.

III

(BIG HIGH SONG FOR SOMEBODY)

F
Train
Absolutely stoned
Rocking bug-eyed billboards WAFF!
No more bridge than Adam's
off ox
Pouring over 16 2/3ds MPH sodium-

Vapor light yellow light

LOVE YOU!

Got *you* on
like a coat of paint
Steamy girder tile

LOVE YOU!

Cutting-out blues
(Tlaxcala) left me
like stoned on the F-train
whole week's load ready
for that long stretch ahead
Prisoners jailed
SHBAM
Train chained to this train
boring through diamonds
SQUALL

LOVE YOU!

Barreling zero up Balcony Street
Leaning from ladders
Same angle of lean; different cars
The Route of the PHOEBE SNOW

LOVE YOU!

Blue-black baby
16-foot gold buddha in your arms
Taking you with me!
Straight up Shattuck Avenue
Hay-burning train, bull-chariot
With bliss bestowing hands

LOVE YOU!

And I'm the laughing man
with a load of goodies for all

Bridge still stands, bulls may safely graze,
Bee-birds in the frangipani
clock

LOVE YOU!

Sourdough Mountain Lookout

Tsung Ping (375–443): "Now I am old and infirm. I fear I shall no more be able to roam among the beautiful mountains. Clarifying my mind, I meditate on the mountain trails and wander about only in dreams."
—in *The Spirit of the Brush,* tr. by Shio Sakanishi, p. 34.

FOR KENNETH REXROTH

I always say I won't go back to the mountains
I am too old and fat there are bugs mean mules
And pancakes every morning of the world

Mr. Edward Wyman (63)
Steams along the trail ahead of us all
Moaning, "My poor old feet ache, my back
Is tired and I've got a stiff prick"
Uprooting alder shoots in the rain

Then I'm alone in a glass house on a ridge
Encircled by chiming mountains
With one sun roaring through the house all day
& the others crashing through the glass all night
Conscious even while sleeping

Morning fog in the southern gorge
Gleaming foam restoring the old sea-level
The lakes in two lights green soap and indigo
The high cirque-lake black half-open eye

Ptarmigan hunt for bugs in the snow
Bear peers through the wall at noon
Deer crowd up to see the lamp
A mouse nearly drowns in the honey
I see my bootprints mingle with deer-foot
Bear-paw mule-shoe in the dusty path to the privy

Much later I write down:
        "raging. Viking sunrise
        The gorgeous death of summer in the east"
(Influence of a Byronic landscape—
Bent pages exhibiting depravity of style.)

Outside the lookout I lay nude on the granite
Mountain hot September sun but inside my head
Calm dark night with all the other stars
HERACLITUS: "The Waking have one common world
But the sleeping turn aside
Each into a world of his own."

I keep telling myself what I really like
Are music, books, certain land and sea-scapes
The way light falls across them, diffusion of
Light through agate, light itself . . . I suppose
I'm still afraid of the dark

        "Remember smart-guy there's something
        Bigger something smarter than you."
        Ireland's fear of unknown holies drives
        My father's voice (a country neither he
        Nor his great-grandfather ever saw)

        A sparkly tomb a plated grave
        A holy thumb beneath a wave

Everything else they hauled across Atlantic
Scattered and lost in the buffalo plains
Among these trees and mountains

From Duns Scotus to this page
A thousand years

                ("... a dog walking on his hind legs—
                not that he does it well but that he
                does it at all.")

Virtually a blank except for the hypothesis
That there is more to a man
Than the contents of his jock-strap

EMPEDOCLES: "At one time all the limbs
Which are the body's portion are brought together
By Love in blooming life's high season; at another
Severed by cruel Strife, they wander each alone
By the breakers of life's sea."

Fire and pressure from the sun bear down
Bear down centipede shadow of palm-frond
A limestone lithograph—oysters and clams of stone
Half a black rock bomb displaying brilliant crystals
Fire and pressure Love and Strife bear down
Brontosaurus, look away

My sweat runs down the rock

HERACLITUS: "The transformations of fire
are, first of all, sea; and half of the sea
is earth, half whirlwind. . . .
It scatters and it gathers; it advances
and retires."

I move out of a sweaty pool
(The sea!)
And sit up higher on the rock

Is anything burning?

The sun itself! Dying
Pooping out, exhausted
Having produced brontosaurus, Heraclitus
This rock, me,
To no purpose
I tell you anyway (as a kind of loving) . . .

Flies & other insects come from miles around
To listen
I also address the rock, the heather,
The alpine fir

BUDDHA: "All the constituents of being are
Transitory: Work out your salvation with diligence."

(And everything, as one eminent disciple of that master
Pointed out, has been tediously complex ever since.)

There was a bird
Lived in an egg
And by ingenious chemistry
Wrought molecules of albumen
To beak and eye
Gizzard and craw
Feather and claw

My grandmother said:
"Look at them poor bed-
raggled pigeons!"

And the sign in McAlister Street:

"IF YOU CAN'T COME IN
SMILE AS YOU GO BY
L♡VE
THE BUTCHER

I destroy myself, the universe (an egg)
And time—to get an answer:
There are a smiler, a sleeper, and a dancer
We repeat our conversation in the glittering dark

Floating beside the sleeper.
The child remarks, "You knew it all the time."
I: "I keep forgetting that the smiler is
Sleeping; the sleeper, dancing."

From Sauk Lookout two years before
Some of the view was down the Skagit
To Puget Sound: From above the lower ranges,
Deep in forest—lighthouses on clear nights.

This year's rock is a spur from the main range
Cuts the valley in two and is broken
By the river; Ross dam repairs the break,
Makes trolley buses run
Through the streets of dim Seattle far away.

I'm surrounded by mountains here
A circle of 108 beads, originally seeds
    of *ficus religiosa*
        Bo-Tree
A circle, continuous, one odd bead
Larger than the rest and bearing
A tassel (hair-tuft) (the man who sat
        under the tree)
In the center of the circle,
A void, an empty figure containing
All that's multiplied;
Each bead a repetition, a world
Of ignorance and sleep.

Today is the day the goose gets cooked
Day of liberation for the crumbling flower
Knobcone pinecone in the flames
Brandy in the sun

Which, as I said, will disappear
Anyway it'll be invisible soon
Exchanging places with stars now in my head
To be growing rice in China through the night.
Magnetic storms across the solar plains
Make Aurora Borealis shimmy bright
Beyond the mountains to the north.

Closing the lookout in the morning
Thick ice on the shutters
Coyote almost whistling on a nearby ridge
The mountain is THERE (between two lakes)
I brought back a piece of its rock
Heavy dark-honey-color
With a seam of crystal, some of the quartz
Stained by its matrix
Practically indestructible
A shift from opacity to brilliance
(The Zenbos say, "Lightning-flash & flint-spark")
Like the mountains where it was made

What we see of the world is the mind's
Invention and the mind
Though stained by it, becoming
Rivers, sun, mule-dung, flies—
Can shift instantly
A dirty bird in a square time

Gone
Gone
REALLY gone
Into the cool
O MAMA!

Like they say, "Four times up,
Three times down." I'm still on the mountain.

Sourdough Mountain *15:viii:55*
Berkeley 27–28*:viii:56*

Note: The quotes of Empedocles and Heraclitus are from John Burnet's *Early Greek Philosophy*, Meridian Books, New York.

Metaphysical Insomnia Jazz. Mumonkan xxix.

Of
Course I could go to sleep right here
With all the lights on & the radio going

(April is behind the refrigerator)

Far from the wicked city
Far from the virtuous town
I met my fragile Kitty
In her greeny silken gown
fairly near the summit of Nanga Parbat & back again, the wind
flapping the prayer-flags

"IT IS THE WIND MOVING."

"IT IS THE FLAG MOVING."

Hypnotized by the windshield swipes, Mr Harold Wood:
"Back & forth;   back & forth"

We walked beside the moony lake
Eating dried apricots
Lemons bananas & bright wedding cake
& benefits forgot

"IT IS THE MIND MOVING."

& now I'm in my bed alone
Wide awake as any stone

7:iv:58

20:VII: 58, On Which I Renounce the Notion of Social Responsibility

The minute I'm out of town
My friends get sick, go back on the sauce
Engage in unhappy love affairs
they write me letters & I worry

Am I their brains, their better sense?

All of us want something to do.

I am breathing. I am not asleep.

In this context: Fenellosa translated *No* (Japanese word)
as "accomplishment"

(a pun for the hip?)

Something to do

"I will drag you there by the hair of your head!"
& he began doing just that to his beautiful wife
Until their neighbors (having nothing better to do)
Broke it up

If nothing else we must submit ourselves
To the charitable impulses of our friends
Give them a crack at being bodhisattvas
(although their benevolence is a heavy weight on my head
their good intentions an act of aggression)

Motion of shadows where there's neither light nor eye to see
Mind a revolving door
My head a falling star

7:v–20:vii:58

All About Art & Life

a compulsion to make
marks on paper

whatever good or bad

"& as for meaning
let them alone to mean
themselves"

or that I'm ill
out of adjustment
not relating with real situation in living
room I just left below
i.e. two other people, friends of mine
reading books

a shock out of the eye-corner
Dome & cornices of Sherith Israel
blue sky & fog streaks
(reminiscences of Corot, Piranesi)

to mean themselves
Adam & Eve & Pinch-Me

walks out of silence, monotony
many colors dangling & sparkling

(TINKLE?)

there. You know. Uh-huh.
we kill ourselves making it

PICTURE: a wood-engraving by Bewick
GIANT WOOLY COW

PICTURE: children, their faces concealed
by their hats which are heads which are
flowers

PICTURE: Leonardo: *Madonna & Child, with*
S. Giovanbattista

PICTURE: Ladies in marble palace with fountains
located high in Canadian Rockies a
peacock light the color of burning
incense

PICTURE: a room, & through the door a hallway
with a small round or octagonal window

PICTURE: 2 Bedouins praying in sand/ocean a camel
with square quizzing-glass on head

PICTURE: All of us when we were young before you
were born

2 PICTURES: Battle scenes (medieval-type) in high
plaster relief curved glass not lens, no
sound

LARGE PICTURE: C. S. Price: Indian women who might
be mountains picking huckleberries in
mountains that might be Indian women

PICTURE : 5 Persimmons (Chinese)

52 PICTURES: (Mexican provenance) playing-cards, each
one different, repellent & instructive

PICTURE: 360 degrees: the world is outdoors it is
both inaccessible & unobtainable
we belong to it

. . . most of your problems will disappear if you sit still (privately, *i.e.* in solitude) 1 hour per day without going to sleep (do not speak, hum or whistle the while). . .

The orders of architecture we are to suppose symbols of the human intellect & inspiration (in this case, severe Romano-Judaic)

"a symbol doesn't MEAN
anything
it IS
something . . . relationship of that kind doesn't exist
except in the old philosophy whose vocabulary
you insist on using . . ."

MANIFESTS itself
whether I write or not
we call it good, bad, indifferent as
we feel ourselves exalted or brought down
it has its own name but never answers
never at home
& we want a stage for our scene
(wow)
as if Shakespeare
LIED

---

all of us end up

Zero for Conduct

You bet.

Why bother to say I detest liver
& adore magnolia flowers
Liver keeps its flavor the blossoms
drop off
& reappear, whoever
cares, counts, contends

I said to the kitten rolling the glass
"Kitty, you're stupid"
Thoughtlessly: the cat's growing
exercising & I merely talking to hear my head rattle

What opinion do you hold on Antinomianism?
It makes me nervous trying to remember what it was
& which side of the argument Milton took
        also rattles
                Not I love or hate:

        WHAT IS IT I'M SEEING?

                &

            WHO'S LOOKING?

        It comes to us straight & flat
        My cookie-cutter head makes shapes of it

                CHONK: "scary!"
                CHONK: "lovely!"
                CHONK: "ouch!"

                        but any of us is worth more
                        than it
                        except that moment
                        it walks out of me, through me

& you ask, Where does it come from
Where did I go

Some people got head like a jello mold
It pours in & takes one shape only
Or instantly becomes another flavor
                raspberry to vanilla
                strawberry to vanilla
                orange to vanilla, etc.

Some legendary living ones can take it or leave it alone
They go on planting potatoes, writing poems, whatever they do
Without hangups
Minimum bother to themselves & all the rest of the world
And anyone observing them a little may
        turn all the way
                        ON

Meanwhile, psychologists test us
                & get a bell shaped curve
They know something or other I could tell them any time

All this is merely

GRAMMAR

The building I sit in
A manifestation of desire, hope, fear
As I in my own person, all the world I see . . .

Water drops from tap to sink
Naturally the tap's defective or not completely "OFF"
Naturally I hear: My ears do what they're made for

        (a momentary reflection—will my brain
        suffer a certain amount of water erosion
        while I sleep?- - -)

OUT

28:viii:59–9:ix:59

. . . .

From Every Day, *1965.*

The Lotus Sutra, Naturalized

I got drunk your house
You put that diamond my shirt pocket
How am I supposed to know?
Laying there in drunk tank
                strange town don't nobody know

Get out of jail at last you say
"You already spend that diamond?"
How am I going to know?

27:III: 64

Absolute Realty Co.: Two Views

I.

THE GREAT GLOBE ITSELF

I keep hearing the airplanes tell me
The world is tinier every minute
I begin believing them, getting scared.
I forget how the country looks when I'm flying:
Very small brown or green spots of cities on the edges
of great oceans, forests, deserts

There's enough room. I can afford to be pleasant & cordial to you
. . . at least for a while . . .
Remembering the Matto Grosso, Idaho, Montana, British Columbia,
New Hampshire, other waste places,
All the plains and mountains where I can get away from you
To remember you all the more fondly,
All your nobler virtues.

7:v:64

2.

VULTURE PEAK

Although my room is very small
The ceiling is high.

Space enough for me and the 500 books I need most
The great pipe organ and Sebastian Bach in 46 volumes
        (I really NEED the Bachgesellschaft Edition)
        will arrive soon, if I have any luck at all.

Plenty room for everybody:
Manjusri and 4700 bodhisattvas, arhats, pratyekabuddhas,
            disciples, hearers, Devas, Gandharvas, Apsaras,
            kinnaras, gnomes, giants, nauch girls, great
            serpents, garudas, demons, men, and beings not
            human, flower ladies, water babies, beach boys,
            poets, angels, policemen, taxi drivers, gondoliers,
            fry cooks and the Five Marx Brothers

All of us happy, drinking tea, eating Linsertorte,
Admiring my soft plum-colored rug
The view of Mt Diablo.

11:v:64

Mahayana

Soap cleans itself the way ice does,
Both disappear in the process.
The questions of "Whence" & "Whither" have no validity here.

Mud is a mixture of earth and water
Imagine WATER as an "Heavenly" element
Samsara and nirvana are one:

Flies in amber, sand in the soap
Dirt and red algae in the ice
Fare thee well, how very delightful to see you here again!

5:iv:65

. . . .

From Vanilla.

Opening the Mountain, Tamalpais: 22:X:65

Hot sunny morning, Allen and Gary, here they come, we are ready.
Sutras in creek-bed, chants and lustrations, bed of Redwood Creek
John Muir's Woods.

First Shrine: Oak tree grows out of rock
Field of Lazuli Buntings, crow song

Second Shrine: Trail crosses fire road at hilltop
Address to the Ocean,
Siva music addressed to the peaks

Third Shrine: Rock Springs music for Sarasvati
Remember tea with Mike and JoAnn years ago
Fresh water in late dry season

Fourth Shrine: Rifle Camp lunch, natural history:
Allen: "What do wasps do?"
Gary: "Mess around."

Fifth Shrine: Collier Spring, Great Dharani & Tara music

Sixth Shrine: Inspiration Point, Gatha of Vajra Intellectual
Heat Lightning

TO THE SUMMIT: North Side Trail, scramble up vertical North
Knee WHERE IS THE MOUNTAIN?

Seventh Shrine the Mountain top: Prajnaparamita Sutra, as
many others
as could be remembered in music & song

Eighth Shrine, The parking lot, Mountain Home
Sunset Amida going West
O Gopala, &c Devaki Nandi na Gopala
with a Tibetan encore for Tara,
Song against disaster.

RETURN TO CREEKBED, MUIR WOODS: Final pronouncement of the Sutras

We marched around the mountain, west to east
top to bottom—from sea-level (chanting dark stream bed
Muir Woods) to bright summit sun victory of gods and
buddhas, conversion of demons, liberation of all sentient
beings in all worlds past present and future.

. . . .

From The Winter.

The War Poem for Diane di Prima

1.

The War as a Manifestation of Destiny. Whose?

I thought of myself as happily sitting someplace quietly
Reading—but now is multiple
Images of people and cars, through lens-cut flowers of glass fruit dish
Many more worlds.

I would be sitting quietly reading
The 4th platoon helicopter marines firing into the bushes up ahead
Blue and white triangular flags all flap at the same rate,
Esso station across the street (Shirakawa-dori)
Eastern States Standard Oil here we all are,
Asiatically Yours,
Mah-jong on deck of aircraft carrier, Gulf of Tonkin
remember the Coral Sea

I write from a coffee shop in conquered territory
I occupy, they call me "*he-na gai-jin*," goofy-looking foreigner
I am a winner.
The postage stamps read NIPPON, the newspaper is dated
41SHŌWA 7MOON 16SUN
(This is the 41st year of the reign of SHŌWA of that Divine
Emperor, Holy Offspring of the Sun Goddess)
I am a winner, the signs in the streets
carefully written in English:
YANKEE, GO HOME

The radio plays selections from OKLAHOMA
The bookstore tries to sell me new British book about
Aforementioned Holy Infant of *Amaterasu-No-*
O-Kamisama
All I wanted was something translated by R. H. Blyth,
18,000 pounds of napalm and a helicopter,
Why do I keep losing the war? Misplacing it?

The Secretary of State came to town
I wasn't invited to meet him.
The Secretary of Agriculture, the Secretary of Labor,
All nice people doing their jobs, quieting the locals
Answering embarrassing questions:
e.g. *Question*. "What is the Republic of China?"
Answer. "The Republic of China is a medium-
sized island, south of Japan. Portuguese
navigators discovered it 300 years ago. They
called it Formosa. As for Cochin China, now
known as Viet Nam, we are now doing all in our
power to prevent &c. &c."
Question. "Why?"
Answer. "Because we can."

I like to think of myself sitting in some cool place
(It's un-Godly hot here, as they used to say)
Reading Mallarmé: *Le vierge, le vivace et le bel aujourd'hui*

Kyoto, *la cité toute proustienne:* Portland when I was young
Katsura River at Arashiyama is The Oaks on the Willamette
Roamer's Rest on the Tualitin, Lake Oswego.
The clouds conceal Miyako, the Hozu becomes a tidal river
The Kyoto smog hides a flat Oregon beach and the Pacific, just
beyond

Where is home,

"Pale hands . . .
. . . Beside the Shalimar . . ."

Caucasoid, go back to those mountains
Your father is chained there, that rock tilted
Into Chaos, heaved up icy pinnacles and snowy peaks

Astrakhan on the north
Persia on the south
Caspian Sea on the east
Black Sea to the west

From the mouth of the Volga you cross the lake and follow
The Amur River into the Pamir,
Coast along the Black Sea with Medea "in one bark convey'd"
To Athens, Rome, or across the great plateaus and the Hindu
  Kush
To Alexandria-in-the-Mountains,
          "Pale hands . . .
               . . . agonized them in
                 farewell . . ."
Among waterlilies where the Arabs killed Buddha
Tara surged out of that gorgeous blooming tank
Gazelle eyes. moon breasts
Pomegranate cheeks, ivory neck
Navel a deep wine-cup
                    Moon lady
                         Mother of the Sun
Jewel flower music
          A P P E A R I N G

There's no question of going or staying
A home or a wandering
          Here we are

II.

The Real War.

I sit on the shelf outside my door
Water drops down the rain-chain
Some flies outward instead of continuing link by link

IGNORANCE
ACTIVITY
CONSCIOUSNESS
NAME & FORM
SENSE ORGANS
CONTACT
PERCEPTION
DESIRE
BEING
BIRTH
ATTACHMENT
OLD AGE & DEATH

The small
rockpile
anchors
bottom of the
chain also
harbors a couple
shoots of dwarf
bamboo, chief
weed afflicting
gardens hereabouts

*

ÇA IRA,

ça ira!

as the French Revolution goes on teaching us
as the Bolsheviki demonstrated
as that Jesus who keeps bursting from the tomb
("Safe as the Bank of England," people used to say)
several thousand miles and centuries
beyond Caesar his gold, the Civil Service

The Seal on the dollar bill still reads,
NOVUS ORDO SAECULORUM
a sentiment worth at least four-bits
I want THAT revolution to succeed (1776, USA)
The Russians gave up too soon—
The Chinese keep trying but haven't made it yet

POWER,
anyone?
"Grab it & use it to do GOOD;
Otherwise, Evil Men will, &c &c."
Power of that kind, crude hammers, levers
OUT OF STYLE!
The real handle is a wheel, a foot-pedal, an electric switch
NO MOVING PARTS AT ALL
A CHANGE OF STATE

The war is only temporary, the revolution is
Immediate change in vision
Only imagination can make it work.
No more war poems today. Turn off the general alarm.

III.

The War. The Empire.

When the Goths came into Rome
They feared the Senators were gods
Old men, each resolutely throned at his own house door.
When they finally came to Akron, Des Moines, White Plains,
The nomads will laugh as they dismember us.
Other nations watching will applaud.
There'll be no indifferent eye, nary a disinterested ear.
We'll screech and cry.

A friend tells me I'm wrong,
"All the money, all the power's in New York."
If it were only a matter of money, I'd agree
But the power's gone somewhere else . . .

(Gone from England, the English now arise
Painters and singers and poets leap from Imperial tombs
Vast spirit powers emanate from Beatle hair)

Powerful I watch the shadow of leaves
Moving over nine varieties of moss and lichen
Multitudes of dragonflies (all colors) the celebrated
Uguisu bird, and black butterfly: wing with trailing edge of
    red brocade
(Under-kimono shown on purpose, as in the *Book of Songs*)

I sail out of my head, incandescent meditations
Unknown reaches of clinical madness, I flow into crystal world
    of gems, jewels
Enlightened by granite pine lake sky nowhere movies of Judy
Canova

I'll return to America one of these days
I refuse to leave it to slobs and boobies
I'll have it all back, I won't let it go

Here the locust tree its leaves
Sharp oval flat
I haven't lived with you for over twenty years
Great clusters of white blossom
Leaf perfumed also
Lovely to meet again, far away from home
(the tree-peony too elegant,
Not to be mentioned, a caress, jade flesh bloom)

My rooms are illuminated by
Oranges and lemons in a bowl,
Power of light and vision: I'll see a way . . .

Nobody wants the war only the money
fights on, alone.

31:v:66–25:viii:66

. . . .

From Decompressions, *1977.*

Walking Beside the Kamogawa, Remembering Nansen and Fudo and Gary's Poem

Here are two half-grown black cats perched on a
lump of old teakettle brick plastic garbage
ten feet from the west bank of the River.
I won't save them. Right here Gary sat with dying Nansen,
The broken cat, warped and sick every day of its life,

Puke & drool on the *tatami* for Gary to wipe up & scold,
"If you get any worse I'm going to have you put away!"
The vet injected an overdose of nemby and for half an hour
Nansen was comfortable.

How can we do this, how can we live and die?
How does anybody choose for somebody else.
How dare we appear in this Hell-mouth weeping tears,
Busting our heads in ten fragments making vows &
promises?

Suzuki Roshi said, "If I die, it's all right. If I should
live, it's all right. Sun-face Buddha, Moon-face Buddha."
Why do I always fall for that old line?

We don't treat each other any better. When will I
Stop writing it down.

Kyoto 14:iv:69

POSTSCRIPT, 17:iv:69 (from De Visser, Vol. I, pp. 197–198), 20 Commandment of the *Brahmajala Sutra* (Nanjo 1087): ". . . always practise liberation of living beings

(*hō jō,* 放生)"

. . . .

Like his friend Gary Snyder, Whalen spent summers working as a fire lookout. In this excerpt, from an interview conducted by Aram Saroyan in 1972, Saroyan has asked Whalen to expand on a "visionary experience" he mentioned in passing.

Well, one time, for example, I was working in the Forest Service up in Washington, and—Jack Kerouac has described this, has described the place in *Desolation Angels*, I guess—it was a big guard station that was built on a raft on Ross Lake, way up by the Canadian border. And we used horses to pack people into the lookouts from that raft, and one night all the horses were on a raft that was tied up next to ours, and in the middle of the night one of the horses fell off, with a great splash, because they had all been jumping around—I don't know what got at them, the moon or something—and the horses were all dancing and singing, and one of them got excited and went overboard. And so I got up out of bed, and some other guys got up, and we were all rushing around trying to find the horse that had fallen overboard. Well, I was the one that found her. She was a horse with one eye called Maybelle, and here she was in the water, so that people yelled at me, and I said, "I found it." And they said, "Well, hold up her chin, and we'll get a rope on her." And so, the packer brought the rope and wrapped it around the horse a little bit, around its throat sort of, kind of tied it up so I could hang onto it easier. And then he went off to get a boat, and I was kneeling over the edge of this raft in my underwear, and holding this horse under the chin, and the rope in the other hand, and the sense—you know, it was two o'clock in the morning, and it was a beautiful summer night, and the mountains were all around, and the lake, and this horse, and me—and I suddenly had a great, weird, kind of satori, a sort of feeling about the absolute connection between me, and the horse, and the mountains, and everything else . . .

. . . .

An excerpt from an interview conducted by Yves Le Pellec in 1972 at the San Francisco Zen Center.

LE PELLEC: He [D. T. Suzuki] played an essential role in introducing Zen to the West, didn't he?

WHALEN: Oh yes, he practically invented it for the West. His books began coming out in the twenties and he went on until he died. Actually there had been some German,

Russian, and French people who had written a little about it but in English nobody knew much about it at all until Suzuki Daisetz began writing his essays. Of course he had a lot of Zen training, he knew what he was talking about. During the fifties and sixties a great many people wrote a great deal about Zen, large parts of which were either lifted out of Suzuki Daisetz' books or made up out of a very short experience in Japan, accounts that were rather hazy and misleading and that jump to a whole lot of false conclusions. Anyhow the clearest and best account is Gary's [Snyder's] essay about the sesshin in *Earth House Hold* [. . .]

LE PELLEC: I suppose those [Whalen's] stays in Japan were essential as far as your knowledge of Zen is concerned.

WHALEN: Oh yes, I had not heard of Zen until I was in college. The last year I was in college I was living in a big house with Gary and Lew Welch and a whole flock of other friends, and Gary discovered the writings of D. T. Suzuki in the college library and began bringing them home. It sort of renewed my interest in Buddhism. It seemed much simpler, at least easier for me to come to terms with, than classical Pali Buddhism, the Buddhism of the Theravada which is still practiced in Ceylon and Thailand and Burma, and Java. Zen seemed to cut away many extravagances and get down to the point of emancipation and energy and cutting loose from all your emotional problems. Everything that used to hang you up goes away or at least you can deal with it in some other way. There is also the problem of right now, what are you doing right this minute and how do you get through that and how can you make it alive, vivid, solid? In Zen there is a great deal to understand—the long historical tradition, the connections with the various sutras and so forth—but the Zen experience cannot be explained, you have to be it, you have to practice it. . .

LE PELLEC: [. . .] Norman Mailer was very much attacked for his essay on hipsters, *The White Negro,* and many critics of the time wrote that the violence of the hipster was in germ in the beat mystique. Do you think that a poem like "Howl" for instance could in any way justify such ideas?

WHALEN: As an explanation of what we were feeling about America at that time "Howl" is certainly very clear. But it is only violence against the grammarians [laughs!] . . . It was purely literary, it's still a big misunderstanding . . . Here we're sitting and there are those people in the Pentagon who are able to push buttons and make catastrophic things happen. But all we can push is words. At the same time the regular poetical Establishment, Robert Lowell and company, all that level of guys who were professors and who were thought of in the public mind as respectable poets and so forth were writing grammatical English poetry which rhymed and lay on the page very stiff and quiet. We were trying to write in the way we spoke and in the way people around us were speaking. Also we were saying "Come on, everybody is being broken down by the system, nobody is having fun, why is nobody dancing and singing and taking dope?" Probably the only violent feelings were against the government and against social conditions that were ruining people's lives and creating Negro and Mexican ghettos, a government that makes terribly stringent laws against the use of marijuana while it conducts iniquitous wars all over the world all the time talking about peace and saving people from communism. So we had to say: "This is bad, wake up, don't let yourself be drawn into this fraudulent system and into these damn wars."

LE PELLEC: Were you conscious at that time that you were out to change the American consciousness?

WHALEN: Oh yes!

LE PELLEC: Or was this message made clear by the young people who followed you afterwards?

WHALEN: Sure, it's the same people, the same age group more or less that carry on the same thing and it's been going on longer and better now than it ever used to. But in the twenties people were already revolting against puritanism and against prohibition. For many years in this country you couldn't buy a copy of Rabelais. It was considered an unsuitable book that could damage your moral character. Same thing with Joyce. For many years this silly puritanical police morality blocked up all kinds of artistic and intellectual communication. So the idea of not being able to use about two thirds of the language was one of the things that we wanted to break out of and we used all possible words which had never been printed before [. . . .]

LE PELLEC: But don't you think that in American poetry a rather frequent use of colloquial language was made by earlier poets like T. S. Eliot, though he is often considered academic and highbrow by the new poets.

WHALEN: Oh yes. Eliot was of great importance to me when I was young.

LE PELLEC: What about Whitman?

WHALEN: He was a major influence. His essays—*Democratic Vistas* and the Prefaces to *Leaves of Grass*—are very sharp social criticism of what he saw going on in America. Emerson and Thoreau were also saying: the system is no good, wake up! They had read translations of Hindu classical religious writings and were quite influenced by them and then Thoreau influenced Mahatma Gandhi with his theory of civil disobedience.

. . . .

From The Kindness of Strangers: Poems 1969–1974.

Tassajara

What I hear is not only water but stones
No, no, it is only compressed air flapping my eardrums
My brains gushing brown between green rocks all
That I hear is me and silence
The air transparent golden light (by Vermeer of Delft)

Sun shines on the mountain peak which pokes
The sun also ablaze &c.
Willard Gibbs, Hans Bethe, what's the answer
A lost mass (Paris gone)
Shine red in young swallow's mouth
Takagamine Road

The water suffers
Broken on rocks worn down by water
Wreck of THE DIVINE MIND on the reef called Norman's Woe
"Suddenly, ignorance," the *Shastra* says.
Moon arises in my big round head
Shines out of my small blue eyes
Tony Patchell hollers "Get it! Get it!"
All my treasure buried under Goodwin Sands

. . . .

From an interview with Lee Bartlett conducted in 1975.

BARTLETT: What is your connection with the Zen Center?

WHALEN: Well, what I'm doing right now is an American version of formal Zen training with a Zen roshi, my friend Dick Baker. After I came back from Japan in 1971 I was living in Bolinas, and it was very noisy and crowded there. Around New Year's in 1972 Dick Baker and his wife and daughter paid me a visit in Bolinas. I told him I wanted to get out, so he invited me up to the Zen Center. He said all I'd have to do is sit once a day—I told him that I did that anyway. I slowly got involved with the Zen Center, and after I had been here about a year I asked to be ordained a monk.

The main reason I've stuck with the outfit is that we're doing that thing Gary Snyder talks about all the time—offering an alternative society, offering a different way of handling life in the United States other than getting a job with Standard Oil and after thirty-five years getting a gold watch. We're trying to work out something else. We have an old pattern, what is essentially an Indian-Chinese-Japanese paradigm [. . . .]

BARTLETT: How did someone from Oregon get turned on to Zen in the first place?

WHALEN: Well, I first got interested in Buddhism and Hinduism just after I got out of high school, in 1941 I think. I stumbled across Madame Blavatsky's work in the library. It didn't take me long to figure out where she was getting her material—out of the classical Indian philosophies, the Vedas and so on. That changed my life about as much as anything ever did, then. I began to take a wider interest in everything. . . .

BARTLETT: You were raised a Christian?

WHALEN: A Christian Scientist, which is theologically a very vague position. It's very unsystematic, somehow hooked up with the magic of disease and the magic of healing. I started wondering what this religion business was about, and began visiting various churches of friends of mine. I thought it was very interesting, but when I found out about Oriental religions, they seemed to make much more sense than the Christian stuff. But I kept wavering for several years.

After I got out of the Army I was living in Portland, Oregon, and quite by accident came upon the Vedanta Society—they had their own captive Swami who had been ordered from India. It was all very nice. You can't imagine how difficult it was for me to get up nerve to talk to the Swami, though. I finally did it; he was extremely kind but I just couldn't make it. It was the usual American vibrations made up of old people who were into the mysteries of the antique Orient. They would play the piano and sing "In a Monastery Garden," which is a terrible old song.

I had been starting to meditate in the way that the Yoga system talked about. There were times when I discovered that something really does happen to your head when you do try to sit. You change, somehow. Your attitudes change. So I was more and more persuaded that those Orientals had something. A couple of years later I met Gary Snyder, who had found these essays by Daisetz Suzuki in the library, and I got into reading them. I thought they were great entertainment—the first thing I had ever read or heard about Zen.

Well, we all came down here to San Francisco. I came first, while Gary went to the University of Indiana. He didn't stay there long because there weren't any mountains, and ended up at Cal enrolled as a special student in Oriental languages. I was busy trying to be a writer, trying to write poems and a novel. All the time I was wondering about Zen, what about Buddhism? I just didn't do much about it, except that once in a while I would try to sit. Then, about the time that Ginsberg and Kerouac showed up in the mid-fifties, Gary met Albert Saijo, who had been a student of Nyogen Senzaki down in L.A. Albert showed us how to sit properly, how to use a pillow and keep our backs straight, how to sit for long periods at a time. That was very helpful. It was around that time that Gary was invited to go to Japan through the First Zen Institute.

All of these ideas we had about Zen and Buddhism of course began to find their way into the poetry. Gradually, the more we studied and the more we found out about it, it seemed in both its philosophical and historical dimensions extremely interesting. And now here I am—I guess everything does catch up to you in the end.

. . . .

From Enough Said: Poems 1974–79.

"Back to Normalcy"

My ear stretches out across limitless space and time
To meet the fly's feet coming to walk on it
The cat opens an eye and shuts it
That much meaning, use or significance

Wind chime, hawk's cry
Pounding metal generator
Bell and board rehearsing bluejays
Dana, phoning, shouts "You mean fiberglass?"
Telephone grapeleaves shake together
Dull blond sycamore sunshine
Dana says, "All you guys bliss out
Behind the carrot and raisin salad?"
Brown dumb leaves fall on bright ferns
New and thick since the fire.

Tassajara
8–11:XI:77

Dying Tooth Song

Now flesh and bones burn inside my mouth
Ganges gushes from under my tongue
To fall in Siva's hair
Tooth temple of Kali
Skull dance place of Siva

Becoming Yama god of death
I become Yamantaka slayer of death
Endless wheel of waterbuckets turns
Through Babylon zodiac

I stays here turning through life and death
Offering up all this flesh and bones
Round and round

Grass greener than yellower
More birds than bluejays
Railway roar of creek
Not going to Chicago

North mountain peak
A pile of patriarchs' bones
Nyogen, Shunryu, host and guest all one heap

Tassajara
28:II:79

Joanne Kyger
(1934–   )

Joanne Kyger pursued her two interests, poetry and philosophy, when she was a student at the University of California at Santa Barbara. In 1957, Kyger moved to San Francisco, where she immersed herself in the city's increasingly active poetry community, meeting Philip Whalen and Gary Snyder, among others. Kyger moved into East-West House, a large turn-of-the-century building that had been turned into a communal living project, and soon after taking up residence there began studying with Shunryu Suzuki Roshi, who had just arrived from Japan to teach at the Soto Zen Mission, located just around the corner. In 1960, Kyger left for Japan to join Gary Snyder, whom she then married. She lived in Kyoto for four years, during which time she wrote poetry, studied flower arranging, and practiced at Daitoku-ji with Ruth Fuller Sasaki. Her experiences are chronicled in *Japan and India Journals: 1960–64.*

Returning alone to San Francisco in 1964, Kyger began to write prodigiously, as well as give readings and participate in the Berkeley Poetry Conference. Her first book of poems, *The Tapestry and the Web*, was published the following year. In 1975 Kyger went to Naropa Institute, where she met Chogyam Trungpa Rinpoche and, later, the Sixteenth Gyalwa Karmapa, the head of the Kagyu school of Tibetan Buddhism. She now sits at the Ocean Wind Zendo in Bolinas, California. Recent collections of Kyger's poetry include *Going On: Selected Poems 1958–80* and *Just Space: Poems 1979–1989*.

. . . .

Excerpts from the Japan and India Journals: 1960–64. *This selection covers a journey Kyger took to India with Gary Snyder. They were later joined by Allen Ginsberg and Peter Orlovsky.*

January 13, 1962

[. . .] Madras: entering by bus. Wide clean streets, fancy modern shops in one section.

Room in RR Retiring Room, 10 Ruppees, perfectly enormous. Bathroom, with hot running water—for a short time. Ate Bombay style meal with chappaties in a restaurant. Very good on open roof.

At Higgenbotham Book Store: a copy of *Howl* among Indian art books, Kerouac's *Scripture of Golden Eternity* in books on geography of India next to pamphlet on fruit crops.

Sunday. January 14, 1962

[. . .] Dance concert by two Maharaja's daughters. One very much better than the other. Ankle bracelets of bells, ornaments in the hair, flowers, vermillion painted fingers, spot on the palm and painted feet.

Upon entering the concert:

Sandlewood cream on the hand
Rose water shaken on the head
& sugar crystal to put in the mouth

Later Swiss fellow joins the party. He has been in Kathmandu and Nepal for several years. And asks Gary what he thinks of *The Dharma Bums.* He had just read it and it seemed pretty incredible to him. "They don't know what they're doing." Gary played dumb.

January 20, 1962. Saturday

Calcutta. Arrived 8 o'clock. Two narrow facing seats. Try to sleep slung between them. We don't have change. An Indian pays for our tea.

The Sikh taxi driver takes us way past Mahabodhi society. We walked back. Gary angry. The Ceylonese Bhikku in charge: who is she. She's my wife. Well *who* is she. What does she do. Letters from everyone. Allen not to meet us until February 28th.

Men squat when they pee.

{In India, after Allen Ginsberg and Peter Orlovsky arrive.}

March 2, 1962.

Rishikesh, left. Moved across the Ganges to Swarg Ashram. Two rooms, for Peter & Allen, and Gary & I. Afternoon walk down to sand and rock point of the Ganges—white glittering sand. A few orange robes spread on rocks to dry. Everyone strips to undershorts, launders and bathes in the river.

March 28, 29, 30, 31, April 1

Visited the Dalai Lama. Allen asks him if he wants to take L.S.D. Climbed and spent the night on a mountain. Smoked opium. Went to a fair in the mountains. Everyone vomited the opium except me and had carbon monoxide poisoning.

April 8

Guided tour bus to Ellora. A young affected guide with an umbrella furled speaks in English but mostly Hindi, constantly urging us to hurry hurry. Completely exhausted, dragging myself through the Buddhist, Brahmin and Jain temples. All of them were painted.

Lunch stop where there is no food to buy.

The Hinayana Buddhas of the Ajanta caves so unrelentingly religious. Puritanical and heavy. No grace at all. Whereas Sanchi had such life. And Ellora (Mahayana) where the Buddhas have a bit more grace—but somehow the caves are over all depressing.

Aurangabad's tomb, a simple plot of ground, covered and surrounded by the English in 1911 with a carved marble screen. Aurangabad, a great and fervent iconoclast sent men out to smash the noses of the Buddhas at Ellora.

Gary leaning, a high tiny speck from the tower at Daultabad Fort.

Come down.

   Then chipmunk approaches
& then runs away. Rats under the toilet pans
   at Ellora
            The flower
   fort.
      Now this path
   the grey lumps, Buddhas

Pattern following
the trident of shiva as
electricity. The
black Ethiopian. The
sheep following. Indian
men tweak each
other on the ear. Their
loud voices, flapping
their hands their English
another course, about emotion

Swimming
up stream against the current.
Breaking against a
law,   the muscles on my
shoulders always tense.

Pulling down all the Hindu
gods, pulling down the
green foliage with her
hand, the bough
brings a Buddha. The
large round breasts of
the woman   I envy.

April 10. Aurangabad

The rest have gone back to Ellora caves for the day. It's a depressing place I stay here. Laundry going in the big silver handled bowl in the bath, the water off at eleven.

Williams, besides the Tapestry, also Kora in Hell. Which I thought for years was a war poem, Korea & Hell and wouldn't look at it. I keep resolving to write to him. He must have bad tempers & have narrow moments, but seems to be a great great man, the most human, showing his vulnerability.

From a letter of Ferlingetti's to Ginsberg: " . . . hope Gary is still there by then. (Your meeting seems to be known all over the US, in the bookstore circuit, that is. Everybody saying Allen got to India to meet Gary yet? Like some kind of International sorcerer swamis' conjunction on Feb 4th maybe . . .)"[. . .]

April 11. 1962

Letter to Nemi April 10, 1962.

[. . .] We met the Dalai Lama last week right after he had been talking with the King of Sikkim, the one who is going to marry an American college girl. The Dal is 27 and lounged on a velvet couch like a gawky adolescent in red robes. I was trying very hard to say witty things to him through the interpreter, but Allen Ginsberg kept hogging the conversation by describing his experiments on drugs and asking the Dalai Lama if he would like to take some magic mushroom pills and were his drug experiences of a religious nature until Gary said really Allen the inside of your mind is just as boring and just the same as everyone else's is it necessary to go on; and that little trauma was eased over by Gary and the Dalai talking guru to guru like about which positions to take when doing meditation and how to breathe and what to do with your hands, yes yes that's right says the Dalai Lama. And then Allen Ginsberg says to him how many hours do you meditate a day, and he says me? Why I never meditate, I don't have to. Then Ginsberg is very happy because he wants to get instantly enlightened and can't stand sitting down or discipline of the body. He always gobbles down his food before anyone else has started. He came to India to find a spiritual teacher. But I think he actually believes he knows it all, but just wishes he *Felt* better about it.

. . . .

From The Wonderful Focus of You, *1980.*

Silver City Overlay for Turkey Buzzard

The past has vanished
The future being unborn has not come
into existence
And the present cannot be fixed as being
in the present

Timeless Sighs

Whither rideth us, huh? to what timeless
shore shall we float
in our quest, our homely quest for carrion
Come back little heart, I miss you.

Hey big bird, you of the squashed consciousness
Here in soft May Bolinas breeze on porch
I want to fly overhead too, with the Crows
Suddenly free
And down comes Mr. Blue Jay
into the grasses, You with the most
silver grey chest
and into the loquat fast what's
happening. And suddenly
the sky changes, and earth gets still.

Waking in the night with sinkings of mortality
I am still, alive, this morning. One would do well
to just look, this place where I begin free

each day to take the path.

. . . .

From Just Space: Poems 1979–1989.

Back to the Life of Naropa

It's ghastly. It's been
going on for some time.
Sitting still for over a year, motionless
stiff as a log. No speech.
No thought. What's going on?
Naropa's teacher is not responding.

But finally he gets up and climbs to the top
of the fancy temple roof. Naropa follows him.
First words uttered: "JUMP!"
Naropa jumps to the ground.
And broken, lays there in terrible pain.
Great Disciple.
His teacher heals him instantly saying:
"You really deserved this, you clay pot!
Thinking there is an *I* inside that body
All birth and death and the stages in between
Must be resolved into the Radiant Light
of emptiness."
And goes back to his silent sitting.

Philip Whalen's Hat

I woke up about 2:30 this morning and thought about Philip's
hat.
It is bright lemon yellow, with a little brim
all the way around, and a lime green hat band, printed
with tropical plants.
It sits on top
of his shaved head. It upstages every *thing* & every
body.

He bought it at Walgreen's himself.
I mean it fortunately wasn't a gift from an admirer.
Otherwise he is dressed in soft blues. And in his hands
a long wooden string of Buddhist Rosary beads, which he
    keeps
moving. I ask him which mantra he is doing—but he tells
    me
in *Zen,* you don't have to bother with any of that.
You can just *play* with the beads.

. . . .

Anything that is *created*
        must sooner or later die.
                Enlightenment is PERMANENT
    because we have not *produced* it
  we have merely *discovered* it.
                        —Chogyam Trungpa
                        Died April 4, 1987

    Many years ago
I am going into San Francisco over Mt. Tamalpais
to read at a big Poetry Reading
given by Chogyam Trungpa in honor of the first visit
        of the Karmapa.
I am very nervous   I wonder if the car
        will make it
    I think I may die at any moment
When I get to the place of the reading
                it is very gracious
        there is a bar set up back stage
The poets are given a little bottle
        with a hand lettered label
    saying "LONG LIFE PILLS"
        FROM HIS HOLINESS KARMAPA"
I am so nervous
I swallow them down right away and feel better *Whew!*

I ask Michael McClure, Aren't you going to take yours?
He says, I'm going to *save* mine.
Years later (still alive) I think of those pills—
They were little seeds
If I'd really done a wise thing
        I would have planted those seeds
          So there would be a whole bunch of seeds
        And everyone could have some
                    whenever they wanted them
So now what have I got?   the little bottle
                                        of this story—
               and its own Empty Space.

Albert Saijo (1927–   )

Born in Los Angeles, Albert Saijo was fifteen when he was interred at Heart Mountain camp during World War II. A teenager and the son of a Christian minister, Saijo did not involve himself in the Buddhist activities sponsored by the camp. It was a full eight years later that he would begin to study with his fellow internee, Nyogen Senzaki.

Saijo returned to Los Angeles after the war, and it was there that he formally met Senzaki through a friend. In 1950, he began to regularly attend the meetings Senzaki held in his tiny room in a dilapidated hotel; Saijo continued to study with him for seven years. However, the increasingly active poetry community of North Beach proved too hard to resist and the young poet moved to San Francisco in the mid-fifties. There he met Lew Welch, Philip Whalen, and Gary Snyder and moved into East-West House. In 1959, Lew Welch introduced Saijo to Kerouac. The three of them then took off on a cross-country journey from San Francisco to New York, composing spontaneous haiku all along the way. When they arrived in Manhattan, they went to a service at the First Zen Institute, but Kerouac, drunk and distracted, spent the evening scribbling notes on Saijo's program. Of all of the Beats interested in Buddhism in the early fifties, Saijo was unique in having had the experience of formal practice. As Philip Whalen remembers, Saijo was the first person to instruct the other poets on how to sit properly.

Saijo continues to write poetry, much of it having to do with ecological concerns. He lives in Hawaii.

. . . .

In Big Sur *Kerouac recounts the trip to the East Coast that he and Saijo ("George Baso") and Lew Welch ("Dave Wain") took in Welch's Jeep.*

And on the trip to New York with Dave and me up front talking all the way poor George just sat there on the mattress for the most part very quiet and told us he was taking this trip to find out if HE was traveling to New York or just the CAR (Willie the Jeep) was traveling to New York or was it just the WHEELS were rolling, or the tires, or what—a Zen problem of some kind—So that when we'd see grain elevators on the Plains of Oklahoma George would say quietly "Well it seems to me that grain elevator is sorta waitin for the road to approach it . . ."

Later the three haiku inspired by Saijo's observation were published in Trip Trap*:*

Albert's Haiku

Grain elevators on
Saturday lonely as
abandoned toys.

Lew's Alternate

Lonely grain elevators
on Saturday
—abandoned toys

Jack's Alternate

Grain elevators on
Saturday waiting for
the farmers to come home

. . . .

This description of how and when Albert Saijo met his teacher was written in 1994, expressly for this volume.

1942—WW2—all Japanese in US herded into concentration camps scattered around the remotest locations of Western US Heart Mountain Relocation Center one square mile fenced in with barbed wire—guard towers with search lights and armed guards—inside 10,000 dispossessed people of Japanese ancestry both US citizens & aliens—beautiful high plateau surrounded by mountains in distance—big sky—I believe it's part of the Big Horn Basin—Heart Mountain itself was a butte-like prominence along a low ridge—it had a strong presence in the landscape NW corner of Wyoming between the towns of Cody and Powell—The Shoshone River was close by the camp—us kids used to sneak under the fence by crawling down a shallow gulch which then deepened and widened & eventually led us to the Shoshone & the mountains beyond—The camp was divided into blocks—Senzaki was in Block 2—I remember becuz Block 2 also had a barrack given over to a group of artists as a studio where my brother spent all of his time—I saw Senzaki walking around the block & here & there in the camp—Each barrack was divided into 1-room apts & at each end of the Barrack were tiny apts for single people—the apts were simply a room with a coal burning stove—the only furnishings metal beds & mattresses—olive green wool army blankets—it's here he held zazen—the parents of a close friend were students of his—it was thru them I knew of Senzaki & learned of something called Zen—I was your dumb teenager & had no interest in such matters so I didn't meet Senzaki in camp.

When did you start to study with Senzaki?

Around 1950 in LA when he held zazen in his small apt top floor (6th floor) in the Miyako Hotel (torn down long ago) at the corner of E. 1st & San Pedro Street smack dab in the middle of downtown LA in the part called Little Tokyo—I met Senzaki through a friend who in turn had a friend who was an elderly lady masseuse—Senzaki often dined at the apt of this lady—one evening I was there with my friend for supper & Senzaki was there too—it was after I met him here that I started to attend his zazen sessions—I attended the twice a week sessions that were for English speakers—Mon & Fri nites as I recall—let me give you a short description of his apartment—the Miyako Hotel was a seedy rundown place—a very tired elevator barely got you to the sixth floor—down a long narrow hallway then to the corner apt—no need knock—just open door & walk in—a main room perhaps 16' x 12' & off this main room was a kitchenette & a bathroom—windows along one wall of the main room overlooked a parking lot—Senzaki's bed was in the main room—in front of the bed to the wall opposite was the zendo—on the wall opposite were book shelves holding his considerable library with an altar in front of the shelves—there were potted philodendrons whose vines climbed among the books—Senzaki was seated in a Roman camp chair in front of the altar—before him was a folding card table & on it was the text of his lecture for that nite—we students sat on wooden folding chairs in rows facing him—perhaps there were 12 regulars at these meetings—zazen started at 7:30 with the recitation of the 4 vows in Japanese—during zazen Senzaki faced the altar—zazen was for an hour—a bell was rung every 15 minutes—zazen ended with the recitation of the 4 vows—Senzaki then read his lesson to us—these were commentaries on different Zen texts such as the Gateless Gate—his command of English was excellent so he could speak on any subject in the tongue—his dentures creaked as he spoke—after the lecture there was always hot Japanese green tea & a Japanese confection—the confection provided by one of Senzaki's Japanese patrons who had a confectionery shop—the meetings closed after the tea & sweets at which time Senzaki would say don't stand around & talk go home—my first impression of Senzaki was of a person totally unlike others—Even as a kid seeing him in camp I could see he walked different & stood different—I did not have to talk to him to know he was in some other space from us others—he was living out of a different place than average & conventional—obviously there was an aura of quiet around him at all times—I'm just beginning now to fully appreciate him—

. . . .

The following two poems, written in 1994, are previously unpublished.

Same Horizon Different View

BODHISATTVA OR ARHAT—NOW TOO MUCH BODHISATTVA
NOT ENUFF ARHAT—BOTH IN SAME PLACE WITH SAME HORIZON
BUT WITH DIFFERENT VIEW—BODHISATTVA LIKES HUMAN
WORLD SO BLONDE HARD ROMANTIC THAT IS MISERICORDIA
OUT OF EXQUISITE SUFFERING—THEY LIKE WHERE SUFFERING

TURNS ANGELIC—THE EDGE OF SAME—BUT BODHISATTVA
RIPE PERISHABLE MUST FALL TO GROUND AND EASY TO
CORRUPTION—NO MATTER—BODHISATTVA LIKES TO GO
AND COME BACK FOREVER & THAT'S A VOW—ARHAT SITS ON
ROCK WITH UNIVERSE SQUEEZED BETWEEN THUMB AND FOREFINGER
— A THIN TWIST OF SMOKE RISES FROM BETWEEN THUMB &
FOREFINGER—NOT HUMAN—NOT ANIMAL—NO BINOMIAL—
—NO ADDRESS—NO TELEPHONE #—NO CREDIT—NO
DEBIT—FAST AGAINST EVERY HOOK—IGNORANT
NOWHERE

Is Language Necessary to Human Existence

LANGUAGE IS A BODY OF SUFFERING & WHEN YOU TAKE
UP LANGUAGE YOU TAKE UP THE SUFFERING TOO—US IN
WORDS IS INNER VOICE THE CONSTANT COMPANION OF
OUR MENTALITY—IT WEIGHS ON OUR CONSCIOUSNESS
LIKE A PROBLEM THAT WON'T GO AWAY—NO DOUBT IT'S HANDY
THE WAY IT TAKES SOMETHING MOVING AND MAKES IT STILL
—AN ARTIFACT THAT CAN BE HELD AND LOOKED AT—
THE LANGUAGE DREAM—IT GOES WITH COUNTING—
BUT LANGUAGE MAKES US INTO EVERY MEANING IT
EXPRESSES SO WE ARE EVERYTHING WE CAN SAY & THIS
IS HEAVY—THAT SOMETHING SO OBVIOUSLY ABSTRACT
SERIAL & RELATIVE CAN BE SO POWERFUL MAKES YOU WONDER
—BUT THE CONSTANT PRESSURE OF WORDS ON PURE MENTALITY
ESPECIALLY MEASURED WORDS FINALLY DRIVES EACH OF US
MAD IN OUR OWN WAY—IF WE COULD SCREAM OUT OUR
INNER VOICE THEN AS IN TOURETTE'S SYNDROME—WHO
HAS NOT BEEN TRAPPED IN A WORD PRISON—WHO DOES
NOT KNOW SPIRALING WORD VERTIGO—YET FOR BETTER OR
WORSE WE MAKE LANGUAGE # ONE TOOL OF MENTALITY—
NO BETTER HERE—MAYBE ALL WORSE—TELL ME A TRUE
BENEFIT DERIVING FROM LANGUAGE—CAN A GOOD COME OF
IT—PURVEYORS OF HIGHEST GOOD GENERALLY SAY WORDS
DESCRIBE NOTHING BUT IGNORANCE—LIKE LAO TZE
SEZ THEM WHO KNOW DON'T SPEAK—A WAG ADDED LATER

LAO TZE SEZ THEM WHO KNOW DON'T SPEAK BUT IT TOOK HIM
5000 CHARACTERS TO SAY IT—HERE IS PARADOX OF
LANGUAGE IT IS ALWAYS A CASE OF THIS STATEMENT IS
FALSE—WE CAN'T TAKE THE TENSION OF UPHOLDING
THIS PARADOX SO WE GO FOR THE FALSE CERTAINTIES
OF SYLLOGISM & THIS IS KILLING US OFF AS AN ANIMAL
—EVEN AS WE SEE IT AIN'T GOOD FOR US WE USE IT
—WE SEE PLAINLY IT POLLUTES MENTALITY STILL
WE'RE ENAMORED OF IT—WE KNOW ABSTRACTIVE LANGUAGE
TO BE THE BASIC CAUSE OF OUR MISREADING OF NATURE
—HOW WE LOST TOUCH—YET THE WAY WE CONTINUE TO
THINK ABOUT IT IS WHAT ELSE IS THERE—PLENTY
PLENTY WHAT—PLENTY MUTE ABSOLUTE

Lew Welch
(1926–1971?)

"I try to write accurately from the poise of mind which lets us see that things are exactly what they seem. I never worry about beauty, if it is accurate there is always beauty. I never worry about form, if it is accurate there is always form." —LEW WELCH

Lew Welch, born and raised in Phoenix, Arizona, served briefly in the air force and then enrolled at Stockton Junior College to study English, music, and painting; there he encountered the work of Gertrude Stein and promptly dedicated himself to becoming a writer. The following year, 1947, Welch transferred to Reed College in Portland, Oregon, where he met and befriended Gary Snyder and Philip Whalen, two poets with whom he shared an interest in Asian thought. In 1949, the three poets met William Carlos Williams, who had been invited to the campus to speak. Williams, impressed with Welch's thesis on Gertrude Stein, encouraged him to try to publish it.

On the strength of Williams's recommendation, Welch decided to move to New York, where he planned to revise his thesis for publication while holding down a day job at a department store. A long way from all of his friends out west, however—and isolated still more when Williams fell ill—Welch soon abandoned this project, eventually enrolling in the master's program (in philosophy and then English) at the University of Chicago. He grew disappointed with the school's dry academic approach to poetry, however, and dropped out and began work in advertising. In 1957 he picked up a newspaper and read about "the Beat Generation"—including his old friends from Reed—and he immediately fired off letters to Whalen and Snyder.

Inspired by their success, Welch moved out to San Francisco, where he wrote more poetry and practiced Zen meditation in Snyder's Mill Valley cabin. Welch soon met Allen Ginsberg, Jack Kerouac, and other writers. In 1959 Welch and fellow poet Albert Saijo drove Kerouac back to New York. In 1960 Welch's first book of poetry, *Wobbly Rock,* was published and he met and became romantically involved with poet Lenore Kandel. Kandel and Welch lived together at East-West House, which, at different times, was also home to Philip Whalen, Albert Saijo, and Joanne Kyger, among others. He and Kandel accompanied Kerouac on a journey to Lawrence Ferlinghetti's cabin in northern California, a trip recorded in Kerouac's novel *Big Sur.*

After Welch's relationship with Kandel ended in the early sixties, he retreated to an abandoned cabin in mountain country, where he composed his *Hermit Poems* and drafted the poems for *Way Back.* In these poems a sense of place is paramount, and much of this poetry seems to reflect the influence of Chinese and Japanese nature poetry. In a preface to a collection of these works, Snyder wrote: ". . . Lew really achieved the meeting of an ancient Asian-sage-tradition, the 'shack simple' post-frontier back country out-of-work workingman's style, and the rebel modernism of art. . . ." Over the next few years, Welch continued to publish, give readings, and regularly teach a poetry workshop. The influence of Welch's study of Zen texts makes itself felt in his later poems, which often present a puzzle or a question posed by a character Welch called the "red monk." Welch referred to these poems as "the first American koans."

While Welch's professional career reached a high point in the early seventies (he had just signed a contract for a collection of his work with a major publisher), his personal life was at a low ebb. Welch had been sinking into a deep depression, perhaps the result of a steady abuse of alcohol. His plan was to build himself a home on land adjacent to Gary Snyder's property; Allen Ginsberg, who had purchased a tract there, offered Welch a piece of it for that purpose. In the early spring of 1971, Welch drove to the site, where he began work on the project, but not long afterward, on May 23, he took his revolver and went into the woods. He left a farewell note, but his body was never found.

. . . .

The following poems come from Ring of Bone: Collected Poems 1950–1971, *which were arranged by Welch into five "books." Welch called this work "a spiritual autobiography arranged in more or less chronological sequence." Although only a small number of the poems are reprinted here, they are grouped according to Welch's order. "Leo" is a name Welch invented for himself and something that he invokes when he refers to the necessary process of uninventing oneself, a process of working with the ego. The final section of the book consists of* "Uncollected Poems," *which were gathered and ordered by Welch's editor, Donald Allen. The first three poems are from Book 1 (1950–60),* On Out.

Entire Sermon By the Red Monk

1.
We invent ourselves.
2.
We invent ourselves out of ingredients we didn't
choose, by a process we can't control.
3.
The Female Impersonator, and the Sadistic Marine can
each trace himself *back* to the same stern, or weak, father.
4.
Usually it's less dramatic. He was only indifferently
a basketball player. Now he is selling cars.
5.
The baby on the floor cannot be traced, *forward,*
to anything.
6.
It's all your own fault then.
7.
On all kinds of baby purpose, you invented whoever
you think you are. Out of ingredients you couldn't
choose, by a process you can't control.

All you really say is, "Love me for myself alone."
8.
It is also possible to *uninvent* yourself. By a process
you can't control.
9.
But you invented Leo. Forget it.

Wobbly Rock

for Gary Snyder

"I think I'll be the Buddha of this place"

and sat himself
down

1.

It's a real rock

(believe this first)
Resting on actual sand at the surf's edge:
Muir Beach, California

(like everything else I have
somebody showed it to me and I found it by myself)

Hard common stone
Size of the largest haystack
It moves when hit by waves
Actually shudders

(even a good gust of wind will do it
if you sit real still and keep your mouth shut)

Notched to certain center it
Yields and then comes back to it:

Wobbly tons

2.

Sitting here you look below to other rocks
Precisely placed as rocks of Ryoanji:
Foam like swept stones

(the mind getting it all confused again:
"snow like frosting on a cake"
"rose so beautiful it don't look real")

Isn't there a clear example here—
Stone garden shown to me by
Berkeley painter I never met
A thousand books and somebody else's boatride ROCKS

(garden)

EYE

(nearly empty despite this clutter-image all
the opposites cancelling out a
CIRCULAR process: *Frosting-snow*)

Or think of the monks who made it 4 hundred 50 years ago
Lugged the boulders from the sea
Swept to foam original gravelstone from sea

(first saw it, even then, when finally they
all looked up the
instant AFTER it was made)

And now all rocks are different and
All the spaces in between

(which includes about everything)

The instant
After it is made

3.

I have been in many shapes before I attained congenial form
All those years on the beach, lifetimes . . .

When I was a boy I used to watch the Pelican:
It always seemed his wings broke
And he dropped, like scissors, in the sea . . .
Night fire flicking the shale cliff
Balls tight as a cat after the cold swim
Her young snatch sandy . . .

I have travelled
I have made a circuit
I have lived in 14 cities

I have been a word in a book
I have been a book originally

Dychymig Dychymig: (riddle me a riddle)

Waves and the sea. If you
take away the sea

Tell me what it is

4.

Yesterday the weather was nice there were lots of people
Today it rains, the only other figure is far up the beach

(by the curve of his body I know he leans against the
tug of his fishingline: there is no separation)

Yesterday they gathered and broke gathered and broke like
Feeding swallows dipped down to pick up something ran back to
Show it
And a young girl with jeans rolled to mid-thigh ran
Splashing in the rain creek

"They're all so damned happy—
why can't they admit it?"

Easy enough until a little rain shuts beaches down . . .

Did it mean nothing to you Animal that turns this
Planet to a smoky rock?
Back among your quarrels
How can I remind you of your gentleness?

Jeans are washed
Shells all lost or broken
Driftwood sits in shadow boxes on a tracthouse wall

Like swallows you were, gathering
Like people I wish for . . .

cannot even tell this to that fisherman

5.

3 of us in a boat the size of a bathtub . pitching in
slow waves . fish poles over the side . oars

We rounded a point of rock and entered a small cove

Below us:
fronds of kelp
fish
crustaceans
eels
Then us
then rocks at the cliff's base
starfish
(hundreds of them sunning themselves)
final starfish on the highest rock then
Cliff
4 feet up the cliff a flower
grass
further up more grass
grass over the cliff's edge
branch of pine then
Far up the sky

a hawk

Clutching to our chip we are jittering in a spectrum
Hung in the film of this narrow band
Green
to our eyes only

6.

On a trail not far from here
Walking in meditation
We entered a dark grove
And I lost all separation in step with the
Eucalyptus as the trail walked back beneath me

Does it need to be that dark or is
Darkness only its occasion
Finding it by ourselves knowing
Of course
Somebody else was there before . . .

I like playing that game
Standing on a high rock looking way over it all:

"I think I'll call it the Pacific"

Wind water
Wave rock
Sea sand
(there is no separation)

Wind that wets my lips is salt
Sea breaking within me balanced as the
Sea that floods these rocks. Rock
Returning to the sea, easily, as
Sea once rose from it. It
Is a sea rock
(easily)

I am
Rocked by the sea

. . . .

From Book II (1960–64), Hermit Poems.

[I Saw Myself]

I saw myself
a ring of bone
in the clear stream
of all of it

and vowed,
always to be open to it
that all of it
might flow through

and then heard
"ring of bone" where
ring is what a

bell does

. . . .

From Book III (1960–64), The Way Back.

The Way Back

He Prepares to Take Leave of His Hut

And They, The Blessed Ones, said to him,
"Beautiful trip, Avalokiteshvara.
You never have to go back there again."

And he said, "Thank you very much, but I think I will.
Those people need all the help they can get."

Not that I'm on the
Other Side of the River, you understand,
except literally.

To get to the shack I found, you have to
cross a rickety bridge of splintered boards, of
cables, rusty, small, not really
tied anymore to Alder trees.

And a Raccoon takes a shit on it,
almost every day, right where I have to
step to get across.

And should I wonder if it's
fear, malevolence, or chance that
makes him do this thing to me,

when nothing's really stained by it,
and yesterday a Butterfly sat down on it

Butterfly on a Coon Turd
A wet, blue, Jay

And even that is just a
pretty imitation of a
state of Mind I don't possess
or even seek, right now, or
wait for anymore.

"Why should it be so hard to give up
seeking something you know you can't possess?"

"Who ever said it was easy?"

. . . .

From Uncollected Poems.

Buddhist Bard Turns Rat Slayer

"Kill, Kill, Kill" Shrieks Wordsmith

I cannot stand your scratch your
nervous skitter twitch of
nose poking through eave-holes scamper
stop scamper over rafters in
dim light of kerosene can't
sleep and it just isn't
cute anymore your

walnuts, tinfoil,
maple leaves, your
shaving brush, you

RAN OVER MY FACE!

I don't know about dogs but
rats ain't got no Buddha nature

DIE!

DIE!

and found one in my trap: immaculate
gray fur, white breast, white
little paws, short tail, mountain-sweet as
everything else is here

(all the others died by
poison

The Cabin

almost too quiet

ever since

In a note to the following poem, Welch identifies the quotation from Kerouac as having its source in The Dharma Bums; *Welch says that it was Kerouac's {Ray Smith's} response to Snyder's {Japhy Ryder's} request that Kerouac help with a little work around their shared shack.*

Leo Gives Himself Yet Another Name

"I'm the Buddha known as
the quitter." —Jack Kerouac

I am the Buddha known as *The Beginner*.

Deep in Zazen, *"The Beginner"* (the words)
hit me, simultaneously, in these four ways:

1) Instigator. Inventor.

2) He who is chosen to start, but cannot
finish, as on a relay team, in track.
Once, after passing the baton, I crossed
in front of another team, and my team
was disqualified, though we actually won,
and would have won whether I crossed over
or not.

3) Eternal novice.

4) He who is doomed to begin again and again and
again.

Commentary by the Red Monk:

In the first place, it was I, not you, who crossed over in front of another team. This is how we learned right conduct. *Remember, instead, how fast we were, and are.*

In the second place, "doomed" is wrong. Avalokiteshvara called it "returning." When "doom" dies in your mind, "beginning" will cease to be painful. Avalokiteshvara chose to begin again and again, though he didn't have to. You said that yourself, in one of your poems. Don't you believe your own poems?

Maitreya Poem

Ron Loewinsohn: *Why is it whenever*
I see a statue of Maitreya,
he's always laughing?

Phil Whalen: *Maybe it's because he's*
not even here yet, and
he's already made it.

•

At last, in America,
Maitreya, the coming Buddha
will be our leader, and,
at last, will not be powerful, and
will not be alone

(powerful, but not as Kings are,
as Johnson tried to be—
who wielded power more than
any other king and,
like the rest,
wielded it wrong)

How perfect!
The last (first?) Emperor of America
a Texas Millionaire!

•

"and will not be alone" means

Each one is one.
There are many of them.

(Gertrude Stein)

Many.
Many many women and men of such a size
they knew what Patchen meant:

it would take little to be free.
that no man live at the expense of another.

(and this is NOT that same old
"Second Coming" poem,

though that story, too, comes out of
what source writes me now)

Take it as a simple prophecy.

•

Look into the cleared eyes of so many thousands,
young, and think:

Maybe that one?
That one?
That one?

And then think:

How can they bear it?

(and vow, as I have, to help them in any way you can)

Slouching
toward Bethlehem
to be born.

•

Look Out. (The secret is looking Out.)

And, never forgetting there are
phoney ones, and lost ones, and foolish ones,
know this:

Maitreya walks our streets right now.
(each one is one.   There are many of them.)

Look out. For him, for
her, for
them, for

these will break America as
Christ cracked Rome

                    (and just tonight
                    another one

                              got born!)

[1967]

. . . .

Excerpts from an interview with Lew Welch conducted by Jack Shoemaker and David Meltzer in 1970, and published in Meltzer's book The San Francisco Poets.

[. . .] I want to tell you what I feel about poetry. I can do it easily with a poem of mine.

I WANT THE WHOLE THING, THE MOMENT
    when what we thought was rock, or
        sea
    became clear Mind, and

what we thought was clearest Mind really
        was that glancing girls, that
            swirl of birds . . .

        (all of that)

AND AT THE SAME TIME that very poem
        pasted in the florist window

(as Whalen's *I Wanted to Bring You This Jap Iris* was)
        carefully re-typed and
    put right out there on Divisadero Street.

        just because the florist thought it
                pretty,

        that it might remind of love,
        that it might sell flowers . . .

The line

Tangled in Samsara!

Later in the same interview, Welch talks about bringing poetry back into the realm of speech:

You have to go out into the street and listen to the way people talk. You have to really listen to the kind of things that people say. You have to listen to the birds that are in the air, the helicopters, the big rush of jets. . . . Listen to this, you can't even talk in my living room without the din of it. You have to have your ears open. You have to have your goddamn ears open or you are not going to be a poet. Or you are not going to be a writer of any importance whatsoever.

[. . .] you have to hear what is. You have to hear how your mother talked. You have to hear how your mother talked in a way that is so straight that it will almost kill you. Not only what she said, but how the language moved in what she said. And how the language affected the people around her. Because that is what is going to affect you. And you have to know what the people in the town talk like. How it is said. You have to know it so perfectly that you can never ever make an error. Even Hemingway made errors, and we must not, if we are poets, ever make an error. It is a very precise art and a strong and a good one. I die behind it . . . its strength and its purpose.

[. . .] I got two free drinks from a guy in Riverside just a few weeks ago. Before the poetry reading there, I asked the guys that were driving me from the airport to the reading to stop at a bar and we would all have a drink together. And as we had a drink, I got all excited . . . I am getting ready for the reading and I happen to mention this to a very groovy bartender why I was in town, and would he like to have a book of mine. He said: "Why sure." And I said, "You can't have it unless I can read it out loud, right here." And he got very nervous because he expected some gloomy poem . . . "I-love-the-night" bunch of bullshit to come out of me. Here it was, eleven in the morning and who was ready for poetry? Who was ready for poetry in a bar in Riverside at eleven A.M. in the morning?

And I read *Courses* to him from start to finish, and he broke up. He thought it was the funniest thing he had ever heard. So I laid the book on him and I said, "See, I work. Like Bobby Burns worked. I am trying to get the poem back into the bar." And he said, "That's a good idea. You should hear most of the shit these people talk around here!"

It could easily follow from such a position that, therefore, poetry would be quite mundane, watered down, made popular. Pop art instead of great art. Now I think that Bobby Burns wrote as fine a set of lyrics as any poet ever wrote. Or even more heavily, probably the greatest poet that ever lived was Milarepa, the great Tibetan Buddhist. All of his teachings are in the form of songs. They are poems that he sang out loud to his students, his disciples, the people in the town.

The poetry of Homer, after all, are simply the songs of a blind old man in a time when there weren't printed books. Men would go around and tell the kings what their history was. Chaucer is the same thing. Chaucer is the man who made poetry of the streets, just as Han-Shan's poetry would be scribbled on shithouse walls. . . . People found them on the rocks.

Han-Shan wrote them on the rocks on the mountains. People would run down to town and say: "Han-Shan's written a new poem!" They would write it on the walls.

Po-Chui, the great Chinese bard . . . his poetry was memorized by all the harlots in China, and was sung by all the whores and pimps. I am not talking about writing down something. I believe if a poem is really well made, it can be strong enough to stand inside the general din of the speaking world.

Lenore Kandel
(1932-   )

Lenore Kandel decided at the age of twelve, from her wide readings in comparative religion, that Buddhism was the way of life she wanted to pursue. In 1959 she began sitting zazen in New York. In the same year, Kandel had three short collections of her poetry published. In 1960 she moved to San Francisco, where she became romantically involved with Lew Welch. Not long after her arrival, she became a resident at East-West House and began to study with Shunryu Suzuki Roshi. It was through Welch that Kandel met Jack Kerouac, who immortalized her in *Big Sur* as Ramona Swartz: "a big Rumanian monster beauty of some kind I mean with big purple eyes and very tall and big (but Mae West big), . . . but also intelligent, well read, writes poetry, is a Zen student, knows everything . . ."

Kandel's work was admired by her own contemporaries and singled out for praise by established poets such as Kenneth

Rexroth. Today she remains best known for her erotic poetry, particularly *The Love Book,* which like "Howl" was deemed pornographic and forcibly removed from Lawrence Ferlinghetti's City Lights Bookshop by the San Francisco State Police. When challenged in an obscenity court, Kandel defended *The Love Book* as the culmination of "a twenty-three-year search for an appropriate way to worship" and an attempt "to express her belief that sexual acts between loving persons are religious acts." Much of Kandel's work carries explicit tantric references. In recent years, she has continued to write poetry and pursue an interest in Tibetan Buddhism.

. . . .

From Word Alchemy, *1967.*

Enlightenment Poem

we have all been brothers, hermaphroditic as oysters
bestowing our pearls carelessly

no one yet had invented ownership
nor guilt   nor time

we watched the seasons pass, we were as crystalline as snow
and melted gently into newer forms
as stars spun round our heads

we had not learned betrayal

our selves were pearls
irritants transmuted into luster
and offered   carelessly

our pearls became more precious and our sexes static
mutability grew a shell, we devised different languages
new words for new concepts, we invented alarm clocks
fences   loyalty

still . . . even now . . . making a feint at communion
    infinite perceptions
I remember
we have all been brothers
and offer   carelessly

Small Prayer for Falling Angels

too many of my friends are junkies
too many of my psychic kin tattoo invisible revelations on
    themselves
signing their manifestoes to etheric consciousness with little
hoofprint scars stretching from fingertip to fingertip
a gory religiosity akin to Kali's sacred necklace of fifty human
heads

Kali-Ma, Kali-Mother; Kali-Ma, Kali-Mother
too many of my friends are running out of blood, their veins
are collapsing, it takes them half an hour to get a hit
their blood whispers through their bodies, singing its own
    death chant
in a voice of fire, in a voice of glaciers, in a voice of sand that
    blows
forever
over emptiness

Kali-Ma, remember the giving of life as well as the giving of
    death
        Kali-Ma . . .
Kali-Ma, remember the desire is for enlightenment and not
    oblivion
        Kali-Ma . . .
Kali-Ma, their bones are growing light; help them to fly

Kali-Ma, their eyes burn with the pain of fire; help them that
    they see
with clear sight

Kali-Ma, their blood sings death to them; remind them of life
that they be born once more
that they slide bloody through the gates of yes, that
they relax their hands nor try to stop the movement of the
    flowing now

too many of my friends have fallen into the white heat of the
    only flame
may they fly higher; may there be no end to flight

Will Petersen (1928-   )

Will Petersen had already launched a promising career as an artist when he was drafted by the U.S. Army in 1954 and required to serve as an education specialist in Japan. Upon his return to the States, Petersen moved to northern California and soon became a member of a Friday night study group that was guided by Reverend Kanmo Imamura and held at the Jodo Shinshu Berkeley Buddhist Church. Regular members of the group included Gary Snyder, Alan Watts, and Philip Whalen. Petersen took over the editorship of the group's magazine, the *Berkeley Bussei,* for one year in 1956. Under his editorship, the magazine published Kerouac's first haiku and a chorus from *Mexico City Blues.* In addition to work by Allen Ginsberg, Whalen, and Snyder, Petersen also wrote frequently for *Bussei* and published poems and other literary journals, and was in attendance on the night of the Six Gallery reading.

In 1957 he returned to Japan to study printmaking and Noh drama. He went on to write plays, translate Japanese texts, and, in the early sixties, serve as managing editor for the influential periodical *Origin*, second series. Petersen stayed in Japan until 1965; when he returned to the States, he continued to make prints, exhibit, teach, and, with his wife Cynthia Archer, run Plucked Chicken Press until his death in 1994.

. . . .

In a letter to Gary Snyder, Jack Kerouac praised an essay written by Petersen: "Phil sent me Bussei *with my poem and haikus. I thought the Will Petersen article the most intelligent and very best thing in there, a really profound Buddhist it takes to say 'where there is no emptiness there is no form' and to gauge that from staring at the rocks of Ryoanji." (Kerouac was later to include Petersen, as Rol Sturlason, in* The Dharma Bums.*) Passages from the essay, which first appeared in the* Berkeley Bussei *in 1956, follow.*

Stone Garden

[. . .] The garden of Ryoanji is generally included in the flat *kare-sansui* style. Carefully raked white sand was an important feature of these "dry landscape" gardens and often served to depict water, which was entirely absent. In effect the plain surfaces of sand were akin to the untouched areas of white paper in *sumi-e* paintings, then the vehicle of such masters as Sesshu. However, like the paintings of Sesshu, or the *haiku* poetry of Basho, the garden is unique—a work of art that stands above its traditions. It is one of the world's masterpieces [. . . .]

It is possible to bring to this simple garden the endless fine points of gardening, compounded with a wealth of religious, mythological or intellectual ideas and historical relevances accumulated over the centuries. Any discussion of the garden of

Ryoanji is in peril if it fails to account for all of these! For example, it was customary to name stones individually after Buddhist divinities and to assign them certain positions. In *kare-sansui* compositions, a triangular grouping, or a group of three stones, often referred to a Buddhist triad. There are echoes, too, of the Mt. Sumeru theme, common in an earlier time. Most commonly, however, the rocks of Ryoanji are said to depict rocks in the river or, on another scale, islands in the sea [. . . .]

Most explanations of the garden are based primarily on the rocks—as forms, figures, objects or shapes. The sand is usually left unexplained. When explained, the sand, serving as vacant space, is referred to as a depiction of the void. The question arises: if it is maintained that the garden is voidness translated into sand, why would not a rectangle of sand alone express this concept? Why the rocks? And why their careful choice and arrangement, if we are to grasp this sense of emptiness?

It is at this point that we come to one of the basic paradoxes of Buddhist thought: Only through form can we realize emptiness. However, "emptiness in its absolute sense is not a concept reached by the analytical process of reasoning . . ." but is a statement of intuition or perception . . . "a fact of experience as much as the straightness of a bamboo and the redness of a flower." (Suzuki's *Zen Buddhism and Its Influence on Japenese Culture*)

From this "fact of experience" is derived the principle of *sumi* painting. The blank sheet of paper is perceived only as paper and remains as paper. Only by filling the paper does it become empty. Much in the same way the sound of the frog creates the silence in Basho's well-known *haiku*. The sound gives form to the silence—the emptiness. In the Noh play it is through voice and instrument that we are aware of profound silence; elaborately colorful costumes create austere simplicity and bareness; and in the dance, movement creates stillness—and stillness creates movement.

Sunyata, expressed as vacant space in visual art, silence in music, time and spatial ellipses in poetry or literature, or non-movement in dance, requires aesthetic form for its creation and comprehension. As stated above, the idea of emptiness is not a concept reached by analytical reasoning, but one that must be perceived in aesthetic terms. Aesthetic form is pre-requisite to conceptual perception. Thus, unless the frog leaps within a well constructed poem the sound produces no silence [. . .] And without the most careful arrangement of rocks the sand of Ryoanji becomes incomprehensible [. . . .]

Restated: The sunyata of Buddhism is not the emptiness of absence, it is not a nothing existing beside a something, it is not a separate existence, nor does it mean extinction. It is always with individual objects, always co-existent with form, and where there is no form there is no emptiness. Emptiness is formlessness, without selfhood or individuality. "Form is emptiness, and emptiness is form." Beneath these ideas is the Buddhist conception of an object or form as an event, and not as a thing or substance. (Susuki's *Essence of Buddhism*)

In declaring that the garden represents islands in the sea, etc., as is most commonly done, is to be held by form. To say, on the other hand, in more abstract terms, that the sand represents the void, is to ignore the rock. All of these are merely equations in which the garden represents X, the unknown, and X is merely substituted. Regarded as a puzzle, the garden offers no solutions, but presents new questions to meet each answer.

. . . .

These passages are from September Ridge, *a memoir completed in 1991 and as yet unpublished in its full form, in which Petersen pays tribute to his friendship with Gary Snyder. Petersen recounts his introduction to Snyder through the Buddhist study group run by Rev. Ryo Imamura, the sections addressed to "Pete" are passages from Snyder's letters to Petersen. Walter is Walter Nowick Roshi, then a Zen student at the Kyoto temple where Snyder studied.*

1954: SAN FRANCISCO, SEPTEMBER

She, Buddhist minister's wife's sister returning to Berkeley, I, to Gertrude Stein's *no there, there*, no Oakland A's then, nor football, nor Museum of Art, but California College of Arts & Crafts, Veteran's Benefits—

"If that's what you're interested in," Kiyo exuded, "You ought to come (she could hardly contain herself) to our Study Group—Shinshu, Zen. Tibetans—Alex Wayman. He's great! And Alan Watts, on the radio, have you heard? Hakujin, Nisei, all getting together, you have to come, have to meet Gary Snyder."

Here's a snapshot: Alan Watts standing by his father's side; a list of persons who'd each donated 2 dollars, to keep the Berkeley Buddhist Church going.

BERKELEY BUSSEI

Remarkable. An ethnic community church's annual publication is the first to publish poem by G. Snyder, Philip Whalen, Jack Kerouac, essays by Watts & (Rol Sturlason) Petersen, as well as Schopenhauerian Buddhist Thought as Revealed in the Ring of the Niebelungen—what do the devout Shinshu Buddhist churchgoers, culturally confused, think of all this? "I've always liked Wagner," Jane Imamura, our Muse, admits; her daughter, Hiro, classical pianist, adores Elvis.

1955: OCTOBER, EAST BAY

You need a goddam passport to go there, Rexroth complained, but nonetheless, crossed over from The City, served as Master of Ceremonies, coach bringing on the rookies, atop a plywood platform, a space Dark. Black walls. Packed Full. Reconverted auto body shop? Co-op gallery? Mistaken memory? History speaks of a momentous occasion in San Francisco, at the fabled Six Gallery. Gary reading, straightforward. People passing jugs of dago red; Phil shy; McClure insistent—

light light light

. . . in a time of blue suede shoes, of Elvis and rock & roll, Canute against the tide

light light light

almost booed off, Expressionists impatient, wanting wantonness, long before Minimalism, Michael's poem sounds, as I listen now to melting snow

& then the tidal wave, Allen, new in town
clean shaven, in charcoal grey, white shirt & tie, first time we
met, at Gary's, now in blue jeans, rousing all, hooping &
hollering, like a black baptist church's mass, all responding
to *Howl!* out of a dark space, transported—

"Save the invitation," Gary confided: "Some day
it will be worth something."

MAY 1956

Out under the Golden Gate
Aboard the *Arita Maru*
Gary's gone

OAKLAND

Still at Montgomery Ward's loading dock, working overtime,
saving all for boat fare, I room across the street. Christmas
rush—Hiroshi gets hired, moves in; all he
possesses packed into one duffel bag.

On a wall, a scroll.
In a bowl, five oranges.

AT SEA

a vision of back-packing companion,
a dream of high sierra meadow, cool lake,
a dream of dust-free air, in September,
the favored month of Noh, the time
of recurring ghosts, of attachment
& release

JANUARY 1957

. . . Back again! old haunts—It was not immediately I hunted
him up, north, neath gnarled pine

down off the raw veranda wood
Tiger pounced upon me, exuberantly
embraced me, you must
know, no tigers ever existed,
not ever in Japan, only on

tourists' backs, on GI jackets, on
paper-paneled screens
of temple entranceways
ferociously silly, rendered in a cat's dream,
intensely whiskered eyebrows
prefiguring twinkle-eyed

bonze

cup of
tea

RINKO-IN

Gary, Walter, & Walter's piano, dark, looming high, heavily,
on low horizon tatami, co-exist
within "somewhat rundown" ancient pine, gravel path
& wet moss temple compound, Shôkoku-ji
Since 1392
Quakes Fires Wars Rebuilt countless times Past its prime
All the junk that goes with being human
stashed
in the tokonoma,
Zen's
altar

hard rock wavers
tour buses crowd Ryôanji

Even the heavy present seems to fail
This bubble of a heart
highways creep up
the mountains
tour buses

Stashed, in the tokonoma, Zen's true altar—skis.

Temple spaces rented to Christian college boys,
from the red-brick university, adjoining

South, across the bicycle crowded pushcart motor-scooter
three-wheeler
honking truck rattly trolley main drag, serene:
the Ancient Imperial Palace Grounds, a vast
rectangular breathing space

MT HIEI: 1957

At the top, no high Sierra, no fire lookout, but a looking
back, a looking in, into the burning house of being, seeing
the realm of dust —Our age, Somon, solitary, not merely for
a summer, nor for a single tinderbox season, but

seven years
in a temple
older than America

we talk, drink tea, smile
bow, scramble back down
before sundown

no way Gary could know
he'd be dwelling at the foot,

in Yasé hamlet,
and later,

in his
stead,

Pete

STUPA

Off the path, in the moss, a tumble of stone.
We set the stones once again one atop the other.
Good karma, Gary smiled. We hiked on.
Upward. Past fern.

THE SHACK

Gary's immediate query, seeing my scrapwood retreat
barkroofed, back where he'd planted his corn, had I
like Thoreau, counted nails, kept accounts?

ALL THOSE YEARS

we licked roadside trickles, dropping down, cold, clear.
Up on Mount Hiei we lay on our bellies,
lapping rivulets between moss.

22 APRIL 1958

Ah, Pete, we came through.
Made it back to white clean sea-air San Francisco unrolled
or robbed . . .

•

Can't find it.

It's in the dust, in dew, in

moon, in shade of tree & flow of

stream;

"in my kitchen
in a jar"

tokonoma.
Wherever. Anywhere.
Staying overnight with Gary, 1969,
in Midwest college town motel
he makes of dresser top, a shrine

places with casual precision a hand-hidden carved wooden
bear; three, four other discrete objects, making
of this careless space,
his world.

Open the sacred medicine bundle,
unroll the sleeping bag

no one loves rock,
but here we are

under stars
at ease

1989
Evanston, Illinois
Will Petersen

Bob Kaufman
(1925–1986)

After joining the Merchant Marine at the age of thirteen and serving for two decades, Bob Kaufman moved to New York to study at the New School for Social Research. While he was on the East Coast, Kaufman met Allen Ginsberg, Jack Kerouac, and William Burroughs. He later moved to San Francisco, and quickly became a prominent figure in the San Francisco poetry community, frequently reading at the Co-Existence Bagel Shop. Kaufman also helped to edit *Beatitude,* the periodical that took Kerouac's exposition on the term "Beat" for its title. Kaufman's broadsides were published by City Lights, and his first book of poetry, *Solitudes Crowded with Loneliness,* was published by New Directions in 1965. Kaufman frequently got into altercations with the police over free speech. In 1963, after the assassination of President Kennedy, Kaufman launched a protest in the form of silence, by taking what Eileen Kaufman described as a "Buddhist vow of silence," a vow he maintained until the Vietnam War ended twelve years later. He also renounced writing and went into a self-imposed four-year retreat in 1978. Kaufman died in 1986.

Kaufman was raised in a religious household; he attended synagogue with his father, an Orthodox Jew from Germany, as well as church with his mother, a Catholic from Martinique. He also learned about voodoo from his grandmother. Kaufman studied Zen Buddhism, practiced prostrations, and made frequent references to Buddhist thought throughout his writing, particularly in his later work.

. . . .

From Solitudes Crowded with Loneliness, *1959.*

Reflections on a Small Parade

When I see the little Buddhist scouts
marching with their Zen mothers
To tea ceremonies at the rock garden,
I shake my head. . . . It falls off.

. . . .

From The Golden Sardine, *1967.*

Come

Come let us journey to
 the Sky.
I promised the Moon.

All that I come from
All that I have been,
All that I am
All that I come to
All that I touch,
Blossoms from
          a thorn,
AROSEAROSE

Love is the condition
of Human Beings
Being Humans.

To be beloved
Is all I need
And whom I love
Is loved indeed,
There never was a Night that
Ended, or began,
Forms breaking
Structures imaged,
Come love,
Love come.

. . . .

The following three poems are from The Ancient Rain *(1981).*

I am a Camera

THE POET NAILED ON
THE HARD BONE OF THIS WORLD,
HIS SOUL DEDICATED TO SILENCE
IS A FISH WITH FROG'S EYES,

THE BLOOD OF A POET FLOWS
OUT WITH HIS POEMS, BACK
TO THE PYRAMID OF BONES
FROM WHICH HE IS THRUST
HIS DEATH IS A SAVING GRACE

CREATION IS PERFECT

Scene in a Third Eye

on the gray shadow of the darkened city
in lost photographs of other sad visions,
ferrying images of transient ecstasies,
pains, private sadnesses, hid
in smoky towers, secret pockets in clandestine
nations.

what? pushed into hungry mouth's of crowded buildings
retains its form, reason is too unreliable,
memory screwed into hoped-for visions, desire,
twisted beyond recognition, detected in echoed
sound.
shouting crossviews from worn cliffs, dug down
in the wake of violent earthworms, blinded in
refracted corkscrew glares, from coppery phantom
silhouettes of fake existence, pinned into air, stuck in
time.

Private Sadness

Sitting here alone, in peace
With my private sadness
Bared of the acquirements

Of the mind's eye
Vision reversed, upended,
Seeing only the holdings
Inside the walls of me,
Feeling the roots that bind me,
To this mere human tree
Thrashing to free myself,
Knowing the success
Of these burstings
Shall be measured
By the fury
Of the fall
To eternal peace
The end of All.

. . . .

The following poem is previously unpublished.

A Buddhist Experience

Cannot give it a name
or shape, might seek
to find a context to
understand the language
being used, historical
yes, also something else,
how people emerge
from the group, complete
individual, each responding
to some higher stone
of order, unchallenged
in the search for meaning,

in reaching for the pure
relation, to interpret
life and by that
interpretation to live more deeply
in Zen, Zen of the
Real Red bone, like
Coltrane, who is playing
the saxophone, speaking
of life and death, and
what lies in between.

The balloons, rising up
seem to take the poet
to the sky, perhaps the
same sky the little French
boy, they sailed into the
heavens, now the Inyo
Mountains, speak their
meaning. I am the sky
rock, the plunging rock,
waiting to be surrounded
by clouds, to illuminate
the angels patrolling
the earth.

The heavenly brigade
moving mysteriously
through everything,
should I speak to them?
I do, I ask them for a
life that can be lived
in heaven while being
lived on the earth.
I ask them to make this
possible, they speak of
this earthly life
as a transition to
a different experience
someplace else. People

seem to have personal
reasons for whatever
they do.
I must find my
motives.

PART THREE

Echoes

William Burroughs (1914-)

In 1944, when William Burroughs met the other Beats, he was slightly older and more well-read than they were. He took up the role of a mentor and gave the other Beats books such as Oswald Spengler's *The Decline of the West,* which introduced them to the idea of the fellaheen, the down-and-out, that became central to the Beat ethos. His first book, *Junky,* published in 1953, was followed by *The Naked Lunch.* The latter title was Kerouac's and is suggestive of a kind of clarity, a moment of vision. Burroughs says it means "a frozen moment when everyone sees what is on the end of every fork." Published in 1959, *Naked Lunch* won Burroughs an ardent following, and although he has continued to publish many books, it remains the one for which he is best known.

Burroughs never aligned himself with Buddhism, but some of the themes that occupy his work bear striking similarities to principal concerns of Buddhism—in particular, his notion of addiction, which Burroughs has described as not simply something limited to drug addicts, but a general condition of human nature. This finds a parallel with the Buddhist view that desires are inexhaustible. And the literary technique pioneered by Burroughs, the cut-up—the use of random collages of words to create new texts—aims at getting away from "the tyranny of the ego." Burroughs believes that through the creation of literary collages the author is effectively erased. The spontaneity of this practice, as well as its "ego-killing" ideal, are not unlike other Buddhist concerns of the Beats.

Burroughs had read about Buddhism long before the other Beats and found it "interesting" but not a suitable practice for Westerners. (He was also critical of the hybrid Catholic-Buddhist practice that Kerouac embraced.) Despite his misgivings, however, Burroughs frequently gave readings and classes at Naropa Institute and eventually went on a two-week retreat with the Tibetan teacher Chogyam Trungpa Rinpoche.

Burroughs lives in Lawrence, Kansas. His recent works include *Interzone, The Place of Dead Roads, The Adding Machine,* and *The Western Lands.*

. . . .

On August 23, 1954, Jack Kerouac wrote to Allen Ginsberg about a letter he had just received from Burroughs. Kerouac's comments appear in parentheses.

What a magnificent letter I just got from him [Burroughs], one sentence says "He (Paul Bowles) invites the dreariest queens in Tangiers to tea, but has never invited me, which, seeing how small the town is, amounts to a deliberate affront"—

and

"I cant help but feeling that you are going too far with your absolute chastity. Besides, mast'ion is not chastity, it is just a way of sidestepping the issue without even approaching the solution. Remember, Jack, I studied and practised Buddhism in my usual sloppy way to be sure. The conclusion I arrived at, and I make no claims to speak from a state of enlightenment, but merely to have attempted the journey, as always, with inadequate equipment and knowledge—like one of my South American expeditions, falling into every possible accident and error, losing my gear and my way, shivering in the cosmic winds on a bare mountain slope above life line, chilled to the blood-making marrow with final despair of aloneness: What am I doing here a broken eccentric? a Bowery Evangelist, reading books on Theosophy in the public library (An old tin trunk full of notes in my cold water, East Side flat), imagining myself a Secret World Controller in Telepathic Contact with Tibetan Adepts?—Could he ever *see* the merciless, cold, *facts* on some Winter night sitting in the operation room white glare of a cafeteria—NO SMOKING PLEASE"—(me)—bill: "NO SMOKING PLEASE—*See the facts and himself*, an old man with the wasted years behind, and what ahead having seen The Facts? A trunk full of notes to dump in a Henry Street lot? . . . so my conclusion was that Buddha is only for the West to *study* as *history*, that it is a subject for *under standing*, and Yoga can profitably be practiced to that end. But it is not for the West, An Answer, not A Solution. WE must learn by acting, experiencing, and living, that is, above all by Love and by Suffering. A man who uses Buddhism or any other instrument to remove love from his being in order to avoid suffering, has committed, in my mind, a sacrilege comparable to castration." (ya cant castrate tathagatas) (castrate the uncastratable? the invisible love?) (wisible enuf when you open yr eyes and look) (izzasso?) (i have my own doubts, you see, i make these little jokes) "You were given the power to love, in order to use it, no matter what pain it may cause you." (wow) "Buddhism frequently amounts to a form of psychic junk . . . I may add that I have seen nothing from those California Vedantists but a lot of horse shit, and I denounce them without cavil as a pack of frauds." "Convinced of their own line to be sure, thereby adding self-deception to their other failings. In short a sorry bunch of psychic retreaters from the dubious human journey. Because if there is one thing I feel sure of it is this, that Human life has *direction*."

But I dear Allen say, no direction in the void . . .

But Burroughs's original letter doesn't stop where Kerouac cuts him off:

"Even if we accept some Spenglerian Cycle routine, the cycle never comes back to exactly the same place, nor does it ever exactly repeat itself.

Well about enough of that. I am about to become a long-winded German with some philosophy about the direction of life arising from the potentials inherent in the cellular structure of the human time-space traveller. When the potentials of any species are exhausted, the species becomes static (like all animals, reptiles, and other so-called lower forms of life). What distinguished Man from all other species is that he *can not become static, "Er muss streben oder untergehen"* (quotation is from myself in character of German philosopher)—"He must continue to develop or perish." This is going to run to five tremendous volumes. What I mean is the California Buddhists are trying to sit on the sidelines and there *are* no sidelines. Whether you like it or not, you are comitted to the human endeavour. I can not ally myself with such a purely negative goal as avoidance of suffering. Suffering is a chance you have to take by the fact of being alive. I repeat, *Buddhism is not for the West.* We must evolve our own solutions [. . . .]

. . . .

These passages from The Retreat Diaries *are based on Burrough's two-week retreat with Chogyam Trungpa Rinpoche in 1976. James Grauerholz wrote the introduction, a paragraph of which is reprinted here.*

Introduction

This essay, I think, is a major statement of the dilemma any artist faces if he begins to take Buddhism seriously. In Burroughs' case this dilemma was all the more explicit for that his invitation to the retreat was specifically qualified by a request that he not bring a typewriter. He had balked, in a furnished room in Boulder last summer, asking his host Chogyam Trungpa Rinpoche what he should do then if a literarily useful idea came to him on retreat. But when Rinpoche compared Burroughs' typewriter to the carpenter's saw and the chef's utensils, he saw Rinpoche's point and agreed to comply. The idea, of course, was that quiet self-examination and meditation removed from the means of compulsive self-expression were more important to him than any writing he might produce. I believe that Burroughs gave this idea a fair trial.

The Retreat Diaries

Last summer in Boulder I was talking to Chogyam Trungpa Rinpoche about doing a retreat at his Vermont center. I asked about taking along a typewriter. He objected that this would defeat the whole purpose of a retreat, like a carpenter takes along his tools—and I see we have a very different purpose in mind. That he could make the carpenter comparison shows where the difference lies: the difference being, with all due respect for the trade of Jesus Christ, that a carpenter can always carpenter, while a writer has to take it when it comes and a glimpse once lost may never come again, like Coleridge's Kubla Khan. Writers don't write, they read and transcribe. They are only allowed access to the books at certain arbitrary times. They have to make the most of these occasions. Furthermore I am more concerned with writing than I am with any sort of enlightenment, which is often an ever-retreating mirage like the fully analyzed or fully liberated person. I use meditation to get material for writing. I am not concerned with some abstract nirvana. It is exactly the visions and fireworks that are useful for me, exactly what all the masters tell us we should pay as little attention to as possible. Telepathy, journeys out of the body—these manifestations, according to Trungpa, are mere distractions. Exactly. Distraction: fun, like hang-gliding or surfboarding or skin diving. So why not have fun? I sense an underlying dogma here to which I am not willing to submit. The purposes of a Boddhisattva and an artist are different and perhaps not reconcilable. *Show me a good Buddhist novelist.*

When Huxley got Buddhism, he stopped writing novels and wrote Buddhist tracts. Meditation, astral travel, telepathy, are all means to an end for the novelist. I even got copy out of scientology. It's a question of emphasis. Any writer who does not consider his writing the most important thing he does, who does not consider writing his only salvation, I— "I trust him little in the commerce of the soul." As the French say: *pas serieux.*

I was willing to concede the typewriter, but I certainly would not concede pen and paper. A good percentage of my characters and sets come from dreams, and if you don't write a dream, in many cases, you forget it. The actual brain trace of dream memory differs from that of waking memory. I have frequently had the experience of waking from a dream, going over it a number of times, and then forgetting it completely. So during the retreat I kept pen and paper by my bed, and lit a candle and wrote my dreams down when they occurred. As it happens, I got a new episode for the book I am currently writing and solved a problem of structure in a dream recorded in these diaries. I also attempted some journeys out of the body to visit specific people, with results that, while not conclusive (they rarely are), were at least interesting and fruitful. In short, I feel that I get further out through writing than I would through any meditation system. And so far as any system goes, I prefer the open-ended, dangerous and unpredictable universe of Don Juan to the closed, predictable karma universe of the Buddhists. Indeed existence *is* the cause of suffering, and suffering may be good copy. Don Juan says he is an impeccable warrior and not a master; anyone who is looking for a master should look elsewhere. *I am not looking for a master*; I am looking for the *books*. In dreams I sometimes find the books where it is written and I may bring back a few phrases that unwind like a scroll. Then I write as fast as I can type, because I am reading, not writing.

[. . .] During the retreat I wrote down dreams and the elaboration of dreams that takes place spontaneously in the waking state. I used an exercise in association: take a walk and later write down what you were thinking when a deer crossed the road or when you sat down on a rock and killed a biting fly. One of my first acts in my retreat hut was to improvise a fly swatter from an old whisk broom, and I think this no-killing obsession is nonsense. Where do you draw the line? Mosquitoes? Biting flies? Lice? Venomous insects? I'd rather kill a brown recluse spider than get bitten by one. And I will not coexist with flies. Interesting point here: The Miracle of the Centipede which disappeared as I was about to kill it with a sledge hammer. That was a nice miracle. *Chapeau*, Trungpa Rinpoche. Because that centipede was only half an inch long, and they don't get much bigger in that climate. And that's a bearable size—doesn't keep me awake knowing it is in the room, so why kill it? On the other hand, a centipede three inches long is already an abomination in my eyes. Little spider in web at window. He's all right. But I hear a rustling on the shelf above my bed. I light the candle and there is a spider about an inch across and a brown spider at that. Might be a brown recluse. Any case, too big to live in my vicinity. I feel better after it is dead, knowing it can't get on my face while I am sleeping.

The Retreat Diaries are not a sequential presentation. By sequential presentation, I mean Monday with all dreams and occurrences noted, then on to Tuesday and so forth. Here Thursday and Friday may be cut in with Monday, or the elaboration of a dream cut in with the dream itself in a grid of past present and future. Like the last words of Dutch Schultz. Some of Dutch's associations cannot be traced or even guessed at. Others quite clearly derive from the known events of his life. The *structure* is that a man is *seeing a film* composed of past present and future, dream and fantasy, a film which the reader cannot see directly but only infer through the words. This is the structure of these diaries.

[. . .] The Diaries consist of bits of dreams and poetry and associations cut in together; I can't cover every association, just give a few examples. I was thinking about Bradbury Robinson, an English friend who was then going in for mystical Christianity, when a deer crossed the road. Spanish subtitle on the film *Rashomon.* The woodcutter had deceived the police and stolen a ring. And some spaced-out Buddhist has put the fire extinguisher *under* the Coleman stove. I can see burning fluid falling in a sheet of flame while somebody tries to reach the extinguisher. Move the extinguisher to a better place [. . .]

Someone has written on a piece of cardboard in the woodshed: "How can I please myself when I have no self to please?" Sorry, young man, I think you are kidding yourself. As long as you talk to yourself, you have a self. The self is like a pimping blackmailing chauffeur who gets you from here to there on word lines.

"Maya am I? You don't get rid of me that easy."

I have always felt that the essence of self is *words*, the internal dialogue. Trungpa agreed, with reservations, but does not give the matter of words such basic importance as I do. Don Juan, on the other hand, says that suspending the internal dialogue is the crucial step out of a preconceived idea of self. *Tales of Power*, p. 22: "To change our idea of the world is the crux of sorcery. And stopping the internal dialogue is the only way to accomplish it." The exercise he recommends to stop the internal dialogue is to walk with the eyes slightly crossed, covering a 180-degree area, without focussing on anything. This floods out the internal dialogue. Unfortunately I had not read *Tales of Power* at the time of my retreat and have had no opportunity to perform this exercise. It is not really practical in a city, owing to the constant barrage of word and image [. . . .]

MONDAY, AUGUST 11TH, 1975

First day of retreat. Review the process. Beckett asked me to fish in his pond. Kiki has arranged interview with Playboy. In station with Ray M. waiting for train to St. Louis. Little house in New Orleans. In wrong house on Wyoming St., I live on Denver St. Material witness to murder in Spain. Have they caught the murderers. "Yes" a cop says. "I have him at home. You see I used to run a discotheque." Ra Ra Ra Boomderay. I hurry to my blue heaven. Dinner with Bill Willis and Brion at Italian place. Best steak in town at Lucky Nick Dickendorf's. Roman ruins in England. Rented shack on river from D. Camel. Tandem toilet. "Shall we camel?" A toilet in Hell. Fight with the club steward. "I know what your game is." That damned bus. John Brady in New York with Pat. Blank inhuman look. Boy's Town on Price Road. Bradbury Robinson—deer crosses road. Enganado a la policia. Rashomon. It would be good to hear from you. This heath this calm this quiet scene. Why kill snakes? This is Independence Day in Morocco. Ian will be in Paris tomorrow. Part soiled rope. Milk Weed Minnesota. I wear my trousers rolled. Karma is a word. There goes Madrid. The trolley in Alexandria. "Delodge where are the keys?" Dingy station yellow lights. The hour that darkens and grows always later.

TUESDAY, AUGUST 12TH, 1975

Long process in different forms. Infiltrating some branch of the Process. Alan Watson had brought presents from America. Ian there.

WEDNESDAY, AUGUST 13TH, 1975

Samuel Beckett sent letter asking me to fish in his back yard pond. And to accompany him on deep sea diving trip. He would need help.

An Arab beggar at table in Paris. I offered him a sugar lattice pastry which he refused. I said "Va'ton" (Beat it)

Boeing crash in snow covered montains; cinders?

1. Dropped shaving brush which bounced into shrine by sea shell.

2. About to kill a centipede with hammer, by Trungpa's shrine. Centipede disappeared. By the sun: 11:45 A.M. Later saw centipede behind rock sheets.

Things needed. Shaving mirror. Anyone used to shave feels deterioration if he can not. Mirror also essential in case of something in eye. Flyswatter. Fire extinguisher under Coleman stove behind trash bucket. If stove catches fire, dangerous access. Moved by wood stove. Condensed milk. Powdered milk worse than no milk.

I twice missed path in walk through woods to find flowers for green bottle.

THURSDAY, AUGUST 14TH, 1975

Chaos and gun fights. Confused alarms of struggle and flight. Shot cop. Where ignorant armies clash by night.

Kiki had arranged an interview with Playboy. I arrive on horse back. Army saddle. Play boy of the Western World, guitar is I love you. Words are made from breath. Your breath. Words need you. You do not need words. Breath from maid are words. Words are what is not. Knot is what are words. Words knot are what is? What knot words? Our is? What knot is? Our words? What words knot our is? What? Not our words? Is? What is knot our words? Our words is not what?

Saw deer 12 noon by sun. Is word reverse mirror image of what is not? Try Chinese and Egyptian hieroglyphics in mirrors. Saw Ian as imp with red hair and pointed ears.

(To Friday, April 4th:)

The Evening News, August 14th, 1975. China blue half moon in the late afternoon sky. Note for G. Ferguson attached to milk weed. La Cuerda with a gob of mud from tractor. (8.2.7.6 on toilet paper) Sit. Bradbury. The deer. Left hand path around mud puddle. Walked to wall. She dwelt among the untrodden ways but oh the difference to me. Back to sit. Control needs time. Control needs beings with limited time who experience time. And few could know when Lucy ceased to be. Fair as a star when only one is shining in the sky. A violet hidden by a mossy stone, half hidden from the eye. Turn left. Sit. Sun going. LSD story. Mort. Day is done. Gone the sun. From the lake from the hill from the sky. All is well soldier brave, God is nigh. Back over pine needles. Twirling his club down cobble stone streets the sky goes out against his back.

FRIDAY, AUGUST 15TH, 1975

(To contact Brion, 10 P.M.)

In R.R. station with Ray M. and others. I was waiting for train to St. Louis. Meet me in St. Louis Louie, meet me at the fair. Ray had a whole room full of trunks and parcels. Later trying to find out when St. Louis train leaves. No Information. I was going to find out one way or another. Crowd barrier (Plan 28 at a quick glance) I had my ticket. Old steam trains. Dingy station yellow lights. Tickets. When is the next train for St. Louis?

Not much point in one drink.

(To Tuesday, June 3rd:)

St. Ian. St. Jacques. St. Allen.

Ian turning cart wheels in the dale. Ian in Paris today? Where is my little knife? When did I use it last? Can't remember. Let legs guide you toward the dip. Now I remember, to perforate cardboard note for G. Ferguson (wonder where he is?) Yes there it is by the milkweed. Got milk on hands yesterday putting up note. Harbor Beach, little gold knife. Part the soiled rope. Sit. Milk Weed Minnesota. Biggest milk weed and smallest people. Out to dale. Back. How many types of ignorance? The path. I am hungry. Back to hut. I wear my trousers rolled. Do I dare to eat a peach? Are they ripe yet? No.

Lawrence Ferlinghetti (1919-)

Lawrence Ferlinghetti was fairly conventional in his politics when he joined the navy to serve in World War II; after seeing firsthand the devastation of Nagasaki, however, his political convictions took a sharp turn to the left. He enrolled in Columbia University's master of arts program in literature on the GI Bill, and then went to Paris, where he earned a doctorate from the Sorbonne. Ferlinghetti moved to San Francisco and in 1953, with business partner Peter Martin, launched the first all-paperback bookstore in the country, City Lights. The shop quickly became a meeting ground for artists and writers, and the next year Ferlinghetti celebrated the birth of City Lights Books (a publishing venture) with the publication of his own book of poems, *Pictures of the Gone World.* It was the first in the influential Pocket Poets series, which aimed to make poetry accessible, portable, and affordable. Despite his academic credentials, Ferlinghetti embraced the poetry of the street, a poetry that was populist and colloquial.

After hearing Allen Ginsberg read "Howl" at the Six Gallery, Ferlinghetti wasted no time in asking to publish it. And it was the publication of "Howl" and the ensuing obscenity trial which catapulted the Beats to national attention. In the end the judge vindicated the poem, saying: "It ends in a plea for holy living . . ." The poem went into numerous printings, and City Lights Books, Allen Ginsberg's career, and the Beat Generation were launched on a course, from which there could be no turning back.

Ferlinghetti's role as a publisher was powerful. He brought out work by Diane di Prima, Bob Kaufman, and many others. And while he turned down Kerouac's offer to compile an anthology of Buddhist poetry (Kerouac's own mixed with that of Gary Snyder and Philip Whalen), he did offer to publish Kerouac's *The Scripture of the Golden Eternity.* As a bookstore owner he took risks by stocking his shelves with then-incendiary material such as Lenore Kandel's *The Love Book.* Furthermore, Ferlinghetti's poetry, particularly his spontaneous compositions to jazz, was also influential.

In the sixties, Ferlinghetti, a public defender of free speech, became ever more engaged in politics. As an anarchist, he eschewed traditional religions, but found himself attracted to what he called "the anti-authoritarianism of Zen Buddhism." He embarked on a course of sitting meditation in the sixties and experimented with mantra chanting, using both the Hare Krishna mantra and the *Heart Sutra.* This mantra practice found its expression poetically in his collection *Open Eye, Open Heart,* which Ferlinghetti once described as an attempt to create "an American mantra" using English words in rhythmic patterns. Ferlinghetti also studied with the spiritual teacher Jiddhu Krishnamurti in Ojai, California. He became close with Alan Watts, and Ferlinghetti wrote a remembrance of Watts's death ceremony: " . . . they were all now chanting the Great Prajna Paramita Sutra slowly and solemnly and with great force and beauty and I was thinking this should surely change the world as when they chant it altogether at the Zen Center in San Francisco I hope it changes at least the nearby Fillmore ghetto into a place of light & enlightenment where no more hunger or evil will ever exist."

Ferlinghetti's publishing business continues to flourish, as does City Lights Bookstore, now a San Francisco institution. Among Ferlinghetti's recent collections is *These Are My Rivers: New and Selected Poems, 1955–1993*.

. . . .

From Open Eye, Open Heart, *1973*.

True Confessional

I was conceived in the summer of Nineteen Eighteen
(or was it Thirty Eight)
when some kind of war was going on
but it didn't stop two people
from making love in Ossining that year
I like to think on a riverbank in sun
on a picnic by the Hudson
as in a painting of the Hudson River School
or up at Bear Mountain maybe
after taking the old Hudson River Line
paddlewheel excursion steamer
(I may have added the paddlewheel—
the Hudson my Mississippi)
And on the way back she
already carried me
inside of her
I lawrence ferlinghetti
wrought from the dark in my mother long ago
born in a small back bedroom—
In the next room my brother heard

the first cry,
many years later wrote me—
"Poor Mom—No husband—No money—Pop dead—
How she went through it all—"
Someone squeezed my heart
to make it go
I cried and sprang up
Open eye open heart where
do I wander
into the heart of the world
Carried away
by another I knew not
And which of me shall know my brother?
'I am my son, my mother, my father,
I am born of myself
my own flesh sucked'
And someone squeezed my heart
to make me go
And I began to go
through my number
I was a wind-up toy
someone had dropped wound-up
into a world already
running down
The world had been going on
a long time already
but it made no difference
It was new it was like new
i made it new
i saw it shining
and it shone in the sun
and it spun in the sun
and the skein it spun
was pure light
My life was made of it
made of the skeins of light
The cobwebs of Night
were not on it
were not of it

It was too bright
to see
too luminous too numinous
to cast a shadow
and there was another world
behind the bright screens
I had only to close my eyes
for another world to appear
too near and too dear
to be anything but myself
my inside self
where everything real
was to happen
in this place which still exists
inside myself
and hasn't changed that much
certainly not as much
as the outside
with its bag of skin
and its 'aluminum beard'
and its blue blue eyes
which see as one eye
in the middle of the head
where everything happens
except what happens
in the heart
vajra lotus diamond heart
wherein I read
the poem that never ends.

. . . .

From These Are My Rivers: New and Selected Poems, 1955–1993.

Ladakh Buddhess Biker

The Ladakh Buddhess is watching me
with her witchy eyes
on the corner of Columbus & Broadway
A gold button on her temple
between the eyes with the blue pupils
her eyes with blue eyebrows
not designed to blink
her eyelids like fenders
on old Oldsmobiles
her corneas red and blue
as if from loving & weeping too much
over our samsara
Eternally feminist
her headlight eyes beam at me
as if the sight of me
might make her finally
lower those heavy lids
I notice now she's seated on
a huge hog called Harley
her leather legs hugging its body
in a retro lotus position
Suddenly the traffic light changes
and she roars off still unblinking
through the late late traffic
of our Kali Yuga age

A Buddha in the Woodpile

If there had been only
one Buddhist in the woodpile
In Waco Texas
to teach us how to sit still
one saffron Buddhist in the back rooms
just one Tibetan lama

just one Taoist
just one Zen
just one Thomas Merton Trappist
just one saint in the wilderness
of Waco USA
If there had been only one
calm little Gandhi
in a white sheet or suit
one not-so-silent partner
who at the last moment shouted *Wait*
If there had been just one
majority of one
in the lotus position
in the inner sanctum
who bowed his shaved head to the
Chief of All Police
and raised his hands in a mudra
and chanted the Great Paramita Sutra
the Diamond Sutra
the Lotus Sutra
If there had somehow been
just one Gandhian spinner
with Brian Willson at the gates of the White House
at the Gates of Eden
then it wouldn't have been
Vietnam once again
and its "One two three four
What're we waitin' for?"
If one single ray of the light
of the Dalai Lama
when he visited this land
had penetrated somehow
the Land of the Brave
where the lion never
lies down with the lamb—
But not a glimmer got through
The Security screened it out
screened out the Buddha
and his not-so-crazy wisdom

If only in the land of Sam Houston
if only in the land of the Alamo
if only in Wacoland USA
if only in Reno
if only on CNN CBS NBC
one had comprehended
one single syllable
of the Gautama Buddha
of the young Siddhartha
one single whisper of
Gandhi's spinning wheel
one lost syllable
of Martin Luther King
or of the Early Christians
or of Mother Teresa
of Thoreau or Whitman or Allen Ginsberg
or of the millions in America tuned to them
If the inner ears of the inner sanctums
had only been half open
to any vibrations except
those of the national security state
and had only been attuned
to the sound of one hand clapping
and not one hand punching
Then that sick cult and its children
might still be breathing
the free American air
of the First Amendment

Michael McClure
(1932-   )

"Much of what the Beat Generation is about is nature—the landscape of nature in the case of Gary Snyder, the mind as nature in the case of Allen Ginsberg. Consciousness is a natural organic phenomenon. The Beats shared an interest in Nature, Mind, and Biology—areas that they expanded and held together with their radical political or antipolitical state." —MICHAEL McCLURE

Michael McClure moved from Kansas to San Francisco in 1954 to study art, but after a workshop with poet Robert Duncan soon turned his attention to writing. His first reading was as part of the Six Poets at the Six Gallery. The following year, 1956, McClure's first book of poetry, *Passage,* was published. McClure writes primarily about nature, an interest he found mirrored in Asian texts. Buddhism, particularly the Hua-Yen Vision of Indra's Net, informs his work. In this regard, he is representative of the connection the Beats had, ultimately, with environmental movements. He has written that the nonhierarchical, interdependent Buddhist approach to the natural world was the tonic needed by a country plagued by war neurosis: "The awareness that we are all without proportion, and that all living beings are proportionless, seemed natural. We who felt deeply in the cold fifties were either monists or animists."

McClure's prodigious output includes numerous plays, such as *The Beard,* which won off Broadway's Obie award; a spontaneous novel, *The Mad Club*; as well as essays and many volumes of poetry. His recent collections include *Rebel Lions* and *Simple Eyes.*

. . . .

An excerpt from an interview conducted by David Meltzer in 1971, published in Meltzer's The San Francisco Poets, *in which McClure discusses meditation as a way of "clearing the screen":*

The DNA molecule *is* the memory. It is the memory of the meat. Four billion years of memory telling you to be a mammal [. . . .] Besides our body's being a genetic accretion of billions of years, it is the actual accretion of our physical contacts with our environments, our psychological contacts with our propaganda and our intuitions. It's the actual meat on your bones, the constellation of the perception and events, and, in addition, we have a storage center in which the events that we can symbolize and verbalize about are activated. We call it our cortex. There are other parts of the brain too, like that small part of the brain back there in the nasal area. In that area they have come to believe that memory is stored hologramistically. Memory isn't stored in one place but stored constellatively in many places within the mind. Memory multiplies and lights up the edges that the constellation overlaps. The electrical and chemical activity that goes on—several sources of it going on simultaneously

—are constantly interacting. The universe of cells is in constant action.

If we empty this screen [through meditation] then the experience is the universe. The body of the universe manifested in our body [. . . .] A cell in the tip of your finger might be related to an atom in a star in another galaxy in a way we can't conceive of. The universe is an interweaving of such complexity that we are totally unable to conceive of it. You can imagine butterflies flying randomly through a shifting lattice. Can you imagine the multitudes of invisible presences surrounding it?

. . . .

From Jaguar Skies, *1975.*

HWA YEN TOTALISM

MY SWEET LIBERATION
comes out of the conflagration
like a nation
of tiny bees
and gnats
that swarm in trees
and make a living constellation
real as a transparent whale
or narwhal
with a spiral
horn
borne
by
his might
through the tight
side of a sailing ship.

DO

I

KNOW

THIS
TOUCH?

I love black valentines!

- - - - - - - - - - - - - - - - - - - -

Everything is mysterious wine
that drips from a spike
like gems
from a diamond mine
AND
it is stabbed right through
this solid wall
where we stand laughing in a stall
upon the dipping decks.
We know we're not wrecks
but radiant momentary
gods.

. . . .

From Antechamber & Other Poems, *1978.*

Written on the Flyleaf of Ashvagosha's **The Awakening of Faith**

PERFECT ENLIGHTENMENT,
I kneel and pray
to your bright hand and your chin

asking for sugar. Oh, sorrowless state,
happy black face.
Oh, lap-full of pearls . . .
Pillows of eternal green velvet . . .
Formation of nests in continents of sound . . .
Still drapes in the hurricane . . .
Snuffed candle becoming coolness . . .
Tricycles lighted by the glare of sirens . . .
Thou art the better of thyself
here already
and I yearn to make it
to
thee.

1963–1977

. . . .

In Scratching the Beat Surface: Essays on New Vision from Blake to Kerouac, *1982, McClure discusses one of the poems he read at the Six Gallery ("Poem") and a Buddhist interpretation of it.*

POEM

Linked part to part, toe to knee, eye to thumb
Motile, feral, a blockhouse of sweat
The small of the hunt's
A stench, . . . my foetor.
The eye a bridegroom of torture
Colors are linked by spirit
Euglena, giraffe, frog
Creatures of grace—Rishi
Of their own right.

As I walk my legs say to me 'Run
There is joy in swiftness'
As I speak my tongue says to me 'Sing
There is joy in thought,
The size of the word
Is its own flight from crabbedness.'

And the leaf is an ache
And the love an ache in the back.
The stone a creature.

A PALISADE

The inside whitewashed.

. . . .
. . . .
. . . .
. . . .

A pale tuft of grass.

My concerns in this brief lyric are as various as Buddha's Fire Sermon (that the eye is a bridegroom of torture), physical anthropology (that we are linked part to part), and sexuality (that love is an ache in the back). The poem was also concerned with its own structure. I thought of it as a real PHYSICAL OBJECT. I was not just making a lyric about feelings, or about emotions, or objects. I tried to create the poem in the shape of a palisade, a stockade. Influenced by Oriental thought (especially in Oriental painting) I used *ma*, the negative space in landscape, as silence in the poem. There are four lines of dots utilizing silent time as space in the poem. The four lines of dots are followed by an exclamation point. The last line, "A pale tuft of grass," is an image from the stockade but, secretly, a whisper from Whitman.

PART FOUR

Like Minds

Kenneth Rexroth (1905–1982)

"The moon, the mist, the world, man
Are only fleeting compounds
Varying in power, and
Power is only insight
Into the void—the single
Thought that illuminates the heart.
The heart's mirror hangs in the void."
—KENNETH REXROTH

Kenneth Rexroth was a poet, pacifist, anarchist, critic, translator, and the presiding elder of the San Francisco literary community when the Beats gravitated to the city in 1955. Rexroth had moved to San Francisco in 1927 and published his first collection of poetry, *In What Hour,* in 1940. He was famous for hosting Friday night literary evenings, during which he would pontificate on everything from the history of the West Coast to the poetry of Tu Fu. He always made time to welcome and encourage younger poets, and in the early fifties opened his door to Lawrence Ferlinghetti, Gary Snyder, and Allen Ginsberg, among others. Rexroth also agreed to play the role of the "emcee" at the Six Gallery reading. But this alliance with the Beats was not to last long. Whether he was put off by the near-instant success of the Beats (Rexroth was still struggling for recognition) or simply by the boisterous bad manners of the group (Snyder, Ginsberg, Whalen, and Kerouac all showed up very late for a dinner invitation), the split was dramatic. The man who had been called the father of the Beats soon denounced his offspring, loudly and publicly. Although he maintained a warm friendship with a few of the writers on an individual basis, he tried to put as much distance as possible between himself and the Beat Generation.

While Rexroth could disown the younger poets, they could not deny him. Gary Snyder, for one, has credited Rexroth with giving him "the nerve" to draw on Far Eastern material and to incorporate Buddhist references into his work. In addition to Rexroth's own poetry, which was rich in allusions to the East, Rexroth had translated two important and popular volumes, *One Hundred Poems from the Japanese* (1955) and *One Hundred Poems from the Chinese* (1956), to which many poets looked for inspiration. But his influence, at least with regard to Buddhism, remained largely literary. Snyder has said that Rexroth's attitude toward Buddhism was ambivalent.

Whether or not Rexroth engaged in any formal practice in those days (aside from the "empty days" for contemplation, which he mentioned in letters to his publisher, James Laughlin) is not clear. What is apparent is his contempt for many forms of Buddhism and for some Buddhist practitioners: Rexroth frequently railed against Zen, citing its alliance with military power in Japan, and he said of Kerouac that "his Buddha is a dimestore incense burner, glowing and glowering sinisteringly in the dark corner of a beatnik pad and just thrilling the wits out of bad little girls." In 1958, Rexroth told two interviewers that Zen was for "white people" and that the only acceptable form of Buddhism was Shingon.

But time seemed to have mellowed Rexroth. Perhaps as a result of the two years he spent in Kyoto on a Fulbright (1974–75), Rexroth, in his later years, seemed to admit more readily to being influenced by Buddhism, though he still denied having any "doctrinaire belief." In an interview conducted several years after he returned from Japan, Rexroth was asked, "Do you follow a particular spiritual path?" He replied: "I don't like to say I'm a Buddhist—there are an awful lot of funny people running around saying they are Buddhists—but I suppose I am one. I've been steadily drifting toward it for many years."

In short, with respect to Buddhism, Rexroth seems to have played a dual role for the Beats: He was both an ancestor, in that he made some Asian literature and thought accessible early on, and a "like mind," a fellow traveler, who began identifying himself more personally with Buddhism in the seventies, long after many of the Beats had committed themselves to Buddhist practice. Rexroth never went so far as to reject Western theology altogether; his life was a sort of spiritual mosaic, wherein he frequently lit candles on Friday nights and eventually, as his parents had before him, converted to Catholicism (shortly before his death in 1982). His wife, Carol Tinker, claimed that he died a Catholic *and* a Buddhist, saying that Rexroth was essentially a Buddhist, but that he also believed in observing the rituals of the culture to which he was closest by birth.

These selections are taken primarily from Rexroth's later work, in particular the collection *On Flower Wreath Hill,* which Rexroth named after the Avatamsaka, or the "Flower Wreath" Sutra.

. . . .

This six-section poem takes its title from a collection of poetic essays written by Kamond Chomei in the thirteenth century. Hojoki *literally means "the monk's record," or "record of a monk's hut." This poem was originally published in 1949.*

Hojoki

SPRING

Venus in the pale green sky
Where the Pleiades glimmer
Under a bar of dark cloud,
The moon travels through the L
Formed by Jupiter and Saturn
In conjunction below Gemini—
The year marches through the stars
Orion again walks into the sea.
The horned owl sits on the tree
By my hut and watches me
As I gather a handful
Of sticks and boil my rice.
He stays there through the growing dusk,
I can hardly see him when
He flies off in the starlight.

SPRING

Fine warm rain falls through the maple
And laurel leaves, and fills the narrow
Gorge with a pulse like life.
The waterfall is muffled,
And my ten foot square hut lies
In the abysm of a sea
Of sibilant quiet.

AUTUMN

I lay aside the Diurnal
At the light drenched poetry
Of St. Ambrose that converted

St. Augustine to a world
More luminous and more lucid
Than one where light warred with dark.
I ponder what it is I find
Here by my hut in the speech
Of falling water's swift conjunction.
What have men ever found?
I think of Buddha's infinite
Laugh in the Lankavatara,
Lighting up all the universes.
The steep sides of the gorge enclose
Me like the thighs of a girl's
Body of bliss, and illusion,
And law. The end of dry autumn—
The narrow water whispers
Like the rustle of sheer, stiff silk.

SUMMER

A thing unknown for years,
Rain falls heavily in June,
On the ripe cherries, and on
The half cut hay.
Above the glittering
Grey water of the inlet,
In the driving, light filled mist,
A blue heron
Catches mice in the green
And copper and citron swathes.
I walk on the rainy hills.
It is enough.

WINTER

Very late, a thin wash
Of cirrus cloud covers half
The sky and obscures
A three quarter moon.

Since midnight it has turned warmer.
There will be rain before morning.
There is no wind.
Everything holds still
In the vaporous light.
I walk along the stream.
Its voices are rich and subdued.
The alders overhead blend their bare twigs
And catkins with the moonlit clouds
Into one indistinct, netted haze.
The hills, covered with wet young grass,
Are intangible as billows of fog.
The decaying leaves on the path
Break the light into a hazy shimmer.
The thin bladed laurel leaves
Look like Su Tung Po's bamboos.
Two deer bounce away from me
Through the woods, in and out
Of the shadows like puffs of smoke.
The moon grows very dim.
The air does not move at all.
The stream deepens its voices.
I turn to go back to my hut,
And come on the cloudy moon
And the light filled sky
Reflected through the bare branches
In a boundless, velvety pool.
I stand and gaze and remember
That if this were my home country,
In a few hours, slow, still, wet, huge,
Flakes of snow would be falling
Through the windless dawn.

SPRING

I sit under the old oak,
And gaze at the white orchard,
In bloom under the full moon.

The oak purrs like a lion,
And seems to quiver and breathe.
I am startled until I
Realize that the beehive
In the hollow trunk will be
Busy all night long tonight.

. . . .

An excerpt from an interview conducted by David Meltzer in 1971 for The San Francisco Poets.

DM: There is a seemingly different response to spiritual matters in the West Coast; a type of life-style and response more basically rooted to oriental and pre-institutionalized Judeo-Christian concepts [. . .]

KR: One reason is simply that oceans, like the steppes, unite as well as separate. The West Coast is close to the Orient. It's the next thing out there. There are a large number of orientals living on the West Coast. San Francisco is an international city and it has living contact with the Orient. It also has an internal oriental life. Once a week you can go to see a Buddhist basketball game if you want to. There are Buddhist temples all over the place. To a New Yorker this is all ridiculous, the Orient means dimestore incense burners. It is very unreal.

For years I noticed in Pound's "Cantos" two ideograms that were upside-down. I used to pester [his editor, James] Laughlin about this. I used to make fun of it. Ezra [Pound] by this time had gotten very dim-witted, so he didn't notice it. This was after the war. . . . Laughlin said something to Eliot about it, and Eliot burst out laughing and thought it was a great joke. Not that they were upside-down, but that it would worry me. He said, "But, you know, no one pays any attention at all to that sort of stuff. You know, that Chinese thing. Nobody reads Chinese anyway." Eliot's attitude toward Ezra's interest in the Orient was that it was a great deal more ridiculous than his interest in social credit, or his other crackpot ideas.

Large numbers of people have gone to the Northwest and to California to get away from the extreme pressures of a commercial civilization. On the West Coast it is possible to beat the system. It's possible to be a fly alive on the flywheel, which it isn't in New York. I would have been an utterly different human being if I had gone back to New York. That's why I stayed on the West Coast. Of course, there is another aspect to the whole California business: religious communities and new religions and swamis, [. . .] Krishnamurti is a very impressive guy. His stuff is very intelligent. He is no Kahlil Gibran. He has wonderful answers to give.

This is all part of the wartime thing too. Allen Hunter at the Hollywood Congregational Church is the guy who turned on people like Auden, Aldous Huxley, Pravananda, Gerald Heard, and of course, Isherwood, who is still around. All of these people were extremely influential on the pacifist and anarchist movements. This was another focus. And it all fed into the thing that made the San Francisco scene.

People would come down from the CO camps to us in San Francisco, but they would also go down to see Isherwood, or Aldous Huxley, or somebody like that. Something definitely was being built up.

The big influences in the Northwest were Mark Tobey, who was a Bahai, and Morris Graves, who was a Vedantist. They were both very serious about it. Mark Tobey is a big wheel in the Bahai movement, in so far as they have big wheels. And Morris Graves is very serious. A lot of western migration was in the first place to get away from the destructiveness of the big metropoles and then to find new spiritual roots. That's true of all classes of people, not just intellectuals.

I think it's a great mistake to put down the thought of an old retired couple in Moline, Illinois, who decide to get themselves a little house in the rose-colored slums of southern California after going to a Vedanta meeting. There's nothing wrong with that. The guy comes home and says, "Ma, I think I am going to sell the secondhand car business. I think it is a rotten thing. I think we got enough money and we will go to California. I was sure impressed by that Indian fella we heard at that lecture and I think we'll go out to Glendale . . ." What's wrong with this? Is it any different than Allen Ginsberg?

I have always said that the greatest shock Kerouac ever got in his life was when he walked into my house, sat down in a kind of stiff-legged imitation of a lotus posture, and announced he was a Zen Buddhist . . . and then discovered everyone in the room knew at least one Oriental language.

You have to realize too that KPFA [a radio station] fed us an awful lot of this stuff. For years and years, Alan Watts and I were back-to-back on Sunday. Alan was handing out the Sunday sermon. This was all very influential.

. . . .

From On Flower Wreath Hill*, 1976.*

Hapax

The Same Poem Over and Over

Holy Week. Once more the full moon
Blooms in deep heaven
Like a crystal flower of ice.
The wide winter constellations
Set in fog brimming over
The seaward hills. Out beyond them,

In the endless dark, uncounted
Minute clots of light go by,
Billions of light years away,
Billions of universes,
Full of stars and their planets
With creatures on them swarming
Like all the living cells on the earth.
They have a number, and I hold
Their being and their number
In one suety speck of jelly
Inside my skull. I have seen them
Swimming in the midst of rushing
Infinite space, through a lens of glass
Through a lens of flesh, on a cup of nerves.
The question is not
Does being have meaning,
But does meaning have being.
What is happening?
All day I walk over ridges
And beside cascades and pools
Deep into the Spring hills.
Mushrooms come up in the same spot
In the abandoned clearing.
Trillium and adder's tongue
Are in place by the waterfall.

A heron lifts from a pool
As I come near, as it has done
For forty years, and flies off
Through the same gap in the trees.
The same rush and lift of flapping wings,
The same cry, how many
Generations of herons?
The same red tailed hawks court each other
High on the same rising air
Above a grassy steep. Squirrels leap
In the same oaks. Back at my cabin
In the twilight an owl on the same
Limb moans in his ancient language.

Billions and billions of worlds
Full of beings larger than dinosaurs
And smaller than viruses, each
In its place, the ecology
Of infinity.
I look at the rising Easter moon.
The flowering madrone gleams in the moonlight.
The bees in the cabin wall
Are awake. The night is full
Of flowers and perfume and honey.
I can see the bees in the moonlight
Flying to the hole under the window,
Glowing faintly like the flying universes.
What does it mean. This is not a question, but
an exclamation.

. . . .

From On Flower Wreath Hill.

VII

Night shuts down the misty mountains
With fine rain. The seventh day
Of my seventieth year,
Seven-Seven-Ten, my own
Tanabata, and my own
Great Purification. Who
Crosses in midwinter from
Altair to Vega, from the
Eagle to the Swan, under the earth,
Against the sun? Orion,
My guardian king, stands on
Kegonkyoyama.
So many of these ancient
Tombs are the graves of heroes
Who died young. The combinations

Of the world are unstable
By nature. Take it easy.
Nirvana.
Change rules the world forever.
And man but a little while.

VIII

Oborozuki,
Drowned Moon,
The half moon is drowned in mist
Its hazy light gleams on leaves
Drenched with warm mist. The world
Is alive tonight. I am
Immersed in living protoplasm,
That stretches away over
Continents and seas. I float
Like a child in the womb. Each
Cell of my body is
Penetrated by a
Strange electric life. I glow
In the dark with the moon drenched
Leaves, myself a globe
Of St. Elmo's fire.

I move silently on the
Wet forest path that circles
The shattered tumulus.
The path is invisible.
I am only a dim glow
Like the tumbled and broken
Gravestones of forgotten men
And women that mark the way.
I sit for a while on one
Tumbled sotoba and listen
To the conversations of
Owls and nightjars and tree frogs.
As my eyes adjust to the
Denser darkness I can see

That my seat is a cube and
All around me are scattered
Earth, water, air, fire, ether.
Of these five elements
The moon, the mist, the world, man
Are only fleeting compounds
Varying in power, and
Power is only insight
Into the void—the single
Thought that illuminates the heart.
The heart's mirror hangs in the void.

Do there still rest in the broken
Tumulus ashes and charred
Bones thrown in a corner by
Grave robbers, now just as dead?
She was once a shining flower
With eyebrows like the first night's moon,
Her white face, her brocaded
Robes perfumed with cypress and
Sandalwood; she sang in the Court
Before the Emperor, songs
Of China and Turkestan.
She served him wine in a cup
Of silver and pearls, that gleamed
Like the moonlight on her sleeves.
A young girl with black hair
Longer than her white body—
Who never grew old. Now owls
And nightjars sing in a mist
Of silver and pearls.

The wheel
Swings and turns counterclockwise.
The old graspings live again
In the new consequences.
Yet, still, I walk this same path
Above my cabin in warm
Moonlit mist, in rain, in

Autumn wind and rain of maple
Leaves, in spring rain of cherry
Blossoms, in new snow deeper
Than my clogs. And tonight in
Midsummer, a night enclosed
In an infinite pearl.
Ninety-nine nights over
Yamashina Pass, and the
Hundredth night and the first night
Are the same night. The night
Known prior to consciousness,
Night of ecstasy, night of
Illumination so complete
It cannot be called perceptible.

Winter, the flowers sleep on
The branches. Spring, they awake
And open to probing bees.
Summer, unborn flowers sleep
In the young seeds ripening
In the fruit. The mountain pool
Is invisible in the
Glowing mist. But the mist-drowned
Moon overhead is visible
Drowned in the invisible water.

Mist-drenched, moonlit, the sculpture
Of an orb spider glitters
Across the path. I walk around
Through the bamboo grass. The mist
Dissolves everything else, the
Living and the dead, except
This occult mathematics of light.
Nothing moves. The wind that blows
Down the mountain slope from
The pass and scatters the spring
Blossoms and the autumn leaves
Is still tonight. Even the
Spider's net of jewels has ceased

To tremble. I look back at
An architecture of pearls
And silver wire. Each minute
Droplet reflects a moon, as
Once did the waterpails of
Matsukaze and Murasame.
And I realize that this
Transcendent architecture
Lost in the forest where no one passes
Is itself the Net of Indra,
The compound infinities of infinities,
The Flower Wreath,
Each universe reflecting
Every other, reflecting
Itself from every other,
And the moon the single thought
That populates the Void.
The night grows still more still. No
Sound at all, only a flute
Playing soundlessly in the
Circle of dancing gopis.

. . . .

The following is a reprint of "The Jewel Net of Indra," an interview with Rexroth conducted by Rick Fields and Eric Lerner in 1980 for the Buddhist magazine Zero. *The interview took place in Rexroth's Santa Barbara home in a large workroom, "a rough, wooden outbuilding to the trellis-surrounded house," that was filled with high bookshelves, three or more desks, various typewriters, tape recorders, and piles of manuscripts.*

INTERVIEWER: In both your life and your work there seems to be an implied connection between a certain kind of political awareness, planetary consciousness and a mode of artistic expression. How is this association informed by the underlying religious, or contemplative sensibility that appears throughout your work?

REXROTH: The questions you raise are about a world which to me is essentially illusory. That doesn't mean that it doesn't have reality in the ordinary sense of the word but it has no substantiality. The substantial thing in life is the religious experience itself. This is the essence of the teaching of Buddha: that the religious experience is self-sufficient. Behind it lies no god, no immortality, none of these things. He always refused to answer questions on these subjects: "What happens after nirvana?" "Is there a God?"—the answers are not relevant. And as for politics? A life lived according to the Buddha law will not need much from politics. If Christianity was put into effect tomorrow every state on earth would collapse within twenty-four hours. My interest in politics is largely that either of a journalist, an analyst of what is happening, or that its interest is unreal. Many years ago I was sitting in Café Dome with Eric Severeid who was then young and full of piss and vinegar and I said, "Why don't you tell it how it is? How they run things?" And he said, "Look Rexroth you're a journalist, a columnist, just as well as me, and you know perfectly well that if we got up on a lecture platform at a university and told the audience exactly how the world is run and what kind of people run it, they'd call for the men in white, and they'd lock us up and we'd never get out and we'd be diagnosed as hopeless paranoiacs." Well in recent years some of this has come out, since Watergate broke the pucker string.

I have never, no that's not true, I *have* met idealistic, misguided, politicians. Some of them of considerable power. One is a friend of mine, a perfectly sincere man, a congressman. But by and large, just as there are no honest cops, an honest man is not to be found in the profession. See, we not only live in a world of unreality, but we live in a world of lies. People say, "What do you mean by the social lie?" And I say, "It usually begins at home, when Momma says, 'Daddy never masturbated in his life.'" The Freudians could build the entire structure of a sociology on that. And we live in a society where the worst rises to the top. By and large a police sergeant is not as good a man as a patrolman; and a lieutenant not as good a man as a sergeant; and a captain is not as good a man as lieutenant; and a chief is worst of all. And people say, "You don't really mean our president?" Well just figure out how that compounds, increases geometrically. That's like putting one bean on the first checkerboard square and two beans on the next and four beans on the next, finally you have millions of beans. Well you're doing the same thing in politics. Imagine how many beans you've got on the presidency? I simply have no belief in those things.

INTERVIEWER: Is there a consistent position for anarchists to take these days?

REXROTH: Sure I just took it. I don't like to call it anarchist.

INTERVIEWER: What word would you use instead?

REXROTH: What's the difference in that and being a Buddhist? A person who lives the Buddha life to the best of his ability does not need the state and does not need law. That's a different thing from being a political anarchist. This person certainly does not need politics. He may engage in political actions when a Buddhist community is being persecuted as in South Vietnam. But that's a different matter. And also you can't expect every monk in South and East Asia to be a model of Sakyamuni. Buddhism really isn't even passive resistance, it's ignoring the state, in all of its ways. It's ignoring the social lie.

This does not mean that individual Buddhist sects and individual Buddhists are not extremely political. Much of Japanese Zen is identified with the great rich, and with the officer caste who are its supporters. And the identification is perfectly correct. This is the reason why Americans who used to come to Japan announcing, "I'm a Zen poet," discovered that they met no important Japanese poets, to whom Zen is quite distasteful politically. But this does not mean that people like D. T. Suzuki, sensei, was a fascist, black dragon or anything like that. But Suzuki Zen is very much like Martin Buber's Chassidism. It bears very little resemblance to what you find in Daitoku-ji, any more than Martin Buber's *Teachings of a Chassidic Master* resemble the people that you'd meet at 34th St. and 7th Ave. in New York.

On the other hand I have no use for hippy and beat Zen because it's essentially antinomianism. I was playing the Five Spot, a café in New York some years ago, and the chief beatnik was standing at the bar. We hadn't opened yet. And a court officer came in to serve this fellow with a summons for child support and alimony for his wife and child, both of whom had tuberculosis. When he was handed the summons he announced, "This doesn't mean anything to me, I'm a Zen Buddhist." And he tore it up. The owner said, "I don't give a damn if you're Mary Baker Eddy and a Christian Scientist. Get out of here." That's what the kids all over the world have eaten up: Buddhism means irresponsibility. Well, it so happens that the Buddhist law for the layman in the simplest Theravada sects has between 40 and 48 commandments, all of which include the Mosaic code except sabbath and business about God. So to say, "I'm a Buddhist, I don't believe in the Ten Commandments," is not Buddhism. Buddhism includes the Ten Commandments and surpasses them. So I think this stuff is largely pernicious.

INTERVIEWER: Is there an alternative to hippy Zen which clearly misses the point in one direction and the government sponsored institutions of Buddhism which miss from the other?

REXROTH: The power of a personality, of the so-called historic Sakyamuni is so great that it is irrepressible. And in a Tibetan lamasery, representing what westerners call the most decadently superstitious form of Buddhism, you will still find the Buddha life being lived, as you will find it at Daitoku-ji, or not find it. The peculiar thing is that why are they called Buddhists? Look at the Amida Buddhists of Japan, the Pure Land sects like Jodo Shinshu. The historical Buddha Sakyamuni scarcely exists in the sutras of Pure Land. And yet all you have to do is go right here in California to the local Japanese Jodo Shinshu temple and you find people who are essentially trying to live a life modeled on the Buddha life. Now an interesting thing has happened. You see most Caucasian American Buddhists have had very little connection with the organized religions of Buddhism. They came at it through Zen, almost entirely, until recent developments. They don't know that all through the Buddhist sects there has grown up synthetic Buddhism, which in fact greatly resembles the sort of thing which all good Buddhologists put down. In the Buddhism of the Rhys Davids, the English man and wife who translated the sacred books of Theravada Buddhism years ago, Sakyamuni is pictured as something of a liberal socialist, a social worker. The curious thing is that even in the Jodo Shinshu, the Pure Land sect which is the largest Buddhist group in Japan, you find instead this synthesized type of Buddhism. It takes philosophy from Ashvagosha and Nagarjuna and everybody under the sun, and Kobo Daishi and western philosophy, which has very little appeal to them. It's considered bad manners in Japan to talk profoundly. This greatly puzzles westerners who go over to Buddhist conferences and no great mysteries of life are discussed.

I went to stay one time in Japan, at Koyosan which is the big temple complex of the Shingon sect of Buddhism. Now Shingon, which was founded by Kobo Daishi, is also known as Kukai, is esoteric Japanese Buddhism. It is essentially Japanese tantrism. The temple at Koyosan is on a mountain quite a ways from Kyoto. It might be easier to walk there than to go by bus and train and when I arrived there, with my wife, it was all covered with snow. We were ushered into a room and served tea by a novice and my wife commented on the beautiful facsimile prints of great Japanese paintings. "Facsimile?" I said, "You're sitting in a room walled with about a million dollars." Anyway this very nice man came in, the guest master of the place, and he began talking to us. He has been all around the world studying. He promised to come and see us here but he hasn't shown up yet. And what did he talk about? Now this, you have to remember, this temple is the grave of Kobo Daishi, Kukai, the famous founder of Shingon. Shingon is close to Tibetan lamaism. It has ceremonies which greatly resemble puja worship. They're very Indian. It's full of all kinds of extraordinary creatures, Bodhisattvas and devas. In their ceremony when you go in from the center of the altar, toward the Dainichi, Vairochana, you shed the aspects, from the guardian gods at the gate to the Adi Buddha, who in the mandala is usually painted as a blue or black figure, embracing a black or blue female consort, Prajna. This is the Adi Buddha, who is beyond knowledge, beyond qualification and beyond names and beyond conditions, beyond existence—does not exist in anything resembling our sense of the word, "exist."

But our conversation with this monk, the guest master of Koyosan, who was about 35 or 40, was about various places he'd studied at in America, like that ecumenical theological school in Berkeley. And we passed the time of day, talked about the beauty of the snow. We talked of various other things in that vein. Kobo Daishi's prose writing which you can get anywhere is platitudes; but that's just its point, so is Buddhism. There is really nothing profound in the Buddha Word. But Kobo Daishi wrote ten transcendental poems in Chinese which have profoundly influenced me. And which I am tempted to translate if I am not satisfied with the translation being done by a friend of mine. These have a symbolic profundity. But it is a profundity which is not analyzable or quantifiable. You see Buddhism teaches the opposite of Kierkegaard or the Christian existentialists. Man is not utterly contingent on an absolute creator, because there is no creator, there is no absolute, there is no contingency. And the thing that is called a soul is a bundle of skandhas, characteristics which pass through a dissolution, dissolve. People then ask you what reincarnates? If you believe in reincarnation, then what reincarnates? Well reincarnation was universally believed in Buddha's time, was accepted as a fact. You don't have to believe in reincarnation. What is the karma, what is the karma that passes? Well that is what reincarnates. And reincarnates indefinitely until it is dissolved.

Now if you ask a Jodo Shinshu abbot, of the Pure Land sect, "Do you really believe in this paradise of Amida? Do you really believe in a creature named Amida, somebody named Kannon (Avalokiteshvara)? Do you believe in these buddhas and bodhisattvas?" I'll never forget, I was in a seminar up in the mountains, on Buddhism and the leading Jodo Shinshu abbot was there, this woman asked this question, and he said, "These are conceptual beings."

She didn't ask any more questions. Now, as for Zen, well my real objection to Zen, particularly to Rinzai, is strain. I don't believe you have to do any of these things. Yogic exercises are interesting, especially when young. I've done them all, but you very soon realize that they don't mean anything. These are ladders that don't even go to jodo, you're better off in Amida's paradise. They're trips that don't go anywhere. The measure of the defect of vision is visions. And no Buddhist said that, St. John of the Cross said that. And the more trips we have, the further away we're getting. My daughter who is a ballet dancer, who is much more agile than I am, can put her legs behind her head in lotus position and stand on her hands but she's never thought that has got her even as near to illumination as a couple of dots of acid. Illumination doesn't come out of bottles and it doesn't come out of gymnastics, and it doesn't come out of prana and it doesn't come out of strange breathing. All you do is hyperventilate yourself. It's good to sit in meditation. It's good to count your breaths, it's good to say anything repetitiously, you can say, "hail Mary, full of grace" if you want. But you approach illumination as though an invisible mist was coming up behind you and enveloping you. And unless that happens you are nowhere near illumination. Now you can concentrate certain nervous energy, which we're now discovering through acupuncture. You can concentrate that nervous energy in the mysterious square inch of Taoism, between the eyes. But on the other hand you can be sitting on a stupa, at ease entering a world of peace. It probably takes a long time to learn that, I don't know when I first learned it. I've held those ideas for several years now, but I'm 72 years old.

Yet, I feel there is a reality in the world, and in this way I suppose I disagree, though it's hard to imagine, with the historical Sakyamuni who is largely the creation of scholarship. I believe that there is a community in the world, a community of love. It is a community of contemplators. And the only reality is a perspective, but the perspectives are infinite because the contemplators are infinite. And this is the teaching of the Avatamsaka Sutra, the Kegonkyo, which occurs over and over in my poems. And my poems have become very small. I've told people, "You know, when I was last in Japan, I had a transsexual operation but I only had a limited amount of money, so I couldn't afford to have my beard taken off." I've come to write more and more like a Buddhist nun. At least a Japanese woman. I think that the ideas of the Kegon, and of Kobo Daishi, the founder of Shingon, influence me more and more, although I have no doctrinaire belief. In the Avatamsaka Sutra there is this vision of infinity, an infinitude of buddha worlds, each one reflecting the other . . .

INTERVIEWER: "The Jewel Net of Indra."

REXROTH: You read that poem of mine? See, this volume is called *On Flower Wreath Hill,* which is what Kegon means. At the end of it I'm walking above where I live in Kyoto, through the forest around through the graves, past the ruins of a mound of a princess, who must have died an enormous time ago and I sit on a toppled stupa, as did Ono no Komachi in a famous Noh play. In that moment I become as in a Noh play, as it were, possessed by Ono no Komachi, and there in the poem, is a long passage which echoes things that are said in a free form, but primarily in the three Ono no Komachi Noh plays. Then the last part goes "Mist drenched . . .

[*See* On Flower Wreath Hill, *VIII, pp. 334–35 from "Mist-drenched" to "dancing gopis"—Ed.*]

Well that more or less sums it up.

INTERVIEWER: When did you first come in contact with the Avatamsaka Sutra? Recently?

REXROTH: No, no. Buddhological literature seems to have increased geometrically, but after all, before the war there was all kinds of it.

I'm especially devoted to a completely conceptual entity. Marichi-ten who is an Indian goddess of the morning star of the first ray of dawn and is as such the consort of Surya, the sun god, and then of Vairocana and is one of the ten gods of Shingon. Most of my poetry now to a greater or lesser degree is visionary. I just wrote this. It was typed this morning:

Midnight I walk out in the garden
After a hot bath
In yukata and clogs
I feel no cold
But the leaves have all fallen
From the fruit trees
And the cotti hang there all alone
Filled with frosty moonlight
Suddenly I am aware
There is no sound
Not of insects,
Nor of frogs,
Nor of birds,
Only the slow pulse of an owl
Marking time
For the silence.

INTERVIEWER: I wanted to ask you about this poem, "Void Only," if you might comment on the last lines of it.

Time like glass
Space like glass
I sit quiet
Anywhere anything
Happens
Quiet loud still turbulent
The serpent coils
On itself
All things are translucent
Then transparent
Then gone

Only emptiness
No limits
Only the infinitely faint
Song
Of the coiling mind
Only.

REXROTH: You see, what the poem really says, because it's got everything in it, the Kundalini Serpent does not need to rise, it just coils around, just lays down there goes to sleep. Void only and mind only, are the same doctrine. Now here the thing is translated into, I suppose what you would call a form of erotic mysticism. I should really read the other poem that goes with it. They got separated.

Suchness

In the theosophy of light,
The logical universal
Ceases to be anything more
Than the dead body of an angel.
What is substance? Our substance
Is whatever we feed our angel.
The perfect incense for worship
Is camphor, whose flames leave no ashes.

Now curiously enough those lines, those last lines come from Sai Shonagon and are completely frivolous. The empress asks her, "Go get some incense." And the maid said, "What one should I get?" And the empress said, "Get camphor, it doesn't leave any ashes. It's best for worship." And I thought about this and I thought this was a profound remark. Then it goes on to "Void Only" where it's eroticized. It's in another volume and got separated.

I cannot escape from you
When I think I am alone,
I awake to discover
I am lost in the jungle

Of your love, in its darkness
Jewelled with the eyes of unknown
Beasts. I awake to discover
I am a forest ascetic
In the impenetrable
Void only, the single thought
Of which nothing can be said.

I think that in the Buddhist mission if you have enough honest and illuminated teachers to go around the civilization can be greatly influenced. I don't notice, however, that Buddhism ever stopped centuries of civil war for sport in Japan. They didn't have anything to fight about. They did it for fun. It's true! From the fall of the Heian empirate to the founding of the Shogunate what were they really fighting about? For giggles. Then of course Bushido is the ethics of the unemployed soldier. Because after Ieyasu on they didn't have anything to fight about either, except once in a while to chop off the head of a peasant who didn't bow low enough. So the idea that a community of illumination and insight, can *change* the world is an illusion. But it can probably save it. Because when the contemplative life dies out the civilization dies with great rapidity. It takes no time at all. Dead. Somebody asked Jacques Maritain, "What keeps civilization going? You've made such a case for its collapse."

He said, "The prayers of the contemplatives in the monasteries." Everybody thought it was very silly. But it's true. When the flame goes out, then there's nothing but darkness. But I don't think that this can reform the world.

INTERVIEWER: Is this contemplative tradition alive in America today?

REXROTH: Why sure it's alive. Look at all the people who went through the movement who are now in communes or off in various Zen establishments or who have gone to the Far East. It's all over the place. Now, they may fall for terribly phoney things like Rev. Moon. You have to realize that scattered through all these movements are racketeers.

You can't struggle with them. You have to overcome by your example and by your words. This leads you into a certain amount of what might be called hostility, but what can you do about fraud? What are you going to do? Just let it pass? Because it will pass. When I was a boy before the first war there were a lot of these people running around. A lot of them had mothers who looked very much like the lady on the Aunt Jemima package but these people wore turbans and they had crystal balls and they put on mystical performances on the vaudeville stage and elsewhere. They were known as ragheads on the menopause circuit. Well we're up to our ass with ragheads on the menopause circuit today. But they pass. This passes. That's one thing about evil, it's always with us and it always passes.

INTERVIEWER: Do you recognize in contemporary poetry or art or anywhere else similar feelings to your own that are being expressed?

REXROTH: Krishnamurti. Well, you *could* call Krishnamurti an archetype of the raghead on the menopause circuit, but he isn't. All you have to do is read Krishnamurti or talk to him. It's the real thing. As for poetry, no I don't know anyone. Philip Whalen to a certain extent. To quite an extent. One of the great things about Philip Whalen is that so much of his poetry is comic. And on the brink of a very large percentage of the great visions in the Mahayana sutras is a laugh. Just one hell of a joke. Kashyapa lifted a flower, Buddha laughed. Vision. And this is one of the best things about Philip's poetry.

The bodhisattvas of the world are not just the gilded figures in temples. They are like the twelve zaddics in Judaism or the hidden imman in shi'ism. Nobody knows who they are; they live unknown. This is really a fundamental idea of Buddhism, that one should make the greatest possible effort to live unknown. What comes to you comes, as it is expressed in Taoism, as water comes down the hill and washes around the mountain. I have never made the slightest effort to advance myself as a writer, I don't make any effort to make money. Now you're very fortunate with your writing if you can live that way. But the quest for power, the quest for vanity, the quest for all the things of the world that are illusions of illusions are completely contradictory to Buddhism. There is that familiar teaching about the student who mistook a rope in the grass for a snake. Well the snake here is unreal, but the rope has reality only in a derivative sense. And what power can get you, what fame can get may be a dangerous cobra. Or it may be illusory rope, but that's all it is.

Anne Waldman
(1945-   )

"American wags listen
The East is yearning for resurrection
The West is underdeveloped
I want to ride you out here
under Big Sky"

—ANNE WALDMAN

Born after World War II, Anne Waldman came of age in a literary and political landscape that had already been radically transformed by the Beat Generation. Exposed to Beat writing early on, Waldman responded to its musical, jazzy rhythms, its performative element, and its spontaneity. She decided while still a teenager that poetry would be her path, too.

In the summer of 1965, Waldman journeyed across the country, propelled by the news that an important poetry conference was to be held in Berkeley. Waldman was eager to hear the poets who were having such a significant impact on her writing—among them Allen Ginsberg, Robert Duncan, Charles Olson, Jack Spicer, and Lenore Kandel. The experience had a profound effect: After the reading she "envisioned a compassionate human cadre of like-minded illuminati and practitioners of the art who could really 'hear the new music in their nervous systems.'" What also hit home was the political and spiritual quality common to all the poets and the role they assumed as outspoken rebels challenging the status quo. Amid a wave of antiwar protest, civil rights issues, psychedelia, and women's liberation, Waldman sought to contribute by finding an outlet for the voices of the poets. When she returned to New York, she cofounded *Angel Hair* magazine and worked on the Poetry Project of St. Mark's-in-the-Bowery Church, which hosted regular readings.

Waldman had her first taste of "watching her mind" in a comparative religion course at her progressive Quaker high school, which involved students participating in "silent meetings," meditation, for an hour. After the meditation, Waldman recalls there was a time to "speak out our secret observations, doubts, delight." She adds: "These were surprisingly secular occasions. Awareness practice with simplicity and rigor. No hierarchy, no priests." She was not yet twenty when she met a living Buddhist lineage holder, the Tibetan teacher Geshe Wangyal, who was then teaching in the small town of Freewood Acres, New Jersey.

In 1970, she met Chogyam Trungpa at his Tail of the Tiger retreat center [later renamed Karme Choling] in Barnet, Vermont. She stayed two weeks and began to think about performing her poetry in terms of breath and mantra chanting. In 1973 she took teachings for a month in India and took refuge with Chatral Rinpoche. In 1974, Waldman was invited to Boulder, Colorado, along with Allen Ginsberg and Diane di Prima, for the first program of the Naropa Institute. When Waldman arrived Chogyam Trungpa asked if she and Ginsberg would design a poetics department in which poets could learn about meditation and meditators could learn about poetry. He described this as a "one-hundred-year project, at least." The same evening the Jack Kerouac School of Disembodied Poetics was born. The school was named in Kerouac's honor because, Waldman has written, "he had realized the first Buddhist Noble Truth, the truth of Suffering, and had written the spontaneous *Mexico City Blues*, an ecstatic series of choruses inspired by Buddhist thinking ('first thought, best thought'), be-bop, and his own lively poet-mind. Also a writer both generations of peers—my own and Allen's—might agree upon." The school had its first full summer program in 1975, and Waldman has maintained her high level of involvement ever since. Her output as a writer has been prolific: recent collections include *Helping the Dreamer: Selected Poems from 1966–1988, Iovis, Troubaritz,* and *Kill or Cure.*

. . . .

From Baby Breakdown, *1970.*

Pictures from Tofukuji

FOR PHILIP WHALEN

The Buddha is dying

& all the people are crying

as well as all the animals

I see elephant, leopard

jaguar, dove, turkey, monkey, camel, fox, squirrel

to name a few . . .

as well as the clouds & trees & breeze — all this "world" creation

shaking with sorrow

immutable sun in the sky just as it should be

shine on

but what about the hand who draws these quaking lines?

disappearing behind the clouds

behind the celebration of

Buddha's Paranirvana
completely behind it?

*

The smaller picture shows metaphysical Buddha

& the two great bodhisattbas—Manjusri with lion
& Avalokitesvara with elephant
& lots of other guys who know what they're doing there
all sitting & standing on some amazing series of cliffs

ascending clear into your daily consciousness

*

We know what we're doing too
carrying firewood from the barn
taking a walk in the bountiful snow
or simply going out to fetch the mail from the large metal
box by the road:
811 Fireplace Road

These pictures come all the way from Kyoto, Japan

where resides the man who sent me them

. . . .

From Skin Meat Bones, *1985.*

Why I Meditate

A REPLY FOR ALLEN GINSBERG

I sit because I'm wing'd with awe
I sit because the poetry scene got sour in America in 1980
I sit because Milarepa did
I sit because Padmasambhava buried the Bardo Thotrol in the
  Gampo Hills & gave endless transmission to discover how death
  is liberating
I sit because Yeshe Tsogyal appeared in a dream & showed me
  her cervix like an ocean
I sit because the Dakinis dance over my forehead
I sit because thoughts chase thoughts
I sit in Puri they won't let me in the Hindu temple
I sit in Bodnath under the 8 eyes of the great stupa
I sit in Calcutta like being in Preta realm
I prostrate 1,000 times under the descendant of Buddha's
  bodhi tree
I sit like a frog on Cherry Valley's poetry farm
I sit by her hospital door, breathe in my mother's eyeball
  pain
I sit like an agent provocateur on the Orient Express
I sit like a cow in farmer Lang's meadow
I sit inside the body of a nursing mother
I sit to scandalize
I sit because I won't take it lying down
I sit to test old friends & loves
I sit because passion burns me up
I sit because I'm a paranoid speed freak
I sit because I deserted the poetry wars
I sit to be exile from Ego's land.

. . . .

The following poem is intended to be read aloud, singing the words "skin," "Meat," and "BONES" as notes: "skin," high soprano register; "Meat," tenor; "BONES," basso profundo. The three different registers should be markedly distinguishable.

skin
                    Meat
                                        BONES   (chant)

I've come to tell you of the things dear to me
& what I've discovered of the skin
                                        Meat
                                    BONES

your body waking up so sweet to me   skin

dawn light it's green   skin

I'm in hungry repose
                    Meat

it's getting close to motion   O skeleton
                                                BONE

you might stretch it now   skin

so warm, flesh

and lasting awhile
                BONE

clock like a BONE creaking
memory like a BONE creaking

little laughter lines around the eyes skin
& how the mouth's redder than the rest Meat
or nipples off purple rib cage of
BONES

It's morning anywhere!

O sitting and lying around in my weary tinsel skin
got to get up and walk around in my cumbersome skin
put on lightweight cotton skin
& shuffling skin slippers

the light's going to make it raw skin
or vulnerable Meat
or hard
BONES

I could pierce it skin
I'll grow new skin, undergo big character change

please get under my skin take hold of me
interest or annoy me intensely

jump me out of my skin!

no skin off your nose, buster
he's thin-skinned, she's thick
dermis & epidermis mating

Allen's nephew once had a skin
head
haircut

O POOR FLAYED DEER WITH GENTLE HAIR

film on surface of milk this morning

only skin deep

let's go to the oily skin flick

TENDENCY OF HIGH FREQUENCY ALTERNATING CURRENT
TO FLOW THROUGH THE OUTER LAYER ONLY OF A CONDUCTOR

okay, you've wounded me, but it's only skin deep

I'm sitting down in my sweet smelling clammy skin
to eat some juicy MEAT!

one man's meat is another man's poison

animal flesh is tasty

HAD A DREAM THE MEAT WAS TURNED INSIDE OUT,
FLOWERS BLOOMING THERE

Had a dream the jackals came (this was in India)
to collect the Meat of my father's forefingers

O cloud shaped like a tenderloin steak

tree Meat

Meat of Buddha

Had a Meat sandwich   had a Meat day
everyone was carrying their Meat around, flinging
it in the breeze

Small town, downtown, spring: time to show off your Meat
go home when it's dark and sit down with the

BONES

I live in a bare BONES room
he's working my fingers to the BONE
my friend Steven is living close to the BONE
I'm BONING up on my Dante, William Carlos Williams,
Campion and Gertrude Stein

Why is he such a bonehead? won't listen to a thing I say
Why are they so bone idle? won't do a thing I say
I'M GONNA POINT MY ABORIGINE BONE AT YOU & GET YOU WISER!

I've got a BONE to pick with the senator

I've got a BONE to pick with the Pentagon

The BONE of contention has to do with whether or not
we get a lease

Our old '68 Ford's an old BONE-shaker

Ivory, dentine, whalebone, dominoes, dice, castanets, corset
are some of the things made of BONE

but after I die make of my BONES, flutes
and of my skin, drums
I implore you in the name of all female deities wrathful &
compassionate

& PROTECT ENDANGERED SPECIES ALSO!

. . . .

From the collection entitled Makeup on Empty Space.

Makeup on Empty Space

I am putting makeup on empty space
all patinas convening on empty space
rouge blushing on empty space
I am putting makeup on empty space
pasting eyelashes on empty space

painting the eyebrows of empty space
piling creams on empty space
painting the phenomenal world
I am hanging ornaments on empty space
gold clips, lacquer combs, plastic hairpins on empty space
I am sticking wire pins into empty space
I pour words over empty space, enthrall the empty space
packing, stuffing jamming empty space
spinning necklaces around empty space
Fancy this, imagine this: painting the phenomenal world
bangles on wrists
pendants hung on empty space
I am putting my memory into empty space
undressing you
hanging the wrinkled clothes on a nail
hanging the green coat on a nail
dancing in the evening it ended with dancing in the evening
I am still thinking about putting makeup on empty space
I want to scare you: the hanging night, the drifting night,
the moaning night, daughter of troubled sleep I want to scare
you
you
I bind as far as cold day goes
I bind the power of 20 husky men
I bind the seductive colorful women, all of them
I bind the massive rock
I bind the hanging night, the drifting night, the
moaning night, daughter of troubled sleep
I am binding my debts, I magnetize the phone bill
bind the root of my pointed tongue
I cup my hands in water, splash water on empty space
water drunk by empty space
Look what thoughts will do   Look what words will do
from nothing to the face
from nothing to the root of the tongue
from nothing to speaking of empty space
I bind the ash tree
I bind the yew
I bind the willow

I bind uranium
I bind the uneconomical unrenewable energy of uranium
dash uranium to empty space
I bind the color red I seduce the color red to empty space
I put the sunset in empty space
I take the blue of his eyes and make an offering to empty space
renewable blue
I take the green of everything coming to life, it grows &
climbs into empty space
I put the white of the snow at the foot of empty space
I clasp the yellow of the cat's eyes sitting in the
black space I clasp them to my heart, empty space
I want the brown of this floor to rise up into empty space
Take the floor apart to find the brown,
bind it up again under the spell of empty space
I want to take this old wall apart I am rich in my mind
    thinking
of this, I am thinking of putting makeup on empty space
Everything crumbles around empty space
the thin dry weed crumbles, the milkweed is blown into
    empty space
I bind the stars reflected in your eye
from nothing to these typing fingers
from nothing to the legs of the elk
from nothing to the neck of the deer
from nothing to porcelain teeth
from nothing to the fine stand of pine in the forest
I kept it going when I put the water on
when I let the water run
sweeping together in empty space
There is a better way to say empty space
Turn yourself inside out and you might disappear
you have a new definition in empty space
What I like about impermanence is the clash
of my big body with empty space
I am putting the floor back together again
I am rebuilding the wall
I am slapping mortar on bricks
I am fastening the machine together with delicate wire

There is no eternal thread, maybe there is thread of pure gold
I am starting to sing inside about empty space
there is some new detail every time
I am taping the picture I love so well on the wall:
moonless black night beyond country-plaid curtains
everything illuminated out of empty space
I hang the black linen dress on my body
the hanging night, the drifting night, the moaning night
daughter of troubled sleep
This occurs to me
I hang up a mirror to catch stars, everything occurs to me out in the
night in my skull of empty space
I go outside in starry ice
I build up the house again in memory of empty space
This occurs to me about empty space
that it is nevered to be mentioned again
Fancy this
imagine this
painting the phenomenal world
there's talk of dressing the body with strange adornments
to remind you of a vow to empty space
there's talk of the discourse in your mind like a silkworm
I wish to venture into a not-chiseled place
I pour sand on the ground
Objects and vehicles emerge from the fog
the canyon is dangerous tonight
suddenly there are warning lights
The patrol is helpful in the manner of guiding
there is talk of slowing down
there is talk of a feminine deity
I bind her with a briar
I bind with the tooth of a tiger
I bind with my quartz crystal
I magnetize the worlds
I cover myself with jewels
I drink amrita
there is some new detail
there is a spangle on her shoe

there is a stud on her boot
the tires are studded for the difficult climb
I put my hands to my face
I am putting makeup on empty space
I wanted to scare you with the night that scared me
the drifting night, the moaning night
Someone was always intruding to make you forget empty space
you put it all on
you paint your nails
you put on scarves
all the time adorning empty space
Whatever-your-name-is I tell you "empty space"
with your fictions with dancing come around to it
with your funny way of singing come around to it
with your smiling come to it
with your enormous retinue & accumulation come around to it
with your extras come round to it
with your good fortune, with your lazy fortune come round to it
when you look most like a bird, that is the time to come
    around to it
when you are cheating, come to it
when you are in your anguished head
when you are not sensible
when you are insisting on the
praise from many tongues
It begins with the root of the tongue
it begins with the root of the heart
there is a spinal cord of wind
singing & moaning in empty space

. . . .

An excerpt from "Poetry as Siddhi," an essay.

The pivotal word for me, in terms of how I relate my Buddhist practice to a practice of writing, is "energy." The energy itself manifests in a basic sense as passion, which is one of the ingredients in the *doha* [songs of enlightenment] form. The Tantric understanding of energy is actually related to the experience of duality, contrast, extremes. From the Tantric perspective first it would appear that you exist as a solid entity, and others outside you are separate and solid as well. In fact you see your own thoughts as solid, as "real." You create elaborate structures out of thin air but what you come to in practice is to see the deceptive nature of these kinds of projections. Once you start to examine your own mind you see how insubstantial thoughts are, which is not to denigrate them but simply to see them as they are. We are all just conglomerates of psychological tendencies, very tenuous as a matter of fact. You start to see the emptiness, the emptiness of "ego," in oneself and in others. You start to see through the thickness of those fabrications. "I write because we're all gonna die" said Jack Kerouac. Many writers have had that "satori"-like insight, a realization of impermanence, of the terrible beauty and fragility of our existence. It propels them to write, possibly in the hope of giving weight and meaning to experience, of acknowledging the moment as it's passing. But on a deeper level in the writing you are performing a necessary ritual, just as in practice you ritualize your breathing. In a sense, the ritual helps you to really understand breath, or in further practices beyond sitting meditation you understand how energy works. You meet your yidam, or your basic nature. The act of writing also shows you who you are, what life is, what time is, what sound is. You are writing inside your own death. This is not morbid but, on the contrary, inspiring. All meditation, all writing starts with the contrast.

The deceptive existence of "you" and "others" seems to rub together, and that interests me—how and where the rub takes place between my so-called "self," or whatever that consciousness or perception is, and the phenomenal world. I'm interested in the words and the images and arrangements and collidings that occur, that come out of this chaos. There is an unconditioned spark happening, and how you relate this experience can actually exist inside language itself, in how the sounds collide. All this seems related to many Tibetan Buddhist practices, which are themselves explorations and transformations of energy. Energy is energy. It is nonconditioned except through our neurotic and grasping egos. This pure self-existing energy is also the potential of what in Sanskrit is called *siddhi*, which literally translates as magic. You might consider poetry as a kind of siddhi.

So this ability to use the existing energy of the universe may be where poetry touches on the "play" of duality. How you handle it or transcend it, or feel a gap that arises where duality seems to come to a standstill, that interests me. That powerful spark. The original spark is the spark of insight or realization where the poet or adept or student "gets it," the poem is the celebration or process of that, of the "gap" that can occur. I am intrigued by the history and lineage of a tradition that supports this kind of active practice, which is based on an older oral tradition of storytelling and first-hand rugged experience. It is a communal poetry as well, a public expression of siddhi. It also now seems particularly relevant when considering like-spirited movements, such as the Beat literary movement in America, which has an international appeal and force and is also a public poetry. As *revelatory,* as expansive is perhaps the best way to characterize the Beat poetic legacy. Spontaneous insight, "negative capability," sounding the words where every syllable is sacred are other characteristics of the Beatitude thrust. Burroughs, Kerouac, Allen Ginsberg, Philip Whalen are all practitioners of the holy search for enlightenment—satori—insight. It is no accident that the Jack Kerouac School of Disembodied Poetics took root at the Buddhist-inspired Naropa Institute, founded by Tibetan meditation teacher Chogyam Trungpa who arrived in America "looking for poets."

. . . .

From Kill or Cure, *1994. This poem pays homage to women poets and goddesses and celebrates the power of speech, breath, and poetry to heal, to awaken, and to rail.*

Of Ah Or

I cannot be but
fierce
My tongue—is it so?
& liaison of that tight
pact of
this to that
A bargain
rises
swells
reigns
sends darts North
when it is you,
iced over,
I thrust
in my heart
to consider
All the vowels
sing how to
melt that glare
or
stare into
doubt like
words in a
bubble
Can't back out
now
but sing to you
a fire across
our divide,
my tongue is forked!
Flesh language!
We fall into
pieces of
the painting
to be
put
in motion

Splash or Freeze
of Ah or
Whelp
Tell to
          old Greeks
who knew
to stress
(pounce)
stretch out
as you your limbs
the statues tell us
Move it! Move it!
& the Ode
got danced
Tell it to poet
whatshername
Heliodora?
who sang
& shook her ankles,
swallowed honey
to make
a sweeter sound or
Ah, Macabru
I tune your lyre
Stomp on the page!

Speech you are golden
Speech you crack ope my skull
Speech you lieth not down a while
but even as I dream
you rouse me
Rock bed!
Break into babe increments
prick ear awake
Spit juice in my face
Fricative magic excites
every corpuscle
Implode & regroup
Assail me with

all yr plans
to consider
the length & shadow
of vowels

American wags listen
The East is yearning for resurrection
The West is underdeveloped
I want to ride you out here
under Big Sky
Rail 'gainst acid rain,
cruelty, weird belief systems
Insult those who do you
no good in their squawk & bite

Who serve you poorly in
their bid for glory
condemned
'fore they
even sputter forth

What goddess will abide a dull,
                    ignorant tongue?

I speak it

You play me
that forms it

CODA
Jack Kerouac's Dream

From a previously unpublished dream vision by Jack Kerouac.

Suddenly I woke up and there was Avalokiteshvara smiling at me, one radiant hand laid on my brow like a cool diamond—"What do you want Jack?" he asks me—"I want to help the world"—"But you know that can't be done, it is only a vision and unreal—all those mental sunbeams boy have camped themselves out in one form or another, are you quite satisfied"—He's telling me this nowhere in any particular space—"But I noticed you were restless and wanted to be awakened, but I didn't know why."

"To help the world."

"Do you realize how long you've been gone?"

"Is it too late?"

"In earthly time you've been gone five minutes—there you are still lying on your bed."

I look and see my body there—

"Dead?"

"No, in a trance."

"And if I want now I can take off with you forever?"

"Yes—or stay & help the world—This condition we're in is known as the transcendental grace and you are completely free to help in any way you want, go anywhere, to any of the worlds, in the wink of an eye, less—But I can tell you now that your efforts won't help anybody in particular."

"Why not?"

"Dreams are dreams."

"Have I some kind of choice?"

"Stay in this transcendental state & try to help, or go off now into Nirvana, The Perpetual Insurance, or even go back into your body & live out yr allotted space of days as a human being & do what you can, or do what you like."

"Five minutes! and it seems so long I've been dreaming in blissful golden silence I thought I'd been gone for aeons and aeons of golden ages!"

"That's because there's no time. . . . except to speak of."

"Well can I try to help?"

"Yes."

"Will you help me help?"

"Yes" (smiling) "but it won't do any good or do any harm."

"I want to try it."

"All good souls want to try it, all souls are seen—all have made their original vows—I expected you to ask."

"Where do we go first?"

"It's up to you—do you remember what you wanted to do?"

"Well I wanted to *reassure* everybody that everything is alright, forever & forever & forever."

"Think they don't know it?"

"They don't act like it!"

"Acts are nothing, it's what they *are,* where it *is,* shining empty and awake and shot thru with eternal bliss."

"But can we make them *feel* it?"
"Sensation is unreal."
"Oh let's try."
"Go ahead."

Selected Bibliography

It is not possible to list all of the works that were consulted in the preparation of this volume. What follows here is a brief list of works quoted, cited, and relied upon in writing the introduction and editorial comments. Books and periodicals from which excerpts have been taken are listed separately in the acknowledgments section.

Albanese, Catherine L., ed. *The Spirituality of the American Transcendentalists.* Macon, GA: Mercer University Press, 1988.

Allen, Donald, ed. *Off the Wall: Interviews with Philip Whalen.* Bolinas, CA: Four Seasons Foundation, 1978.

Ando, Shoei. *Zen and American Transcendentalism.* Tokyo: Hokuseido Press, 1970.

Bartlett, Lee, ed. *Kenneth Rexroth and James Laughlin: Selected Letters.* New York: W. W. Norton & Co., 1991.

Blavatsky, H. P. *Isis Unveiled: A Master Key to the Mysteries of the Ancient and Modern Science and Theology.* 2 vols. New York: J. W. Bouton, 1877.

Blyth, Reginald Horace. *Haiku*. 4 vols. Tokyo: Hokuseido, 1949–52.

Burroughs, William S., with Daniel Odier. *The Job: Writings and Interviews*. London: Calder, 1984.

Charters, Ann, ed. *The Portable Beat Reader*. New York: Viking Penguin, 1992.

Charters, Ann. *Kerouac: A Biography*. San Francisco: Straight Arrow, 1973.

Charters, Ann, ed. *Jack Kerouac: Selected Letters 1940–1956*. New York: Viking Penguin, 1995.

Charters, Ann, ed. *The Beats: Literary Bohemians in Postwar America*. Vol. 16, Parts 1 and 2 of *Dictionary of Literary Biography*. Detroit: Gale Research Co., 1983.

Christy, Arthur Edward. *The Orient in American Transcendentalism: A Study of Emerson, Thoreau, and Alcott*. New York: Columbia University Press, 1932.

Di Prima, Diane. *Pieces of a Song: Selected Poems*. San Francisco: City Lights Books, 1990.

Di Prima, Diane. *Selected Poems: 1956–1975*. Plainfield, VT: North Atlantic Books, 1975.

Ellwood, Robert S. *Alternative Altars: Unconventional and Eastern Spirituality in America*. Chicago: University of Chicago Press, 1979.

Ferlinghetti, Lawrence. *City Lights Anthology*. San Francisco: City Lights Books, 1974.

Ferlinghetti, Lawrence, and Nancy J. Peters. *Literary San Francisco*. New York: Harper & Row, 1980.

Fields, Rick. *How the Swans Came to the Lake: A Narrative History of Buddhism in America*, Third Edition. Boston & London: Shambhala Publications, 1992.

Gifford, Barry, and Lawrence Lee. *Jack's Book: An Oral Biography of Jack Kerouac*. New York: Penguin Books, 1979.

Ginsberg, Allen. *Allen Verbatim: Lectures on Poetry, Politics, Consciousness*. New York: McGraw-Hill, 1974.

Ginsberg, Allen. *As Ever: The Collected Correspondence of Allen Ginsberg & Neal Cassady*. Berkeley, CA: Creative Arts Books, 1977.

Ginsberg, Allen. *Collected Poems 1947–1980*. New York: Harper & Row, 1985.

Ginsberg, Allen. *Composed on the Tongue*. Bolinas, CA: Grey Fox Press, 1980.

Goddard, Dwight. *A Buddhist Bible*. Boston: Beacon Press, 1994.

Halper, Jon, ed. *Gary Snyder: Dimensions of a Life.* San Francisco: Sierra Club Books, 1991.

Hamalian, Linda. *A Life of Kenneth Rexroth.* New York: W. W. Norton & Co., 1991.

Harris, Oliver, ed. *The Letters of William Burroughs 1945–1959.* New York: Viking Penguin, 1993.

Hodder, Alan D. *Emerson's Rhetoric of Revelation: Nature, the Reader, and the Apocalypse Within.* University Park: Pennsylvania State University Press, 1989.

Jackson, Carl T. *The Oriental Religions and American Thought: Nineteenth-Century Explorations.* Westport, CT: Greenwood Press, 1981.

Johnson, Kent, and Craig Paulenich, eds. *Beneath a Single Moon: Buddhism in Contemporary American Poetry.* Boston: Shambhala Publications, 1991.

Kandel, Lenore. *The Love Book.* San Francisco: Stolen Paper Review Editions, 1966.

Kerouac, Jack. *Good Blonde & Others.* San Francisco: Grey Fox Press, 1993.

Kerouac, Jack. *Pomes All Sizes.* San Francisco: City Lights Books, 1992.

Kerouac, Jack. *The Scripture of the Golden Eternity.* San Francisco: City Lights Books, first City Lights edition, 1994.

Kyger, Joanne. *Just Space: Poems 1979–1989.* Santa Rosa, CA: Black Sparrow Press, 1991.

McClure, Michael. *Scratching the Beat Surface: Essays on New Vision from Blake to Kerouac.* New York: Penguin Books, 1994.

Meltzer, David. *The San Francisco Poets.* New York: Ballantine Books, 1971.

Miles, Barry. *Ginsberg: A Biography.* New York: Simon & Schuster, 1989.

Miles, Barry. *William Burroughs: El Hombre Invisible, A Portrait.* New York: Hyperion, 1992.

Miller, Perry, ed. *The Transcendentalists: An Anthology.* Cambridge: Harvard University Press, 1950.

Montgomery, John, ed. *Kerouac at the "Wild Boar": & Other Skirmishes.* San Anselmo, CA: Fels & Firn Press, 1986.

Nicosia, Gerald. *Memory Babe: A Critical Biography of Jack Kerouac.* New York: Grove Press, 1985.

Norse, Harold. *Memoirs of a Bastard Angel.* London: Bloomsbury, 1990.

Patri, Umesa. *Hindu Scriptures and American Transcendentalists.* New Delhi: Intellectual Publishing House, 1987.

Prothero, Stephen. "On the Holy Road: The Beat Movement as Spiritual Protest," *Harvard Theological Review* 84:2 (1991) 205–22.

Rexroth, Kenneth. *Between Two Wars, Selected Poems Written Prior to the Second World War.* Athens, Ohio: Labyrinth Editions/San Francisco: Iris Press, 1982.

Saroyan, Aram. *Genesis Angels: The Saga of Lew Welch and the Beat Generation.* New York: William Morrow, 1979.

Schumacher, Michael. *Dharma Lion: A Biography of Allen Ginsberg.* New York: St. Martin's Press, 1992.

Seager, Richard Hughes. *The World's Parliament of Religions: The East/West Encounter, Chicago, 1893.* Bloomington: Indiana University Press, 1995.

Silesky, Barry. *Ferlinghetti: The Artist in His Time.* New York: Warner Books, 1990.

Sinnet, A. P. *Esoteric Buddhism.* Boston: Houghton Mifflin, 1884.

Snyder, Gary. *Earth House Hold: Technical Notes & Queries to Fellow Dharma Revolutionaries.* New York: New Directions, 1969.

Snyder, Gary. *No Nature: New & Selected Poems.* New York & San Francisco: Pantheon Books, 1992.

Snyder, Gary. *The Real Work: Interviews & Talks 1964–1979.* New York: New Directions, 1980.

Suzuki, Daiesetz Teitaro. *An Introduction to Zen Buddhism.* New York: Philosophical Library, 1949.

Suzuki, Shunryu. *Zen Mind Beginner's Mind.* New York & Tokyo: John Weatherhill, Inc., 1970.

Thoreau, Henry David. *Walden: Or Life in the Woods.* New York: New American Library of World Literature, 1955.

Trungpa, Chogyam. *The Myth of Freedom: and the Way of Meditation.* Boston & London: Shambhala Publications, 1988.

Tweed, Thomas. *The American Encounter with Buddhism, 1844–1912, Victorian Culture and the Limits of Dissent.* Bloomington: Indiana University Press, 1992.

Versluis, Arthur. *American Transcendentalism and Asian Religions.* New York: Oxford University Press, 1993.

Waldman, Anne. *Kill or Cure.* New York: Penguin Books, 1994.

Waldman, Anne, and Marilyn Webb, eds. *Talking Poetics from Naropa Institute, Annals of the Jack Kerouac School of Disembodied Poetics.* 2 vols. Boulder & London: Shambhala Publications, 1978.

Welch, Lew. *Ring of Bone: Collected Poems 1950–1971*. San Francisco: Grey Fox Press, 1979.

Whalen, Philip. *On Bear's Head.* New York: Harcourt, Brace & World, Inc./Coyote, 1969.

Wilentz, Elias, ed. *The Beat Scene.* New York: Corinth Books, 1960.

Acknowledgments

One gesture common to all forms of Buddhism is the bow. Hands pressed together and with head lowered, the bow is an expression of appreciation and thanks, a way to show respect and honor. This book itself is a bow, a gesture of gratitude to all those writers of the Beat Generation who were instrumental in introducing the teachings of the Buddha to the West. In addition to the authors themselves, and in particular to Allen Ginsberg, appreciation is due as well to those Buddhist masters who nurtured the interests of the Beats, and those translators whose labors first made Buddhist texts available to an English-speaking audience. Many people have contributed to this book by hunting tirelessly through old files, or by recovering lost photographs and memories. A special debt of gratitude is owed to John Sampas, the Literary Executor of the Estate of Jack Kerouac for his long-standing magnanimity, to *Tricycle*'s agent Kim Witherspoon for her foresight, and to Mary South of Riverhead for taking a chance. For his unflagging kindness and patience, a deep bow to David Stanford.

Many thanks also go to Donald Allen, Frank Olinsky, Rick Fields, Ann Charters, Bob Rosenthal, Althea Crawford, Cynthia Archer, Raymond Foye, and Barry Langford. And thanks also go to the entire staff of *Tricycle: The Buddhist Review* who pitched in whenever needed.

Excerpts from *Visions of Gerard* copyright © Jack Kerouac, 1963. Penguin Books USA, 1990.

Excerpts from *The Scripture of the Golden Eternity* copyright © Jack Kerouac, 1960. City Lights Books, 1960.

Excerpts from *Old Angel Midnight* copyright © Jack Kerouac, 1959. Grey Fox Press, 1993, 1995.

Excerpts from *Desolation Angels* copyright © Jack Kerouac, 1965. Coward-McCann, 1965.

"TV poem" by Jack Kerouac from *Heaven and Other Poems*. (Grey Fox Press), 1977.

"Poems of the Buddhas of Old" by Jack Kerouac from *Pomes All Sizes*. (City Lights Books), 1992.

Excerpts from *The Dharma Bums* by Jack Kerouac © 1958 by Jack Kerouac, © renewed 1986 by Stella Kerouac and Jan Kerouac. Used by permission of Viking Penguin, a division of Penguin Books, USA for territories as follows: U.S., Canada, P.I. Open. Reprinted elsewhere in the English language throughout the world by permission of Sterling Lord Literistic, Inc.

Excerpts from "On the Origins of the Beat Generation" by Jack Kerouac, which originally appeared in *Playboy* and is reprinted in *Good Blonde and Others* (Grey Fox Press), 1993.

"Some Western Haikus" by Jack Kerouac from *Scattered Poems*. (City Lights Books), 1971.

Excerpt from "The Last Word" by Jack Kerouac, which originally appeared in *Escapade* and is reprinted in *Good Blonde & Others* (Grey Fox Press), 1993.

Excerpt from "Mexico Fellaheen" by Jack Kerouac from *Lonesome Traveler* copyright © Jack Kerouac, 1960. Grove Press, 1960.

Excerpt from *Big Sur* copyright © Jack Kerouac, 1962.

Excerpt from "The First Word" by Jack Kerouac, which originally appeared in *Escapade* and is reprinted in *Good Blonde & Others* (Grey Fox Press), 1993.

Excerpts from "The Yen for Zen" by Alfred G. Aronowitz, which first appeared in *Escapade*, are reprinted with the permission of the author.

Allen Ginsberg's letter to Neal Cassady, excerpted from *As Ever: The Collected Correspondence of Allen Ginsberg and Neal*

Cassady (Creative Arts Books), is reprinted by permission of the publisher.

"Sunflower Sutra" from *Collected Poems 1947–80,* © 1955 Allen Ginsberg. Copyright Renewed. Reprinted by permission of HarperCollins Publishers, Inc., for the following territories: World English rights excluding the U.K. and the British Commonwealth. Permission is granted in the U.K. and the British Commonwealth excluding Canada by Penguin Books Ltd.

"What would you do if you lost it?" from *Collected Poems 1947–80,* © 1973 Allen Ginsberg. Reprinted by permission of HarperCollins Publishers, Inc., for the following territories: World English rights excluding the U.K. and the British Commonwealth. Permission is granted in the U.K. and the British Commonwealth excluding Canada by Penguin Books Ltd.

"Ego Confession" from *Collected Poems 1947–80,* © 1974 Allen Ginsberg. Reprinted by permission of HarperCollins Publishers, Inc., for the following territories: World English rights excluding the U.K. and the British Commonwealth. Permission is granted in the U.K. and the British Commonwealth excluding Canada by Penguin Books Ltd.

"Thoughts on a Breath" from *Collected Poems 1947–80,* © 1974 Allen Ginsberg. Reprinted by permission of HarperCollins Publishers, Inc., for the following territories: World English rights excluding the U.K. and the British Commonwealth. Permission is granted in the U.K. and the British Commonwealth excluding Canada by Penguin Books Ltd.

"Mugging" from *Collected Poems 1947–80,* © 1974 Allen Ginsberg. Reprinted by permission of HarperCollins Publishers, Inc., for the following territories: World English rights excluding the U.K. and the British Commonwealth. Permission is granted in the U.K. and the British Commonwealth excluding Canada by Penguin Books Ltd.

"Gospel Noble Truths" from *Collected Poems 1947–80,* © 1975 Allen Ginsberg. Reprinted by permission of HarperCollins Publishers, Inc., for the following territories: World English rights excluding the U.K. and the British

Commonwealth. Permission is granted in the U.K. and the British Commonwealth excluding Canada by Penguin Books Ltd.

"Reflections at Lake Louise" from *Collected Poems 1947–80*, © 1984 Allen Ginsberg. Reprinted by permission of HarperCollins Publishers, Inc., for the following territories: World English rights excluding the U.K. and the British Commonwealth. Permission is granted in the U.K. and the British Commonwealth excluding Canada by Penguin Books Ltd.

"In My Kitchen in New York" from *White Shroud: Poems 1980–85*, © 1986 Allen Ginsberg. Reprinted by permission of HarperCollins Publishers, Inc., for the following territories: World English rights excluding the U.K. and the British Commonwealth. Permission is granted in the U.K. and the British Commonwealth excluding Canada by Penguin Books Ltd.

"Why I Meditate" from *White Shroud: Poems 1980–85* © 1981 Allen Ginsberg. Reprinted by permission of HarperCollins Publishers, Inc., for the following territories: World English rights excluding the U.K. and the British Commonwealth. Permission is granted in the U.K. and the British Commonwealth excluding Canada by Penguin Books Ltd.

"Thoughts Sitting Breathing II" from *White Shroud: Poems 1980–85* © 1981 Allen Ginsberg. Reprinted by permission of HarperCollins Publishers, Inc., for the following territories: World English rights excluding the U.K. and the British Commonwealth. Permission is granted in the U.K. and the British Commonwealth excluding Canada by Penguin Books Ltd.

"On Cremation of Chogyam Trungpa, Vidyahara" from *Cosmopolitan Greetings: Poems 1986–1992* © 1994 by Allen Ginsberg. Reprinted by permission of HarperCollins Publishers, Inc., in the world excluding the U.K. and British Commonwealth. Reprinted in the U.K. and British Commonwealth excluding Canada by permission of Penguin Books Ltd.

"Big Eats" from *Cosmopolitan Greetings: Poems 1986–1992* ©

1994 by Allen Ginsberg. Reprinted by permission of HarperCollins Publishers, Inc., in the world excluding the U.K. and British Commonwealth. Reprinted in the U.K. and British Commonwealth excluding Canada by permission of Penguin Books Ltd.

Allen Ginsberg's lecture "First Thought Best Thought" is excerpted from *Composed on the Tongue* (Grey Fox), edited by Donald Allen. It first appeared in *Loka, 1: A Journal from Naropa Institute* in 1975. It is reprinted by permission of Allen Ginsberg, who retains the rights to this lecture.

The interview with Allen Ginsberg conducted by James MacKenzie is excerpted from *Kerouac and the Beats* (Paragon House), edited by Arthur and Kit Knight.

Allen Ginsberg's introductory essay to Jack Kerouac's *Pomes All Sizes* (City Lights Books) is reprinted by permission of Allen Ginsberg, who retains copyright to the essay.

The excerpt from Allen Ginsberg's lecture given in Vienna, 1994, is reprinted by permission of Allen Ginsberg, who retains the rights to this lecture.

"The Master," "Buddhist New Year Song," "Prajapati," "Rant, From a Cool Place," "Alba, for a Dark Year," "Revolutionary Letter #7," "Revolutionary Letter #13," "Revolutionary Letter #33," "Trajectory," "Sixth Notebook Incantation," "Brief Wyoming Meditation," "No Problem Party Poem," "Visit to Katagiri Roshi," and "Life Chant" by Diane di Prima are reprinted by permission of the author, who retains the copyright in each instance. The excerpt from the lecture entitled "Light/and Keats," which previously appeared in *Talking Poetics From Naropa Institute: Annals of the Jack Kerouac School of Disembodied Poetics,* Vol. 1, edited by Anne Waldman and Marilyn Webb and published by Shambhala Publications, is reprinted with the permission of Diane di Prima, who retains copyright to all material. All rights reserved by the author.

"The Fire Sermon," "Kali Yug," and "The House is on Fire," by Harold Norse are reprinted by permission of the author, who retains copyright in every case.

Gary Snyder's poems "Riprap" and "Piute Creek," both appear in *Riprap and Cold Mountain Poems* © 1958, 1959, 1965

Gary Snyder. Reprinted by permission of North Point Press, a division of Farrar, Straus and Giroux, Inc., in the following territories: the United States, its dependencies, Canada, the Philippines, and the open market throughout the world excluding the United Kingdom and British Commonwealth, in English only. Permission for English language in the remaining world territories including Britain and the British Commonwealth granted by the author.

"We Make Our Vows Together with All Beings" appears in *Left Out in the Rain* © 1986 Gary Snyder. Reprinted by permission of North Point Press, a division of Farrar, Straus and Giroux, Inc., in the following territories: the United States, its dependencies, Canada, the Philippines, and the open market throughout the world excluding the United Kingdom and British Commonwealth, in English only. Permission for English language in the remaining world territories including Britain and the British Commonwealth granted by the author.

An excerpt from "Blue Mountains Constantly Walking" appears in *The Practice of the Wild* © 1990 by Gary Snyder. Reprinted by permission of North Point Press, a division of Farrar, Straus and Giroux, Inc., in the following territories: the United States, its dependencies, Canada, the Philippines, and the open market throughout the world excluding the United Kingdom and British Commonwealth, in English only. Permission for English language in the remaining world territories including Britain and the British Commonwealth granted by the author.

An excerpt from the section "Burning" in Gary Snyder's *Myths and Texts* © 1978 by Gary Snyder; "Buddhism and the Coming Revolution" an excerpt from *Earth House Hold* © 1969 Gary Snyder; "LFMBR" and "Dusty Braces," both excerpted from *Turtle Island* © 1974 Gary Snyder; and an interview with Gary Snyder conducted by Peter Barry Chowka excerpted from *The Real Work* © 1980 Gary Snyder are all reprinted by permission of New Directions Publishing Corp. for English language throughout the world.

Gary Snyder's "Ripples on the Surface" excerpted from *No Nature: New and Selected Poems* © 1992 Gary Snyder. Reprinted by permission of Pantheon Books, a division of Random House, Inc., for English language throughout the world.

"Three Variations, All About Love," "Sourdough Mountain Lookout," "Metaphysical Insomnia Jazz. Mumonkan xxix.," "20:VII:58, On Which I Renounce the Notion of Social Responsibility," "All About Art & Life," "The Lotus Sutra, Naturalized," "Absolute Realty Co. Two Views," "Mahayana," "Opening the Mountain, Tamalpais: 22:X:65," "The War Poem for Diane di Prima," "Walking Beside the Kamogawa, Remembering Nansen and Fudo and Gary's Poem," "Tassajara," " 'Back to Normalcy,' " and "Dying Tooth Song" by Philip Whalen reprinted by permission of the author, who retains copyright in every case.

Interviews with Philip Whalen conducted by Aram Saroyan, Lee Bartlett, and Yves Le Pellec are excerpted from *Off the Wall* (The Four Seasons Press) edited by Donald Allen.

Excerpts from *The Japan and India Journals: 1960–64* and "Silver City Overlay for Turkey Buzzard," "Back to the Life of Naropa," "Philip Whalen's Hat," and an untitled poem by Joanne Kyger are reprinted by permission of the author, who retains copyright in every case.

Albert Saijo's memoir, the excerpt from *Trip Trap*, "Same Horizon Different View" and "Is Language Necessary to Human Existence" are all reprinted by permission of the author, who retains copyright in every case.

"Entire Sermon by the Red Monk," "Wobbly Rock," "[I Saw Myself]," "He Prepares to Take Leave of His Hut," "Buddhist Bard Turns Rat Slayer," "Leo Gives Himself Yet Another Name," and "Maitreya Poem," © 1979 by Donald Allen, Literary Executor for Lew Welch Estate. Reprinted by permission of Grey Fox Press.

The interview with Lew Welch conducted by David Meltzer and Jack Shoemaker is excerpted from David Meltzer's *The San Francisco Poets* (Ballantine).

"Enlightenment Poem" and "Small Prayer for Falling Angels" by Lenore Kandel reprinted by permission of the author, who retains copyright in each case.

Will Petersen's "September Ridge" and portions of "Stone Garden" are reprinted by permission of Cynthia Archer, executor of the Estate of Will Petersen. Portions of "September Ridge" appeared previously in *Gary Snyder: Dimensions of a Life* (Sierra Club Books), edited by John Halper. "Stone Garden" originally appeared in *Berkeley Bussei.*

"Come" and "A Buddhist Experience" reprinted by permission of Eileen Kaufman for the Estate of Bob Kaufman. The Estate retains the copyright.

"Reflections on a Small Parade" is excerpted from *Solitudes Crowded with Loneliness* © *1959* Bob Kaufman and is reprinted in English throughout the world by permission of New Directions Publishing Corp.

"I am a Camera," "Scene in a Third Eye," and "Private Sadness" are excerpted from *The Ancient Rain: Poems 1956–1978* © 1981 by Bob Kaufman and is reprinted in English throughout the world by permission of New Directions Publishing Corp.

Excerpts from William Burroughs's *The Retreat Diaries* (including a paragraph from James Grauerholz's introduction) © 1976 by William Burroughs, reprinted with the permission of Wylie Aitken & Stone, Inc.

The portion of the letter from William Burroughs to Jack Kerouac is excerpted from *The Letters of William S. Burroughs: 1945–1959* by William S. Burroughs, edited by Oliver Harris. Copyright © 1993 by William S. Burroughs; Introduction Copyright © 1993 Oliver Harris. Used by permission of Viking Penguin, a division of Penguin Books USA Inc., for the following territories: U.S., Canada, P.I. Open. In the U.K. and Commonwealth excluding Canada, this excerpt is reprinted by permission of the British publisher, Picador.

"True Confessional" is excerpted from Lawrence Ferlinghetti's *Endless Life.* Copyright © 1973 by Lawrence Ferlinghetti. Reprinted by permission of New Directions Publishing Corp. in the English language throughout the world.

"A Buddha in the Woodpile" and "Ladakh Buddhess Biker" are excerpted from Lawrence Ferlinghetti's *These Are My Rivers.* Copyright © 1993 by Lawrence Ferlinghetti. Reprinted by permission of New Directions Publishing Corp. in the English language throughout the world.

"Hwa Yen Totalism/My Sweet Liberation" is excerpted from Michael McClure's *Jaguar Skies.* Copyright © 1975 by Michael McClure. Reprinted by permission of New Directions Publishing Corp. in the English language throughout the world.

"Written on the Flyleaf/of Ashvaghosa's/The Awakening of Faith" is excerpted from Michael McClure's *Antechamber and Other Poems.* Copyright © 1978 by Michael McClure. Reprinted by permission of New Directions Publishing Corp. in the English language throughout the world.

"POEM" in addition to an excerpt from *Scratching the Beat Surface* by Michael McClure are reprinted by permission of the author who retains copyright.

An excerpt from interviews with Michael McClure and Kenneth Rexroth were conducted by David Meltzer and appeared in David Meltzer's *The San Francisco Poets* (Ballantine).

"Hojoki" from *Kenneth Rexroth's Collected Shorter Poems.* Copyright © 1949 by Kenneth Rexroth. Reprinted by permission of New Directions Publishing Corp. in the English language throughout the world.

"Hapax," "Flower Wreath Hill (Sections VII and VIII)" from Kenneth Rexroth's *Flower Wreath Hill.* Copyright © 1979 by Kenneth Rexroth. Reprinted by permission of New Directions Publishing Corp. in the English language throughout the world.

Interview with Kenneth Rexroth conducted by Rick Fields and Eric Lerner first appeared in the magazine *Zero* and is reprinted by permission of Rick Fields.

"Pictures from Tofukuiji" from *Baby Breakdown* by Anne Waldman and the excerpt from "Poetry as Siddhi" are reprinted by permission of the author, who retains copyright.

"Makeup on Empty Space," which originally appeared in *Helping the Dreamer* (Coffee House Press, 1989), by Anne Waldman. Copyright © 1989 by Anne Waldman. Reprinted by permission of Coffee House Press.

"skin Meat BONES" and "Why I Meditate," which originally appeared in *Skin Meat Bones* (Coffee House Press, 1985), by Anne Waldman. Copyright © 1985 by Anne Waldman. Reprinted by permission of Coffee House Press.

"Of Ah Or" from *Kill or Cure* by Anne Waldman. Copyright © 1994 by Anne Waldman. Used by permission of Viking Penguin, a division of Penguin Books USA Inc., in the English language throughout the world.

Unpublished dream by Jack Kerouac reprinted by permission of Sterling Lord Literistic, Inc.